SEVEN WAYS OF KNOWING

Teaching for Multiple Intelligences

A Handbook of Techniques for Expanding Intelligence

Second Edition

David Lazear

with Foreword by
Howard Gardner

Skylight Publishing
Palatine, Illinois

In chapter 1, "Search for Love." From *The Complete Poems of D.H. Lawrence,* collected and edited by Vivian de Sola Pinto and F. Warren Roberts. Copyright © 1964, 1971 by Angelo Ravagli and C.M. Weekley, Executors of the Estate of Frieda Lawrence Ravagli. Reprinted by permission of the publisher, Viking Penguin, a division of Penguin Books USA Inc.

In chapter 6, the ZOOLEY, excerpted from the IMPACT Program (Improve Minimal Proficiencies by Activating Critical Thinking), Copyright 1986 by S.L. Winocur. Reprinted by permission of the author and publisher, Phi Delta Kappa.

Seven Ways of Knowing:
Teaching for Multiple Intelligences
Second Edition, Fifth Printing

Published by IRI/Skylight Publishing, Inc.
200 East Wood Street, Suite 274
Palatine, Illinois 60067
800-348-4474 or 708-991-6300
FAX 708-991-6420

Editing: Carla Bellanca Kahler, Sharon Nowakowski, Robin Fogarty
Book Design: David Stockman, Bruce Leckie
Illustration: David Stockman
Type Composition: Donna Ramirez
Production Coordination: Ari Ohlson

Printed in the United States of America
Library of Congress Catalog Card Number: 91-67598

ISBN 0-932935-39-7

1147-10-93

TABLE OF CONTENTS

I have no doubt whatever that most people live…in a very restricted circle of their potential being. They make use of a very small portion of their possible consciousness…much like a person who, out of the whole body organism, should get into the habit of using and moving only the little finger. We all have reservoirs of life to draw upon of which we do not dream.

—William James

FOREWORD

Science usually progresses, but its course is unpredictable and uneven. When Alfred Binet and his colleagues attempted to measure intelligence for the first time, almost a century ago, this effort was positive scientific development. However, psychologists involved in the Binet effort soon made two crucial blunders: 1) They assumed that intelligence was a single entity; 2) They assumed that intelligence could be measured by a single paper-and-pencil instrument.

It has taken Binet's successors nearly a century to appreciate fully the limitation of these two assumptions. My book *Frames of Mind* is part of a larger effort in which many scientists have been involved to "pluralize" the notion of intelligence, and to demonstrate that intelligences cannot be adequately measured by short-answer, paper-and-pencil tests. Future progress in "intelligence theory" depends upon better conceptualizations of intelligence, and superior methods of measuring and enhancing human intellectual capacities.

In the years since the publication of *Frames of Mind,* my colleagues and I have made some progress on the conceptualization of intelligence. In the 1983 volume, I treated "intelligence" as a property—or, more precisely, a set of human potentials—that exists largely inside the head of the isolated individual. But along with many other researchers, I now feel that intelligence is better viewed as "contextualized" and "distributed." *Contextualization* means that we must conceive of intelligence in terms of the particular social and cultural context in which an individual lives; *distribution* means that a significant part of an individual's intelligence exists outside his or her head, inhering in the human and material resources that he or she has (or can make) available.

To concretize these new terms, let me take the example of spatial intelligence—roughly, the kind of intelligence displayed by people like Frank Lloyd Wright, Bobby Fischer, or Leonardo da Vinci. Whether and to what extent one uses one's spatial potential depends upon the place where one grows up: Are there games of chess? Is the life of an architect or sailor an option? Do teachers model how to reason in visual-spatial images? And the extent to which one uses one's spatial intelligence depends equally on the existence of artifacts like diagrams, video, compasses, and anatomical digests, as well as on the availability of individuals who can help one remember and invent spatial analogues and representations.

In addition to these modest theoretical advances, the theory of multiple intelligences has also been taken in new, more applied directions. A pioneering and skillful example of this endeavor is David Lazear's *Seven Ways of Knowing.* In this book, David Lazear introduces each of the several intelligences; helps the reader gain familiarity with their operation; presents numerous rich examples, games, exercises, and brainteasers—all in a happy effort to arouse and direct the person's full arsenal of intelligences. Lazear's work in *awakening, amplifying, teaching,* and *transferring* intelligences is original and helpful. I especially applaud the use of journals in which one can reflect about the use and evolution of one's intelligences. Such reflective activity is most important if one is going to be able to deploy one's intelligences constructively in the future—after one has closed the pages of this book. Also, worthy of special attention is Lazear's cross-cultural background, which allows him to cull examples from a wide range of settings and the extremely useful bibliographical essay at the end. These features are fine examples of the contextualizing and distributing potentials for intelligence, to which I referred above.

It sometimes surprises readers to learn that, as the author of the theory of multiple intelligences, I have no special allegiance to the notion of seven intelligences, let alone the seven specified in *Frames of Mind* and *Seven Ways of Knowing*. I am confident that if there are seven intelligences, there must be more; and I am sure (as David Lazear seems to be) that each of these intelligences has subcomponents as well. My goal is to convince readers of the *plurality* of intelligence and to offer a reasonable list of what the several intelligences might be. Also, I should stress that, except in the rarest case, intelligences work in combination. All of us possess these intelligences and all of us can use them productively. Where we differ from one another is in our particular combinations of intelligences and in the ways in which we most comfortably deploy them. If reading about the theory helps a reader—or his or her students—gain better access to a number of ways of knowing, the theory will have achieved its most important practical effect.

Naturally, both the theorist and the practitioner in me asks this question: What next for the theory of multiple intelligences?

My own hope is that the theory can enter the classroom, and, more broadly, the education of all individuals, in a more complete way. It's my belief that virtually any topic and any concept can be approached in a number of ways, and that optimal teaching makes it possible for the largest range of students to learn about the range of human knowledge. Put more concretely, I'd like to think that any topic worth mastering—from Newton's laws of mechanics to perspectival drawing to an understanding of political revolutions—can be presented more effectively if the theory of multiple intelligences is drawn on pedagogically. Teachers should be able to present these materials using several intelligences; and learners—intrapersonally intelligent about themselves—should be able to bootstrap themselves to superior understanding in a way most appropriate to their own cognitive profile.

Toward the end of this book David Lazear offers some intriguing hints about how the theory can be used in order to convey the traditional curriculum. In the future, I hope that both he and other workers influenced by a multiple intelligences perspective can carry this effort further. Bracing as it is to behold one's own array of intelligences, it is even more energizing if one can bring them to bear effectively at school, at home, at the work place, and in those regions of creative imagination which are so important to each of us.

Howard Gardner
Harvard Project Zero and
Boston Veterans Administration Medical Center
Cambridge, Massachusetts
November 1990

PREFACE

During the first twenty years of my professional life I worked with an international human development organization called the Institute of Cultural Affairs (ICA). In my capacity as Director of Research, Training, and Staff Development, I had the rare privilege to live in four different nations and conduct training programs for educators, local village people, and private business in some ten others. I owe a huge debt of gratitude to the many people I met and worked with during this time. I am certain that I learned much more from them than I was able to give back in any of the so-called "training" programs I was conducting.

It was during this period of my life that I became fascinated with the multiple ways of knowing, perceiving, and understanding life that I encountered in these cultures. In each I was intrigued by the variety of ways that people approached the task of living. I discovered very different ways of perceiving reality than my own. I experienced a wide variety of innovative approaches to problem solving that had never occurred to me in my most creative moments. And I encountered cultures that have sets of values very different from our own. In all of this, I began to realize there were realms of knowledge and understanding that I had never experienced, but that were second nature to many peoples of the world.

When I returned to the United States for an extended period of time, I had three additional experiences that literally changed the future directions of my life. One was meeting Dr. Jean Houston and having the opportunity to participate in the *Human Capacities Training Program* conducted by the Foundation for Mind Research in New York State, and the *Mystery School* which explored different religious and cultural traditions. Jean helped me unlock latent dimensions of myself and my own capacities, many of which were mirrored in my previous encounters with other cultures and people around the world. The second was reading Dr. Willis Harman's book *Higher Creativity* and visiting the Institute of Noetic Sciences in San Francisco. Working with Willis in several workshops and conferences gave me new insights into the wellsprings of my own creative potentials as well as the motivational spark to begin exploring these dimensions within myself. The third was reading the research work of Dr. Howard Gardner into the phenomenon of multiple intelligences. I was first introduced to Gardner's work by Dee Dickinson, founder of New Horizons for Learning in Seattle and by Linda Campbell, president of New Horizons, who helped me employ multiple ways of knowing in a conference I was designing. Gardner's invaluable research with Harvard's cognitive research effort, *Project Zero*, has given me both a rational framework for more profoundly understanding my own cross-cultural experiences and a wealth of application ideas and suggestions for anyone concerned about the task of education today. These experiences have come to fruition in this book.

After reading this book, if you are so inclined, I would love to hear from you! Write me with your comments about what was helpful and your adventure stories, including results you've seen from using this material in the classroom. In applying multiple intelligences to education today and learning how to use them with your students you will learn much about yourself. In this work, I firmly believe that you are on the cutting edge of multiple intelligence research. The next book on this subject should be written by you about your own lives and applications. So, as you go through this book, try to activate each of your intelligences and discover the benefits of a multiple intelligence approach to your own life's journey. Happy exploration!

I wish to give special thanks to Jim Bellanca and Robin Fogarty of The IRI Group for their encouragement and prodding to turn my vision of a handbook of strategies for teaching for multiple intelligences into a reality. Also, special thanks to Jim Reedy for his support, questioning the practicality of my ideas, and especially patience as I was consumed in the rigors of authorship.

David G. Lazear
Chicago, Illinois
1990

Awakening, Teaching, and Expanding Intelligence

An Introduction to Multiple Intelligences Theory

So many things fail to interest us, simply because they don't find in us enough surfaces on which to live, and what we have to do is to increase the number of planes in our mind, so that a much larger number of themes can find a plane in it at the same time.

—Ortega y Gasset

Recent discoveries about the nature of human intelligence and its limits have literally "blown the lid off" all previous understandings of humanity and its potentials, including the following:

■ **We have the ability to enhance and amplify our intelligence.** No longer is intelligence seen as fixed at birth. In our past thinking, intelligence was something with which you were born and with which you were stuck for life. There was really nothing you could do about it. Today, however, we know that the only limits to our intelligence are self-made and related to our beliefs about what is possible.

■ **Not only can intelligence change, it can also be taught to others.** At any age, and at almost any ability level, one's mental functioning can be improved. In fact, we can all learn to be more intelligent by discovering how to activate perception and knowing on more levels of our being than we usually use.

■ **Intelligence is a multiple reality that occurs in different parts of the brain/mind system.** There are many forms of intelligence, many ways by which we know, understand, and learn about our world. Most of these go beyond those which dominate Western culture and education and they definitely go beyond what our "I.Q. tests" can measure.

■ **While the intellect is pluralistic, at some level it is one.** When we have a problem to solve or a project to accomplish, all of our intelligences work together in a well-orchestrated, integrated way. The stronger intelligences tend to "train" the weaker ones to do their part in solving the problem or accomplishing the project.

A man and a woman are walking together down the street. The woman's step is 2/3 that of the man's. They start off together on the left foot. They want to keep walking together. How many steps will they *each* have to take before their left feet hit the ground at the same time again? (Take 3 minutes to work.)

Try to solve the above problem in *any way you can*. As you work, *watch what you are doing* to get an answer.

STOP and notice the strategy you are using to find an answer. What approaches are you trying? The answer is not important—but awareness of how you sought one is!

This exercise has been used with hundreds of people participating in various seminars and workshops. Without fail, people utilize a wide range of strategies when faced with a problem:

- Some close their eyes and try to imagine the man and woman walking.

- Some draw pictures or stick figures on their paper.

- There are always some who want to get up with a partner and step it out around the room (although the assumed constraints of the seminar situation usually prevent them from actually doing so!).

- Still others try various mathematical formulas, equations, and calculations, usually working with an "x" factor.

- Some have even been observed trying to beat out the rhythm of the steps with their hands on a table top or in their lap.

- Others simply sit there, meditating on the problem, hoping the answer will suddenly "come to them" from inside (and often it does!).

- And, of course, some simply can't resist discussing the problem with their neighbors.

When faced with a problem, we have various ways of approaching it to which we are almost naturally drawn. Maybe it is a learning/knowing strategy that has worked in the past. Maybe it is simply an approach with which we are comfortable, or one that life has taught us we can trust. For whatever reasons, this experience takes us to the heart of current research on the nature of human intelligence—the mystery of how we know, learn, and understand ourselves and the world around us.

WHAT IS INTELLIGENCE ANYWAY?

According to Dr. Howard Gardner, a pioneer in the contemporary understanding of multiple intelligences and director of Harvard's cognitive research effort *Project Zero*:

> An intelligence entails the ability to solve problems or fashion products that are of consequence in a particular cultural setting. The problem-solving skill allows one to approach a situation in which a goal is to be obtained and to locate the appropriate route to that goal. The creation of a cultural project is crucial to capturing and transmitting knowledge or expressing one's views or feelings. The problems to be solved range from creating an end to a story to anticipating a mating move in chess to repairing a quilt. Products range from scientific theories to musical composition to successful political campaigns.[1]

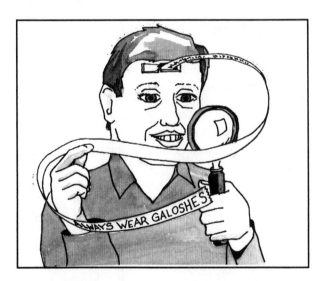

In other words, we call someone "intelligent" if they can solve problems that face them in their lives and if they are able to produce things that are of value to our culture. It is the discovery of the wide variety of ways by which the human brain/mind system approaches these tasks that has broken open multiple intelligences research, and with it, all of our previous assumptions about intelligence. Along with the discovery of intelligence as a multiple reality, whole ranges of potentials and capacities beyond anything we have previously imagined or dreamed have been opened to us. Gardner's research has identified seven intelligences—seven distinct ways that we learn and know about reality—and he believes there may be more (see diagram on page xv).

MULTIPLE INTELLIGENCES OVERVIEW

Verbal/Linguistic Intelligence

Verbal/linguistic intelligence is responsible for the production of language and all the complex possibilities that follow, including poetry, humor, storytelling, grammar, metaphors, similes, abstract reasoning, symbolic thinking, conceptual patterning, and of course, the written word. Verbal/linguistic intelligence is awakened by the spoken word; by reading someone's ideas or poetry; and by writing one's own ideas, thoughts, or poetry.

To activate this intelligence:

- Read a story you enjoy and write your own sequel—"What happens next?"

- Listen to someone expound on their ideas and have a discussion with them.

- Learn the meaning of one interesting, new word each day and practice using it.

- Make a speech on a topic about which you have a great deal of interest and excitement.

- Keep a journal or log in which you write your reflections about events from the day.

Logical/Mathematical Intelligence

Logical/mathematical intelligence is most often associated with what we call "scientific thinking" or deductive reasoning. However, inductive thought processes are likewise involved. Inductive thinking is the ability to make objective observations, and, from the observed data, draw conclusions, make judgments, and formulate hypotheses. Deductive thinking is the ability to observe and understand details as part of a general pattern. Logical/mathematical intelligence is activated in situations requiring problem solving or meeting a new challenge. This intelligence involves the capacity to recognize patterns, to work with abstract symbols such as numbers and geometric shapes, and to discern relationships and/or see connections between separate and distinct pieces of information.

To activate this intelligence:

- Create a four-point outline on your hobby with each point having four subpoints, and each subpoint having four sub-subpoints.

- Practice analytical thinking by comparing and contrasting two objects; for example, five unique characteristics of a typewriter, five of a computer, and five the two objects have in common.

- Create a convincing, rational explanation for something that is totally absurd; for example, the benefits of the square basketball.

- Participate in a project requiring use of the "scientific method." If you are *not* a cook, try making brownies from scratch following a recipe.

Verbal/linguistic intelligence and logical/mathematical intelligence form the basis for all current intelligence tests, standardized achievement tests, and college entrance exams we use in Western systems of education.

Visual/Spatial Intelligence

Visual/spatial intelligence deals with such things as the visual arts (including painting, drawing, and sculpture); navigation, map-making, and architecture (which involve the use of space and knowing how to get around in it); and games such as chess (which require the ability to visualize objects from different perspectives and angles). The key sensory base of this intelligence is the sense of sight, but also the ability to form images and pictures in the mind. Our childhood daydreaming, when we pretended we could fly or that we were magical beings, or maybe that we were heroes/heroines in fabulous adventure stories, used this intelligence to the hilt.

To catalyze your visual/spatial intelligence:

- Work with "artistic media" (such as paints, clay, colored markers, and pens) to express an idea or opinion; for example, what you think the 21st century will be like.

- Do intentional daydreaming; for example, dream about the ideal vacation spot with as much visual detail as you can muster.

- Practice internal imagination exercises—visualize yourself in a different period of history or have an imaginary conversation with your hero/heroine, a character from literature, or a historical figure.

- Use various "design skills" such as drawing, architecture, diagrams, or creating a poster to convey your ideas or thoughts to others.

Body/Kinesthetic Intelligence

Body/kinesthetic intelligence is the ability to use the body to express emotion (as in dance and body language), to play a game (as in sports), or to create a new product (as in devising an invention). Learning by doing has long been recognized as an important part of education. Our bodies are very wise. They know things our minds don't and can't know in any other way. For example, if I gave you a piece of paper and asked you to lay out the keyboard of the typewriter, **without moving your fingers,** could you do it? Probably not. But your fingers know the keyboard without even pausing. People such as actors, clowns, and mimes demonstrate the endless array of possibilities for using the body to know, understand, and communicate, often in ways that deeply touch the human spirit.

To call this intelligence to the fore:

- Perform a dramatic enactment; "role play" an idea, opinion, or feeling. Play charades using current events or modern inventions.

- Play non-competitive games that involve physical activity and a lot of motion; for example, learn names in a group through physical gestures.

- Practice activities that require physical activity such as folk dancing, jogging, swimming, and walking. Try walking in different ways to match or change your mood.

- Carefully observe yourself involved in everyday physical tasks such as shoveling snow, mowing grass, washing dishes, or fixing your car to become more aware of what your body knows and how it functions.

Musical/Rhythmic Intelligence

This intelligence includes such capacities as the recognition and use of rhythmic and tonal patterns, and sensitivity to sounds from the environment, the human voice, and musical instruments. Many of us learned the alphabet through this intelligence and the "A-B-C song." Of all forms of intelligence identified thus far, the "consciousness altering" effect of music and rhythm on the brain is the greatest. Just think of how music can calm you when you are stressed, stimulate you when you're bored, and help you attain a steady rhythm in such things as typing and exercising. It has been used to inspire our religious beliefs, intensify national loyalties, and to express great loss or intense joy.

To activate your musical/rhythmic knowing:

- Listen to different kinds of music to shift your mood; for example, play relaxing, instrumental music before or during a stressful, anxiety-producing activity (such as taking a test).

- Use singing to express an idea (even in the shower!). Use a popular tune and create a simple song about your family.

- Hum to create different kinds of vibrations inside of your head; for example, try the vowels one at a time, using different volumes and pitches.

- Play tapes of various sounds from nature (such as the ocean tides, a waterfall, wind gusts, and animal sounds). Ask yourself what you can learn from the rhythms and patterns of nature.

Interpersonal Intelligence

Interpersonal intelligence involves the ability to work cooperatively in a group as well as the ability to communicate, verbally and non-verbally, with other people. It builds on the capacity to notice distinctions among others, for example, contrasts in moods, temperament, motivations, and intentions. In the more advanced forms of this intelligence one can literally pass over into another person's life context (that is, stand in their shoes) and read their intentions and desires. One can have genuine empathy for another's feelings, fears, anticipations, and beliefs. This form of intelligence is usually highly developed in such people as counselors, teachers, therapists, politicians, and religious leaders.

To awaken this intelligence:

■ Get into different structured situations in which reliance on other people is required for successful completion of a project (such as any kind of team activity or committee work).

■ Practice listening deeply and fully to another person. Cut off the "mind chatter" that usually occurs when you are listening to someone else talk and stay focused only on what they are saying.

■ Try to guess what someone else is thinking or feeling based on various non-verbal clues, then check your accuracy with that person.

■ Explore different ways to communicate with someone else, for example, facial expressions, body posture, gestures, sounds (including but not limited to spoken words).

Intrapersonal Intelligence

Intrapersonal intelligence involves knowledge of the internal aspects of the self such as knowledge of feelings, the range of emotional responses, thinking processes (metacognition), self-reflection, and a sense of or intuition about spiritual realities. Intrapersonal intelligence allows us to be conscious of our consciousness; that is, to step back and watch ourselves as an outside observer does. Our self-identity and the ability to transcend the self are part of the functioning of intrapersonal intelligence. It likewise involves our capacity to experience wholeness and unity, to discern patterns of our connection with the larger order of things, to perceive higher states of consciousness, to experience the lure of the future, and to dream of and actualize the possible. According to Gardner, this intelligence is the most private and requires all other intelligence forms to express itself, such as language, music, art, dance, symbols, and interpersonal communication.

To activate intrapersonal intelligence:

■ In the midst of a routine activity practice acute mindfulness (that is, intense awareness of everything going on, e.g., thoughts, feelings, physical movements, and inner states of being).

■ Practice watching your thoughts, feelings, and moods as if you were a detached, outside observer. Notice patterns that kick into gear in certain situations, for example the "anger pattern," the "playfulness pattern," or the "anxiety pattern."

■ Objectify your various thinking strategies and patterns, such as your problem-solving strategies, your crisis-thinking modalities, and your processes for analytical thinking.

■ In 25 words or fewer write your answer for the question "Who am I?" Keep working on it until you are satisfied. Look at it again each day for a week, making revisions that you feel are needed.

Logical/Mathematical Intelligence

Often called "scientific thinking," this intelligence deals with inductive and deductive thinking/reasoning, numbers and the recognition of abstract patterns.

Visual/Spatial Intelligence

This intelligence, which relies on the sense of sight and being able to visualize an object, includes the ability to create internal mental images/pictures.

Body/Kinesthetic Intelligence

This intelligence is related to physical movement and the knowings/wisdom of the body, including the brain's motor cortex, which controls bodily motion.

Musical/Rhythmic Intelligence

This intelligence is based on the recognition of tonal patterns, including various environmental sounds, and on a sensitivity to rhythm and beats.

Verbal/Linguistic Intelligence

This intelligence, which is related to words and language—written and spoken—dominates most Western educational systems.

Intrapersonal Intelligence

This intelligence relates to inner states of being, self-reflection, metacognition (i.e. thinking about thinking) and awareness of spritual realities.

Interpersonal Intelligence

This intelligence operates primarily through person-to-person relationships and communication.

7

WAYS OF KNOWING

MULTIPLE INTELLIGENCES

GOOD NEWS! EXTRA! EXTRA! READ ALL ABOUT IT!

The good news is that **each of us has all of these intelligences**, but not all of them are developed equally. Thus, we do not know how to use them effectively. In fact, it is usually the case that one intelligence is much stronger and more fully developed than the others. But this need not be a permanent condition. We have within ourselves the capacity to activate all of our intelligences. In so doing, we open an amplified world of sensing, feeling, and knowing. In her book *Life Force*, Jean Houston states it as follows:

We are as different from each other as snowflakes; and each of us has, especially in childhood, a special penchant for different ways of exploring our world. In order to preserve the genius and developmental potential of childhood, one must quite simply give the universe back to the child, in as rich and dramatic a form as possible.

Multiperceptual learning, we have found, is a key to this gifting. In school curricula and programs. . . the child is taught to think in images as well as in words, to learn spelling or even arithmetic in rhythmic patterns, to think with his whole body—in short, **to learn school subjects, and more, from a much larger spectrum of sensory and cognitive possibilities.** [2] (emphasis mine)

In the past, I had the privilege to live and work in a number of different cultures around the world. One of the most interesting, in light of the present discussion, was Africa. I lived in Zambia where I was involved in a village development project. When the village council gathered to solve problems or to discuss a challenge facing the village, they used a multiperceptual approach similar to that described above. The meeting started with everyone sitting in a circle, then:

■ Going around the room in turn, each person would state their opinion about the problem or issue in question. Each could speak their mind without fear of recrimination or being made fun

of. They were concerned about getting all of the data and perspectives on the problem articulated as clearly as possible.

- After listening, they would get out drums and rattles and beat the rhythm of the problem or issue; some would create songs about it—often ridiculous songs that made fun of it.

- Eventually, some would begin to dance the problem, literally trying to "embody" the movements and actions of the problem or issue.

- Some would draw pictures of the problem in the dirt floor of the village meeting hall, and others would add their ideas to the pictures.

- Finally, the village headman would say, "OK, quiet now. Go inside and think about the problem!" Everyone would close their eyes and meditate on it, visualize it, or enter into a trance and dream about it.

- After this period of silence, they would often break into groups of two or three and share what had "come to them" in the silence.

Can you guess the net result of all of this? **Yes—a solution or a breakthrough!** While a full answer to why and how this happens can't be given at the present time, research has shown that when we engage multiple levels of our psyche in knowing, perceiving, and problem solving, much more of our innate, often unconscious, wisdom and intelligence is evoked, and suddenly **we know more than we thought we knew.** This is an example, *par excellence,* of what has been discovered in the sophisticated laboratories of Western brain/mind research.

HOW WERE THE INTELLIGENCES DISCOVERED?

The term "multiple intelligences" and the classification of seven distinct ways of knowing resulted from the research work of Dr. Howard Gardner, director of Harvard University's cognitive research project known as *Project Zero.* Gardner investigated the development of human cognitive potentials in both normal and gifted children. He was also involved in studies of the breakdown of intelligence capacities due to brain damage. This research was done at the Boston University School of Medicine and Veteran's Administration Medical Center of Boston. From these investigations several criteria emerged that a "candidate" for an intelligence had to meet.

These criteria form an important, testable, scientific base from which the present theory emerged:

- **Biological origin.** This is the biological/physiological tendency to participate in a particular way of knowing and problem solving such as body movement, communication with others, inner imagery, use of rhythm and sound, etc. Each of these tendencies is rooted within our biology as humans. Likewise, an intelligence has a distinct developmental journey, which ranges from novice to master.

- **Universal to the human species.** Each particular way of knowing and problem solving is found in every culture, regardless of socio-economic and educational conditions. Although certain skills are more highly developed in some cultures than in others, and in some distinct groups within a given culture, the occurrence of an intelligence is nevertheless universal. Likewise, the roots of an intelligence are traceable to our earlier evolution as a species.

- **Cultural valuing of the skill.** Each particular way of knowing is supported and reinforced by human culture and is part of the wisdom a culture transmits to its young. For example, the development of language may be writing in one culture, hieroglyphics in another, oratory in still another, and sign language in another. Nevertheless, in each, formal language is highly valued and is part of an individual's education and socialization.

■ **Identifiable neurological base.** For each intelligence there is an identifiable core operation or set of operations in the brain that can be "activated" or "triggered" by certain external or internal information. For example, a neurological core of musical/rhythmic intelligence can be seen in the brain's sensitivity to pitch and tonal relationships just as phonic sensitivity is a core operation of verbal/linguistic intelligence. An intelligence is testable by both experimental psychology and, at least in principle, by traditional I.Q. assessment methods.

■ **Capable of symbolic representation.** Each intelligence can be encoded in symbols or in some culturally contrived system of meaning, such as word symbols, picture symbols, music symbols, or numeric symbols. This capability is the key to transmitting and teaching intelligence. Intelligence that cannot be taught and transmitted is really of little value to a culture.

TEACHING FOR MULTIPLE INTELLIGENCES

■ What can we do to "turn on" or awaken our vast intelligence potentials?

■ Once we've awakened them, how do we keep them awake and strengthen them?

■ What does is take to teach intelligence to someone else?

■ What can we do to use multiple intelligences in the learning process?

■ How can we engage more levels of intelligence in our daily living?

The answers are not as difficult or as strange as you might think. In fact, you already unconsciously know how to access all of these ways of knowing and learning. The remainder of this book is about how to awaken more of your intelligence potential, and, once awakened, how to keep it awake, expand it, consciously use it for learning and teaching, and transfer it into everyday life. Here I want to present a model that is the basic structure for the chapters that follow. The model represents four dynamic processes involved in effectively teaching for multiple intelligences.

In the chapters that follow you will be more fully introduced to the seven intelligences, and you will have the opportunity to participate in numerous intelligence exercises for use alone and with your students.

In some ways, dealing with intelligence in this manner is a bit artificial, for in reality, human intelligence is an integrated whole that cannot be separated into seven—or any number—of distinct processes. As you will discover, each of the so-called "intelligences" activates and involves more than itself. However, for the sake of analysis and to emphasize the importance and possibilities of an expanded approach to education today, I deal with each intelligence as though it were a separate entity unto itself.

HOW TO USE THIS BOOK

What follows is a synthesis of research findings from a wide variety of "intelligence explorers," including educators, psychologists, medical doctors, philosophers, and human potential investigators. The overall design of the book is based on Howard Gardner's research as presented in *Frames of Mind: The Theory of Multiple Intelligences. Sevens Ways of Knowing*

What does it take to teach intelligence?

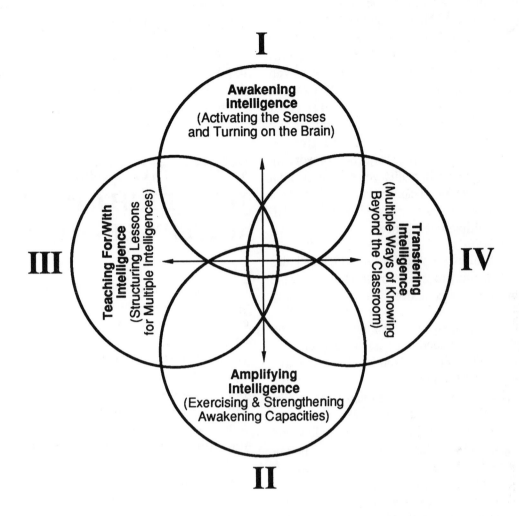

Awakening Intelligence	Teaching For/With Intelligence
I. Since each of the intelligences is related to the five senses, a particular intelligence can be activated or triggered through exercises and activities that use the following sensory bases: sight, sound, taste, touch, smell, speech, and communication with others, as well as "inner senses" such as intuition, metacognition, and spiritual in-sight.	III. This stage involves learning how to use, trust, and interpret a given intelligence in actual knowing, learning, and understanding tasks. In this book, teaching intelligence will be approached from the perspective of classroom lessons that emphasize and use different intelligences in the teaching/learning process.
Amplifying Intelligence	**Transferring Intelligence**
II. This involves practices for expanding, deepening, and nurturing an awakened or activated intelligence. As with any skill, our intelligence skills not only can be awakened, but they can also be improved and strengthened if we use them on a regular basis. Like any skills, however, they will also go back to sleep if not used.	IV. Here we are concerned with the integration of an intelligence into daily living, and its appropriate application to solving problems and meeting the challenges we face in the so-called "real world." The goal of this stage is for the intelligence to become a regular part of our cognitive, affective, and sensory perception of life.

represents an effort to bridge Gardner's research for practical applications in the classroom. Thus *Seven Ways of Knowing* is highly experiential in its approach. This is not a book on the theory of multiple intelligences, although various theories of intelligence as a pluralistic phenomenon are woven throughout its chapters. In order to get the most out of this book, you must engage both yourself and your students in the different intelligence exercises and practices presented. Although the layout of the chapters may suggest a certain sequence for working with the intelligences, in reality you can jump into a chapter at whatever point catches your interest. This is a handbook of ideas and strategies for teaching OF and WITH multiple intelligences.

Each chapter follows a basic format, which includes the four dynamic processes for teaching multiple intelligences discussed above.

The exercises presented at the beginning of chapters 1 through 7 are intended to be quick "triggers" for accessing or *awakening* a given intelligence mode. Thus they have the flavor of fun, almost game-like activities. The next section on *amplifying* intelligence offers practices that involve intentional and systematic techniques for improving, expanding, and enhancing specific intelligence capacities or potentials. Each chapter also presents a model, content-based lesson that emphasizes and uses a particular intelligence in the *teaching/learning* situation of the school classroom. These lessons attempt to demonstrate how daily classroom lessons may be structured to address the multiple levels of intelligence that are present in any and every group of students who appear before you in a given day. At the end of each chapter is a *transfer strategy* that focuses on intelligent behavior beyond the classroom, and on bridging the intelligences into daily experiences. These exercises tend to be more introspective and more oriented toward personal potential actualization.

Chapter 8 goes beyond the exercises, practices, and lessons and suggests future applications for the "Multiple Intelligences School" in such areas as lesson planning, curriculum design, educational structures, and intelligence testing/assessment.

The research appendix references key research findings from a wide variety of fields of exploration.

Following the appendix is a reflection log which offers you a multiple intelligences way to reflect on your experience of the book.

The most important suggestion I can offer for effectively using this book is have fun with it! If you're not enjoying it, you're probably doing something wrong.

GETTING STARTED (OR JUMP RIGHT IN—THE WATER'S FINE!)

Following is an exercise that gives you the opportunity to survey your own intelligence capacities. This exercise is built on the principle of the "multi-modal" approach to knowing I encountered in the African village. In it you will be using different intelligence modalities to explore an issue or challenge facing you in your life at the present moment. Give each part of the exercise a try, even if some seem a little strange and unfamiliar. See what happens. See what you can learn and experience when you "step beyond the boundaries" of your ordinary, accustomed ways of knowing.

Partnering Your Intelligence Development

As we move toward the twenty-first century, the world seems to be growing more diverse and complex with each day. If we are to live effectively in this new world and play a role in co-creating the future, we must learn how to access previously untapped parts of our being, both individually and collectively.

This exercise will lead you through a process of experientially understanding your full range of intelligence capabilities, as well as give you some clues on how to further develop and expand your multiple intelligences.

[Note: This exercise may be done as one lengthy exercise or as a series of brief experiences. However you decide to do it, I suggest that you focus on the same topic throughout the exercise.]

Verbal/Linguistic Intelligence

■ On a piece of paper, make a list of at least five key issues, concerns, or challenges that you are facing in your life at the present moment.

■ Circle one that you would like to use and further explore throughout this exercise.

■ Write this issue, concern, or challenge at the top of a second sheet of paper and then begin listing, in a random fashion, all of your associations with it—e.g. feelings, thoughts, images, colors, smells, sounds.

■ Read over your list and turn your issue into a short "once upon a time story," with you as the hero/heroine.

■ When you have completed the story, read it *aloud* to yourself as if you were hearing it for the first time. What happened to your perception of the issue as you did this?

Logical/Mathematical Intelligence

■ Now set aside the story and return to the list of associations you created above. Go back through your list looking for associations that are somehow related to each other. Put a symbol (e.g. O, Δ, †, Ω, *, etc.) by the items you sense are commonly related.

■ For each grouping of items, create a summary title that describes the items in the grouping. *[NOTE: You may want to re-list the items that comprise a particular grouping under their related symbol so you can see them together.]*

■ Can you see any connections or relationships between the various groupings? If so, note these and create a bridging/connecting statement between them.

■ Pause and reflect on what you have learned about your issue. How has working with it in this way of knowing changed your perspective? What insights have you gained?

Visual/Spatial Intelligence

■ Now, set aside the work you have been doing above. Take another piece of paper and reflect on the issue, concern, or challenge, this time drawing pictures, images, shapes, patterns, designs, and colors to express your different moods and feelings. *No words allowed!*

■ The emerging picture, designs, shapes, images,

and colors may not have an obvious connection to the issue at hand, but don't worry about trying to figure this out rationally. Trust your intuitions and let what you are seeing and sensing in your mind's eye flow out through your hands onto the paper in a purely non-verbal form. *[NOTE: So-called "artistic abilities" have nothing whatsoever to do with this activity. Your goal is to express what you are feeling as fully as possible, so don't worry about artistic talent!]*

■ When you feel that the flow of image associations is complete, stop and reflect on what you have discovered using this way of knowing. What new relationships and/or points of connection do you see as you look at your pictures? What things do you see now that you did not sense when working with the verbal/linguistic and logical/mathematical modes?

Body/Kinesthetic Intelligence

■ Set aside the drawing you have been doing above. Stand up and close your eyes. Think about and try to sense movements, gestures, and actions you associate with the issue, concern, or challenge you are working with in this exercise. Imagine what would be going on if it were acted out. What would it be as a dance?

■ Now, slowly begin to move your body in accordance with some of the motions, actions, and gestures you have been sensing and imaging. Start to act out or dance the issue in whatever way makes sense to you—how it feels, what it looks like, the kind of activity, etc.

■ When you feel you have thoroughly explored the issue through physical movements and actions, stop and close your eyes. Visualize yourself going through the movements, actions, gestures, and dance you have just completed. Try to re-experience and remember as vividly as possible your enactment and/or dance in your imagination only.

■ Reflect on your experience. What new dimensions has this made you aware of? What fresh perspectives do you now sense?

Musical/Rhythmic Intelligence

■ Without thinking about it too much, begin beating out the rhythm of your issue on the table or on the floor. Pay attention to the feel and sound of the rhythm, letting it spontaneously change itself as you continue beating. Stay with this long enough to really get a feel for the beat of your issue, concern, or challenge.

■ Now, experiment with some of the sounds or tones you associate with this issue. Let these sounds/tones begin to rise within you. Again, don't think about this too much, just let whatever sounds/tones you feel like making happen. As you did earlier, keep making the sounds/tones long enough to get an inner feeling of the sounds/tones of the issue, concern, or challenge.

■ Finally, choose a piece of music you intuit would be a good piece of background music for this issue, concern, or challenge. Listen to it for a few minutes and then begin reflecting on changes to your understanding of the issue that have occurred as you explored it through rhythm, sound, and music.

Interpersonal Intelligence

■ Choose another person, one you trust and with whom you feel comfortable talking. Ask this person to sit with you so you can tell them about what you have done in this exercise and what you have discovered about the issue, concern, or challenge as you've been exploring it using the different intelligences.

■ Spend a few minutes with this partner, getting centered and attuned to each other. Ask your partner to practice deep listening as you talk about your explorations and discoveries. Your partner may ask questions and interact with you as they sense it is appropriate. Your task is to communicate as fully as possible what you feel has happened to you during the course of the exercise.

- When you have finished, reflect with them about what you have known, sensed, and learned through this interchange with each other. Ask the other person to likewise share their impressions from the encounter. What new perspectives has this interpersonal communication given you on your chosen issue?

Intrapersonal Intelligence

- Lie down on the floor or sit comfortably so that you can completely relax. Close your eyes and breathe deeply from your abdomen. With your mind, carefully watch your breath, following it all the way into your body and all the way back out. Allow yourself to relax more and more with each breath. Let all other thoughts, worries, and anxieties slowly and naturally fall away as you focus on the flow of your own breathing.

- When you sense that you are in a centered, calm state of being, imagine that you are able to step into a time machine and journey hundreds of years into the future. As vividly as you can, pretend that you are actually making this journey into future time. As you journey, however, you mysteriously do not age. With each step into the future you gain the wisdom of the ages, seeing and knowing things beyond a limited, time-bound perspective; you gain insights deeper and more vast than anything you dreamed possible.

- Standing in this future time, look back at yourself in the present with the issue, concern, or challenge on which you have been focusing. From this vast future perspective, far beyond the immediacy of today, imagine that you are a consultant to yourself, giving advice, support, wise counsel, and encouragement to your client who is you! Speak to yourself seriously and with compassion, trying to be of genuine assistance.

- When you feel that this dialogue between the present you and the future you is complete, allow yourself to slowly, and in your own time, return to the now, refreshed, enlivened, and filled with new insight.

- Spend a few minutes recording the learnings and revelations from this journey: write about it, draw it, or meditate on what has happened to your sense of the issue, concern, or challenge.

Congratulations! You made it through the first exercise. Each of the stages of this exercise is a clue to the "inner homework" you can do to develop and expand your intelligence. In doing this, you are, in effect, developing more of your potential as a human being; and thus, you will be operating on more channels of your being.

A good habit to get into would be to use your seven intelligences at least once each day. If you "buy" this, there are at least three money-back guarantees that go along with your purchase:

- You'll find you have more resources to deal with everyday problems.

- You'll find immense changes occurring in your perception and understanding of life.

- And, you just may discover that the fullness and adventure of being human has been given back to you!

NOTES ON
LEFT BRAIN/RIGHT BRAIN

Probably the most popular and widely known finding of contemporary brain research is that our brains have at least two very different ways of processing information. These are connected with the two hemispheres of the brain—the left and the right. One or the other of these sides tends to be dominant in each of us.

The **left brain's** processing is more analytical, linear, and step-by-step: for example, your left brain is active when you're trying to figure out what happened to all your money as you balance your checkbook! The left brain's information processing mode is more verbal, rational, and logical than the right.

The left brain tends to organize new information into pre-existing knowledge patterns, categories, and schemes. This is like a very meticulous person who is forever looking for little boxes on shelves to put things into so they'll make sense and the house will be neat and tidy.

The **right brain's** processing tends to be more integrating, simultaneous, and all-at-once: for example, your right brain reacts when one of your favorite songs plays on the radio, or you are looking at a magazine and suddenly turn the page to a picture of your ideal vacation spot! The right brain is more visual, spatial, symbolic, and aesthetic in the way it processes information.

The right brain can create leaps in knowing, for its vision is panoramic; it can see the larger patterns of things. It can invent ideas that don't fit into any pre-existing pattern or scheme and for which there is not even any previous reference point or experience. This is much like the artist or science fiction writer who creates worlds and universes no one has ever seen but in their dreams, or the musician who evokes deep emotions by putting together various musical tones and patterns.

An edge in current "split brain" research is the integration of the two sides of the brain into a unified whole—**the whole brain.** When this balancing occurs, we begin to participate in a greatly amplified approach to living. For in addition to so-called "hardheaded," rational thinking about our problems and concerns, the realm of intuition, symbols, and the aesthetic joins with our more analytical skills, giving us a deeper, richer experience of being.

SKYLIGHT PUBLISHING

A TECHNIQUE FOR AWAKENING THE SENSES

The ever-increasing complexity of our world is requiring that we humans become equally complex in our capacities for orchestrating this new reality. This means that we must train ourselves to "operate on more channels" or to "cook on more burners" than have been necessary until this present, unique moment in the evolutionary process.

The following exercise is one that approaches this situation from the perspective of the full range of our senses. It is an exercise in awakening the senses and using them in new and interesting ways to understand the world. The exercise moves from more simple activities to greater and greater levels of complexity.

I suggest that you initially spend 2 to 3 days working with each stage of the exercise until you have worked your way through its entirety. Then adapt it and change it to meet your own needs!

IMPROVING AND EXTENDING THE SENSORIUM

During the first several days, focus your attention on the five senses (touch, sight, hearing, smell, taste) and practice improving and extending their capabilities.

> EXAMPLE: Sitting at your desk, give your awareness fully to all the sounds you hear. Then imagine that you have a dial on your sense of hearing. It is now set at number 3. Slowly begin to turn it up from 3 to 5 to 7, up to 10. With each increase, notice what happens to your hearing. Sounds may seem to be clearer and louder. You may begin to hear things now that you didn't hear on the number 3 setting. Then turn the dial back down to 3.

Do this for each of the senses in turn, knowing that you are doing very serious and real neurological re-programming. It may be difficult or seem impossible at first, but don't get discouraged. Just keep practicing several times throughout the day. It will get easier and you may be surprised at how much you can improve the senses.

Record your experience, reflections, and insights.

EXPANDING AND DEEPENING THE SENSORIUM

During the next several days, focus on more then one sense at a time. Develop an awareness of the inter-relatedness of the senses to each other and to the rest of your mind-body system. Begin with two at a time and then add more if this seems right to you.

> EXAMPLE: While eating your lunch, give your attention to the smell of your food. Notice as many different and subtle smells as you can. Then STOP! What sounds did you NOT hear as you were involved in the smelling. Then resume your eating giving your attention to hearing as well as smell. Then STOP! What tastes did you loose because you were also watching your hearing? Keep playing with it until you can retain full awareness of both simultaneously.

Begin with different combinations of two senses. Then, if you want, add a third and fourth and even a fifth sense so that you have all of the senses engaged as fully as you can as you sink your teeth into that egg salad sandwich!

Also allow yourself to notice things that happen in other parts of your mind-body system when you, for example, are involved in the experience of taste. What else is affected? And what happens to your awareness and perception of reality when you consciously bring all the senses into play at the same time?

Write about what you are observing.

DEVELOPING A COMPLEX AND DIVERSE SENSORIUM

During the next several days, experiment with asking the senses to perform in ways that we don't ordinarily ask them to perform.

> EXAMPLE: While riding the bus, begin working with your awareness of a brightly colored piece of clothing that someone is wearing. Let it completely fill your seeing. Then begin to hear the color. Close your eyes and hear it! Then taste it. Smell it. And allow yourself in your imagination to experience the touch of those florescent yellow pants you're looking at!

Once again, experiment with the simultaneous engagement of all the senses, but invent new, interesting, and unusual things to ask them to do, such as hearing your taste, smelling your touch, tasting your sight, etc.

Be sure to take time to record what happens and what you discover.

SENSING INNER REALITIES

One final thing to try is turning all of your senses to the inner world and training yourself to sense inner states of consciousness and awareness.

> EXAMPLE: Sitting alone in some quiet place, speak to your center of hearing and focus it on hearing the rhythms of awakening that are flowing through your being today. As you begin to hear them, turn up the dial so they become clearer and so you really get in touch with the awakening that is trying to happen within you.

Again, make up your own routines here. Some suggestions that others have tried include: sniffing out new realities and new patterns of being emerging in your life; developing deep vision that goes beyond appearances to the very essence of things; and tasting the many different flavors of the life force present in your being.

Carefully record your experiences, discoveries, and insights.

SKYLIGHT
PUBLISHING

Chapter 1

In the Beginning Was the Word. . .

Explorations of Verbal/Linguistic Intelligence

Of such is the kingdom of language. Without language, no humanity. Without written language, no civilization. So much for the past. Need anything be said of the present and the future?—Charlton Laird, *The Miracle of Language*

 There may be no more formative event in our species' long journey to human development than the emergence of language. With the acquisition of language, for the first time in evolution, comes the dawn of self-reflective consciousness and the possibility of complex communication with others. For the first time, such phenomena as long-term memory, abstract thinking and reasoning, poetry, drama, philosophy, story-telling, and of course, writing eventually appear on the evolutionary stage. In his pioneering book on human development, *The Atman Project*, Ken Wilber puts it this way:

> The emergence and acquisition of language is very likely the single most significant process. . .of the individual's life cycle. It brings in its broad wake a complex of interrelated and intermeshed phenomena, not the least of which are new and higher cognitive styles, an extended notion of time, a new more unified mode of self, a vastly extended emotional life, elementary forms of reflexive self-control, and the beginnings of [a sense of] membership.[3]

Suddenly, we are no longer merely victims of our given situation. We can, through language, step outside of our situation, think about it, discuss it with each other, make plans for improving it, then step back into the situation and change it. We become co-creators of the world. A slogan that is popular on many posters today is *"If you can dream it, you can become it!"* In the case of the verbal/ linguistic dimensions of our being we could almost say that **if we can talk**

and write about it, we can create it! In fact, language is like a double-edged creative sword—we create it, then it in turn creates us. As Wilber notes:

> . . .the deep structure of any given language embodies a particular syntax of perception, and to the extent an individual develops the deep structure of his native language, he simultaneously learns to construct, and thus perceive, a particular type of descriptive reality, embedded, as it were, in the language structure itself. From that momentous point on. . .the structure of his language is the structure of his self and 'the limits of his world.'[4]

Probably one of the most powerful illustrations of the power of language to create the world, and the "limits" of that world, was in the early 1960s. John F. Kennedy, speaking to the American public, said that by the end of that decade we would place a man on the moon. The words were said. In 1969 it happened. Also consider the impact and role of Martin Luther King's "I Have A Dream" speech in shaping the civil rights movement. These words may have shaped the future directions of our nation more than any others in recent times.

What are some of the dimensions and capacities of our verbal/linguistic intelligence?

The following set of exercises illustrates some of the capacities we all possess through this way of knowing. You can use them to help your students begin to understand their verbal/linguistic intelligence and to find ways to strengthen it. Go ahead and try some of these, and see what happens!

Understanding Order and Meaning of Words

The intricacy and complexity of verbal/linguistic intelligence can be seen very clearly when we look at poets or novelists at work. They will often spend days, weeks, even months agonizing over finding just the right word or phrase to express precisely what they want to communicate. Words have many shades of meaning attached to them. What is more, when they are juxtaposed with other words, which also have many shades of meaning, composition becomes a very complex (and shady) affair.

The following two exercises work with the flexibility of language through word patterns and meanings. Give them a try, then invent your own!

■ See how many different sentences you can make by rearranging the order of the ten words in the following sentence. How many different meanings can this set of words convey?

The man only wanted to tell the child about this.

- Here is a fun classroom game. Beginning with the following phrase, each student is to name an ailment that is preventing attendance at school today:

Teacher, I can't come to school today because I've got. . . .

The rule is that the ailments must be in alphabetical order. For example, "Teacher, I can't come to school today because I've got allergies." The next student says, "Teacher, I can't come to school today because I've got allergies, and a backache." The next student may say ". . . because I've got allergies, a backache, and a cough."

- Try the game with other topic areas, or maybe adapt it to use a set of vocabulary words you are trying to learn.

xercise

Convincing Someone of a Course of Action

The persuasive possibilities of language, both its spoken and written forms, are called its "rhetorical" function. Rhetoric relies both on the literal meanings of words used in an argument, and on their "emotional meaning" and power to catalyze action. Usually this capacity is highly developed in such people as politicians, religious leaders, and lawyers. However, the three-year old who is trying to get you to give her a piece of candy has also developed amazing rhetorical abilities! Obviously, rational and logical thinking comes into play here as well.

This exercise works with the rhetorical function of language; that is, its ability to motivate and persuade. Try making up solid rationales or convincing reasons why someone should do the following.

- Make a list of at least ten good reasons why every thinking, responsible human being should save all the crumbs left on the table at the end of a meal.

- Create a TV or radio advertisement that convinces people to purchase the latest breakthrough in sports equipment, roller skates with oblong wheels.

- Write a cover letter to go with a mass mailing soliciting financial contributions to the not-for-profit service organization *GOOFEY*—Grandmothers Of Obstinate Foolish Extremist Yuppies.

- Create a political speech for a platform arguing that a "Bill of Wrongs" be amended to the Constitution, that the voting age be changed so that *only* those between ages 5 and 12 can vote, and that we move to a government-subsidized, one-day work week.

- Think of other preposterous things and devise ways to convince others to think as you do.

Exercise

Explaining, Teaching, and Learning

Much of our current education is built on the capacity to explain things to each other using language. Before written language, education was primarily a matter of oral tradition, which included collections of adages, verses, and simple explanations of what was to be taught. With the dawn of written language, not only was education suddenly available to the masses, but new levels of complexity emerged in the linguistic structure and pattern of language, including metaphor, simile, hyperbole, symbolic language, and the realm of the epic myth or poem.

This exercise is about giving clear verbal directions. You will need a partner for this one. Remember, be patient, creative, and have fun!

- The point of the exercise is for you to ONLY give verbal instructions to your partner for performing some action.

- Your partner is to explicitly follow the instructions you give. They may ask questions to clarify, but you may not show them how to do it.

- Here are some ideas of actions to get you started. After doing these, try creating some of your own—
  - tying a man's tie (both bow and formal dress ties)
  - sewing a button onto a piece of cloth
  - braiding three strands of twine
  - separating the yolk and white of an egg
  - tying different kinds of knots in a rope (square knot, slip knot, etc.)

  [NOTE: if you have to perform the action yourself as you explain it to your partner, then turn your back so your partner cannot see you!]

Exercise

Humor

Language allows us to "get distance on ourselves," so to speak, so we can enjoy ourselves and others. It helps us take a step back from the intensity of life and to laugh. The possibilities for humor that our language presents us are almost endless, from the pun, to the misunderstood comment, to the ability to tell about a ridiculous and absurd situation, to the classic riddle. Almost every situation we encounter in our lives has the potential for humor thanks to language.

This exercise lets you play with several delightful aspects of the endless supply of humor available through our language.

- Brainstorm a list of at least fifteen things you can associate with language, such as grammar, syntax, pronunciation, subject, object, predicate, preposition, adverb, adjective, punctuation, etc.

- Choose three or four words from your list and make them into a limerick. The most basic limerick form is five lines in length with the first and second lines rhyming with each other, the third and fourth lines rhyming with each other, and the fifth line rhyming with the first two. For example—

A young foreign student named Jamlar
Always spoke with a well-defined stammer.
Thus, in English he studied
So his speech was not muddied.
Now he speaks with impeccable grammar!

■ Now work with the "pun" possibilities of your list. Try writing a "punny" story incorporating some of the words. For example—

Little Red Riding Hood was going through the woods to visit her Grammar when she was prepositioned by a wolf. . . .

■ See what other funny things you can think of to do with your list.

Exercise

Memory and Recall

Because of language, especially written language, we have the ability to store an immense amount of information in our "memory bank." Some researchers believe that every experience we have ever had in our lives is stored in our memory. They say that we really never forget anything, although recall of some things may be difficult without the right trigger. We experience this when trying to remember someone's name, a phone number, or something we have misplaced. While the information we desire may not be immediately available, it often "comes to us" later when something "jogs our memory."

■ Below is a multiple intelligences crossword puzzle based on concepts and ideas in the first chapter of the book. See how many of them you can get! (answers at end of chapter)

Across

1. The "person-to-person" intelligence
2. The dimension of one of the intelligences which involves sensitivity to sonic vibrations
3. The intelligence aspect related to imagery, drawing, painting, and sculpting
4. The intelligence dimension involving clear and rational thought processes
5. The key to education based on *Seven Ways of Knowing* is called "___ perceptual learning"
6. The dimension of an intelligence involving physical aspects of one's being
7. The intelligence aspect related to movement
8. The intelligence aspect concerned with the spoken word
9. The intelligence aspect concerned with all aspects of formal language
10. The name of Harvard's cognitive research effort (2 words)

Down

1. The introspective intelligence
2. The intelligence aspect that keeps you from getting lost
3. The intelligence dimension that is especially sensitive to sound
4. Intelligence research investigates how we ___ what we ___ (same word for both)
5. The love of patterns is at the heart of this aspect of one of the intelligences
6. There is one of these at the end of each chapter
7. Who pioneered the current theory of multiple intelligences?
8. Intelligence research investigates this
9. The initials for the test that supposedly determines how smart you are

© 1990 David Lazear

"Meta-linguistic" Analysis

Not only can language give us distance from ourselves, but language can look at and analyze itself. Often, when we are talking with another person and do not understand them we'll say "Did you mean X or Y?" In so doing we are asking them to reflect on their prior use of certain words or phrases and to be more precise. This is also the realm of linguistic inference, where we understand another person's intended communication as much by **how** they say what they are saying as by **what** they actually say.

In the following exercise, you will be experimenting with a piece of poetry and the many levels of meaning it is possible to see and experience.

Those that go searching for love
only make manifest their own lovelessness,
and the loveless never find love,
only the loving find love and they never have
to seek for it.[5]

      —D.H. Lawrence

■ Begin by having three different people read the above poem aloud. What do you notice about the different ways people read it (different emphasis, tones, moods, pace, etc.)?

■ Have the poem read in the following ways:
  - as if it were a script in a comedy nightclub
  - as if you have just had a fight with someone you love
  - as if you were speaking to an infant
  - as if it were lines being read by Hamlet
  - as if you were totally, unconditionally bored

■ What happened to the poem? What did you notice?

■ Make a list of other things about which the poem could have been written. Try substituting some of these for the word *love* and see what this does to the poem. For example, have someone read the poem substituting the word *freedom* for *love*—

Those that go searching for freedom
only make manifest their own lack of freedom,
and those who lack freedom never find freedom,
only the free find freedom and they never have
to seek for it.

VERBAL/LINGUISTIC INTELLIGENCE AND THE BRAIN

The sampling of verbal/linguistic capacities illustrated above are located mostly in the temporal cortex of the left hemisphere of the brain. This is the area of the brain known as "Broca's Area."

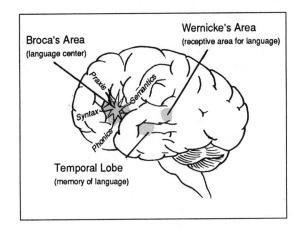

There are at least four interrelated, highly complex processes in the brain that comprise our verbal/linguistic intelligence. Howard Gardner describes these in his book *Frames of Mind* and suggests that we can most clearly observe the primary neurological processes of verbal/linguistic intelligence at work in the poet:

> In the poet. . . one sees at work with special clarity the core operations of language. **A sensitivity to the meaning of words,** whereby an individual appreciates the subtle shades of difference between spilling ink 'intentionally,' 'deliberately,' or 'on purpose.' A **sensitivity to the order among words**—the capacity to follow the rules of grammar, and, on carefully selected occasions, to violate them. At a somewhat more sensory level—a **sensitivity to the sounds, rhythms, inflections, and meters of words**—that ability which can make even poetry in a foreign tongue beautiful to hear. And a **sensitivity to the different functions of language**—its potential to excite, convince, stimulate, convey information, or simply to please.[6] (emphasis mine)

Each of the processes mentioned above is part of the formal study of language. Let us briefly look at them to help us understand some of the complex processes involved in the operation of verbal/linguistic intelligence.

- **Semantics (the meanings of words).** Semantics involves the study of the meanings and connotations of words, including their meaning within the surrounding neighborhood of other words. No word has an *a priori* meaning. Meanings exist only in the mind and only because we have agreed that certain configurations of sound will mean certain things. What this means is that if we were in the situation of starting a new culture, the word *triangle* could as easily be assigned to describe a kind of vegetable as to describe a geometric shape. Imagine going into a res-

taurant and ordering a dish of lightly buttered triangles to go with your steak!

- **Syntax (the order among words within a context).** Syntax involves the rules which govern the ordering of words in speech or composition, as well as their meaning within a particular context. When working within strict grammatical rules, for example, you should not end a sentence with a preposition for it lacks an object; nor should you have a double negative in a sentence. However, when working with a word in a particular context, the rule of relativity is king. Use *what is appropriate to the situation* in which you are writing (or should it be ". . . the situation you are writing IN?!?"). Also consider how the order of words in the following sentences (along with a few grammatical changes) alters their meaning:
  He decided to ask the new girl for a date.

  The new girl decided to ask him for a date.

  He and the new girl decided to date.

  The date was because he decided to ask the new girl.

  He decided to date the new girl.

- **Phonology (the sounds, rhythms, inflection, and meter of words).** Phonology involves the sounds of words, their "musical harmony," inflection, tone, pitch, and their interactional effect on each other. This property of language obviously taps into our auditory sensitivity. What sounds right? What words "go well" with other words? Is this set of words pleasing to the ear? This is the area of linguistic study where *how* something is said is as important to the final meaning as *what* is said (in terms of literal word meanings). Consider all the possible meanings of the following sentence that result by simply changing word **EMPHASIS:**

WHAT do you really want?

What **DO** you really want?

What do **YOU** really want?

What do you **REALLY** want?

What do you really **WANT?**

■ **Praxis (the different uses of words).** Praxis refers to the pragmatic functions to which language can be put. This involves such things as awareness of the different parts of speech and how to effectively employ them in a sentence; understanding the cultural nuances of words and how they have, by custom, come to be used; and various emotive aspects of language, including both tonal qualities and specific words, which can produce an immediate emotional response.

The praxis differences between British and American English illustrate this function. Can you understand what is being communicated in your own language? For example:

- Are the cutlery and serviettes on the table yet?
- Only let the flat to someone who's answered all queries.
- Let me know when the lory arrives.
- Someone has taken the dustbin so please clean the duster outside.

While each of these dimensions of verbal/ linguistic intelligence can in principle be isolated, in reality they all function as an integrated whole. They likewise provide numerous clues for devising strategies to help students who are weak in verbal/linguistic skills.

Awakening Verbal/ Linguistic Intelligence

The previous exercises provide a place for a beginning to activate and get in touch with your verbal/linguistic intelligence. In general, ver-

bal/linguistic intelligence is awakened by such things as rhyme, humor, statements like "Let me tell you a story. . .," telling another about an experience you have had, or trying to persuade or convince someone to do something.

Yet no amount of linguistic analysis can adequately account for or explain the sheer mystery of language. In an early classic about language and its origins, *The Miracle of Language*, Charlton Laird expressed the wonder of the phenomenon of verbal/linguistic intelligence as follows:

> Whatever whimsical gods there be, not the least of their ironies is this, that language, which is often durable as the granite-ribbed hills, is built with air. And this fact must give us pause. In previous chapters we have dealt with words; we have recognized these words as symbols for meaning, and we have dealt with the words as though they had form, and as though this form were expressed in spelling. . . .Words came into being as sound; during most of their history they existed as sound. . . .They are made of air, and in treating them thus far as though they were made from bits of the alphabet, I have done them an injustice, and possibly have led you astray.[7]

Amplifying Verbal/ Linguistic Intelligence

Now that we have awakened verbal/linguistic intelligence as a way of knowing within ourselves, let us begin work to further understand it, to expand it, and to strengthen it so that its full cognitive power is available to us. Once again Ken Wilber's description of these possibilities is illuminating:

> . . .language is the means of *transcending* the simply present world. . . .Through language, one can anticipate the future, plan for it, and gear one's present activities in accordance with tomorrow. That is, one can delay or control one's present bodily desires and activities. . . .Through language and its symbolic, tensed structures, one can postpone the immediate and impulsive discharges of simple biological drives. One is no longer totally dominated by instinctual demands, but can to a certain degree *transcend* them.[8]

Since we live in a culture and society which highly values verbal/linguistic intelligence, it is difficult to approach it with the same sense of discovery as those intelligence modalities with which we are not as familiar and which are not as much a conscious part of our socialization. Western culture tends to evaluate the whole of human intelligence based on one's skill in verbal/linguistic and logical/mathematical capacities. However, few people have developed the verbal/linguistic way of knowing beyond the "lowest common denominator" that is available through public education today.

Three practices follow which can begin to unlock some of the exciting possibilities of your own verbal/linguistic intelligence. As with each of our multiple intelligences, conscious practice and exercise can dramatically improve this way of knowing.

"Calvin and Hobbes"

The first practice is based on one that Dr. Jean Houston uses with participants in human potential workshops. In *The Possible Human* she instructs them as follows:

> Throughout the day, several times an hour, stop whatever automatic, ordinary thing you're doing and become luminous. . . Experience the moment as one in which all of creation is blooming and you are a part of it. . . and do it not in the high moments of ecstasy, but when you are engaged in trivial acts.[9]

This is a little like "Calvin & Hobbes" in the Sunday comics in the newspaper. The ordinary suddenly becomes **EXTRA**-ordinary. Try the exercise and see what can happen to your perception.

In this practice students will try to step beyond taking anything for granted—especially those things which seem quite ordinary and trivial on the surface.

- Make a list of everything you did between getting up and coming to school today. See how many things you can remember no matter how insignificant they may seem.

- Go through your list and circle every fourth item.

- For each circled item make another brainstorm list of the following:
    - the sound of it
    - the sight of it
    - the smell of it
    - the touch of it
    - the taste of it
    - the feelings/emotions of it
    - the thoughts of it

■ Now, choose one of these and write a paragraph about it as if it were the most important, most significant thing that ever has, and ever will happen to you in your entire life. If you need help getting started, try the following:

"There I was minding my own business, getting ready for school, when suddenly...."

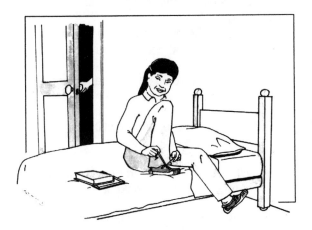

[NOTE: A clue some have found helpful is to use rich, full, sensory-based images from the brainstorm you did above, escalating these to cosmic proportions!]

■ Once you have gotten the hang of it, take a couple of other items from your list and try it again.

■ Conclude the exercise by sharing some of your paragraphs with each other. Write some reflections on what you learned from the exercise.

Reflection on "Calvin and Hobbes" Practice

After doing this practice many people feel like "scales have fallen from their eyes." One man said, "I'm surrounded by a miracle everyday and until now I've been missing it!" Through a practice like this we can experience the power of words to transform the ordinary and familiar into a place of revelation and insight. Yes, it is possible to break the mechanical routines and automated response patterns of our lives. It is possible to approach each moment of each day with a sense of expectancy, wonder, and astonishment.

Ideas for continuing this practice on a daily basis could include:

☐ Create imaginary conversations with different people that catch your attention during the day. Ask them the strange and wonderful questions you would if you had the guts to.

☐ A couple of times during the day, when you remember, STOP and list all the things going on in that moment of which you were not conscious, for example, sounds, smells, thoughts, feelings, tastes. Then continue what you were doing, trying to be more aware of these things.

☐ Try keeping a log of your experiences from day to day. When you "log in" an experience, also list the sound, sight, smell, touch, and taste of it as well as inner feelings, emotions, and thoughts.

☐ At the end of a week, make a list of 10 to 15 distinct events that happened to you in the past week. Arrange these in chronological order and write a "Once upon a time. . ." story about the week.

ractice

Ex Nihilo

The next practice works with the immense creative potentials embodied in our verbal/linguistic knowing. The reality of language allows us to create *ex nihilo*—literally, **out of nothing**. With words, we can create worlds that did not exist before. We can invent extraordinary solutions to ordinary problems that often overwhelm us. And we can talk to ourselves about the variety of perspectives and options facing us when making a difficult decision.

This practice was a favorite of my high school speech teacher. It's great for fostering creativity with language and speaking. Give it a try and see what it can "spark" in your students!

■ Open a dictionary, close your eyes and, in a purely random fashion, put your finger down on the page.

■ Open your eyes and focus on the word to which your finger is pointing. Spend a few minutes familiarizing yourself with the word you have chosen—its correct pronunciation, its meaning(s), and how to use it properly in speech.

■ The word that you have chosen is the topic for a 3-minute persuasive speech. You have 2 minutes for preparation. The speech is to have an introduction, three main points, an illustration or example, and a conclusion.

■ At the end of the speech, you will teach the word, including its pronunciation, meaning(s), and use to the class.

■ Now think of three different upcoming situations in which you could use the word and inject it into conversation.

■ Another "impromptu" speaking exercise would be to have a paper bag filled with a variety of objects. A student reaches into the bag and gets an object and then must make a speech on its usefulness to humanity addressing the following points:

- What if the object were 50 times larger than it is, what could it be used for?

- What if it were 50 times smaller than it is, what could you use it for?

- What if you reversed two of its parts, what could you do with it then?

- What is one improvement you can think of for the object to make it more useful?

- What person(s) would most benefit from this object and why?

You may simply want to do one of these impromptu speeches two or three times a week to keep students on their toes. It might be interesting to have students share what happens when they inject the words into other situations and what they discover happening to their creative verbal/linguistic abilities as they work with this kind of activity. The practice could also be done in smaller groups, allowing more people to participate at a time.

Reflection on Ex Nihilo Practice

Verbal/linguistic capacities involve mostly left-brain hemisphere processes which tend to be more linear, rational, and time-bound than those of the right hemisphere. Therefore, a practice which presents spontaneous and impromptu demands on the left brain, and which asks it to go beyond its usual way of thinking and processing information, causes a great deal of electrochemical activity in the "language organ" of the brain.

This charge can cause creative leaps in thinking as new connections with old information are made, most of which would have never happened without the outside stimulus or provocation of the exercise. In addition to these benefits, it will likewise increase your vocabulary and ability to "think on your feet," thus beginning the weaving of a more complex and flexible linguistic circuitry in the brain.

Ways you could continue to work with this practice every day include:

□ Take the opposite position in a discussion from the one you believe, or outline a defense for something with which you strongly disagree, such as a religious belief, a political viewpoint, or a policy at work.

□ When you are talking with someone and they make a suggestion, practice spontaneously saying (or think about saying) "That's a good idea because. . .!" Do this no matter how outrageous you think their suggestion is.

□ Oliver Wendell Holmes used to require of himself ten impossible thoughts before breakfast each day! Why not try something like this?

□ Get into the habit of making three visionary statements to different people each day, ones that will provoke thinking about the future.

 **Practice**

Journal Writing

The last practice in this section involves the use of language to express inner states of being, feelings, profound thoughts, meaning-full experience, and spiritual insight. There are many experiences that happen to us that are difficult, if not impossible, to put into words. And yet, throughout the ages, men and women have found themselves driven to articulate the inarticulable. In his spiritual classic *Saviors of God*, Nikos Kazantzakis poetically speaks of this experience:

> Ah! Let us gaze intently on this lightning flash, let us hold it for a moment, let us arrange it into human speech.
>
> You shall never be able to establish in words that you live in ecstasy. But struggle unceasingly to establish it in words. Battle with myths, with comparisons, with allegories, with rare and common words, with exclamations, and rhymes, to embody it in flesh, to transfix it!
>
> But it cannot be contained in the twenty-six letters of an alphabet which we string out in rows. . . .[10]

One of the best ways to improve your ability to give full-bodied, juicy verbal expression to your experience is to begin the practice of journal-writing or keeping a reflection log.

Following is a suggested structure for helping students begin a journal or reflection log. Why not give it a try it for three or four weeks and see what happens?

■ To get started, each student will need a loose-leaf notebook with four dividers. In the notebook, behind each divider, place 10 sheets of paper. Label the dividers as follows: Daily Log, Weekly Log, Stepping Stones, and Future Thoughts. Following are suggestions on how to use each section of the notebook.

■ *Daily Log*—At the end of each day write down three things that happened today you want to remember, three things you've been thinking about, and three difficult things about the day. Give the day a name like the title of a novel, TV show, or a song.

■ *Weekly Log*—Sometime on Saturday or Sunday reflect on the past week. Turn the page sideways and draw a line from left to right about one-third of the way down. Divide it into seven sections and label each with a day of the week, starting with Monday, and write in the name you gave each day.

- Now look back at your Daily Log for this week and write down the most important items from each day's entry beneath the line and under the appropriate days.

- Look at the chart you are creating and divide it into two parts. Create a title for each part that communicates what this week was like for you. Then create a title for the whole week: "The great week of...."

■ *Stepping Stones*—This section is for writing about some of the important things that have happened to you, making you who you

are today. These are like stepping stones that got you from there to here!

- When you have a little extra time, look back over your life and brainstorm a list of some key events that have shaped you. For example, an important book you read or a movie that had an impact on your thinking, the death of a close relative, a favorite pet, an especially memorable family trip, etc. Arrange these in approximate chronological order.

- For each event (or stepping stone) write a couple of sentences stating why and/or how that is an important part of who you are.

■ *Future Thoughts*—This section of your notebook is for creative thinking and dreaming about tomorrow, whether tomorrow is next month, next year, or into the next century. Don't worry if things in this section make sense to others. In fact they don't even have to make sense to you! Write in a "stream of consciousness" fashion, letting random thoughts and ideas naturally emerge. Here are several "pump primers" to help you get started on this section:

- When thinking about the future I'm worried about. . . .

- As I think about the 1990s, what if. . . ?

- Wouldn't it be neat if in the future we could. . . ?

- Some ways I think my grandchildren's life will be different from mine are. . . .

Obviously, we have only scratched the surface of the possibilities here. There are many extensions possible even in the simple structure above. For example, you might consider doing a "stepping stone" reflection related to a weekly log: "What have been the stepping stones of this week?" Or you could organize your "future thoughts" reflections by time and create a chart of them like the weekly log in which you project titles for your future life. Really, the only limits to this activity are the limits of your imagination!

Reflection on Journal Writing Practice

It is important that whatever you do with journal writing or the reflection log that you keep it simple, interesting, and fun. I would suggest that you try keeping a journal or log for at least a month and that you write in it a minimum of every other day (obviously daily would be better). Adapt the suggestions above to what is appropriate for you. Create new categories and sections for your notebook. Be creative. There is no right or wrong way to do this. Make it yours—adapt it to what you need and want. An excellent resource for more ideas as well as a more systematic and in-depth journal-keeping process is Ira Progoff's book, *At a Journal Workshop*.

Further suggestions for "journaling" could include such things as:

☐ When you are facing an important decision, pretend each side of the decision is a person and that they are having a conversation about the decision and its possible outcomes. Record this dialogue and let it inform you as you consider what to do.

☐ After viewing a movie, a piece of art, or hearing a musical piece that moved you, spend time debriefing yourself by writing your reflections: What affected you? What were your feelings? Why or in what way was it important to you? Create a name for this experience. Pretend the movie, art, etc. is a person and have an imaginary dialogue with it.

☐ Use a "stepping stone" log to help you analyze such things as your past and present

career path, the life journey and phases of your family, accomplishments and future directions of an organization or club to which you belong, etc.

Teaching and Learning with Verbal/Linguistic Intelligence

So far we have learned various techniques and exercises for awakening verbal/linguistic intelligence and making it ready to work for us. We have likewise participated in a number of practices for strengthening the verbal/linguistic capacities we all possess. In the next section we will work with verbal/linguistic capacities in learning and teaching content-based information. In that these capacities are the foundation for all our education and are the basis for many, if not all, aspects of our daily lives, it may seem strange to present a lesson emphasizing verbal/linguistic capacities. However, the lesson will focus on language as an endless storehouse of creativity. Francis Bacon made the following observation in his essay "Of Studies" from *Century Readings in the English Essay*:

> Reading maketh a full man; conference a ready man; and writing an exact man. And therefore if a man write little, he had need have a great memory; if he confer little, he had need have a present wit; and if he read little, he had need have much cunning to see to know that he doth not.[11]

Story Grid for Creative Writing

The following lesson utilizes a technique developed by the writers of the *Lone Ranger* show. How would you keep the ideas flowing if you had to write a new show every week of every year for over two decades?

This is a language arts lesson which emphasizes creative writing. It utilizes a technique called a "story grid" adapted from *Catch Them Thinking* by James Bellanca and Robin Fogarty.

■ On the blackboard draw a grid like the one below.

■ Now ask students to brainstorm the roles of anyone they would call a *Hero*. For example, doctor, lawyer, Indian chief. Then have them brainstorm *Heroines* and *Villains*. Write these roles on the grid.

■ Brainstorm possible *Conflicts* such as a fist fight, duel, or shouting match, and possible *Settings* for a story such as the OK corral, the West Coast, or the playground.

■ Finally, list possible *Endings* such as "lived happily ever after" or "rode off into the sunset."

■ Choose one student to give the last six digits of his/her phone number.

■ On your story grid circle one item for each column that corresponds to these six numbers.

■ Assign students to groups of four with the following roles: recorder (takes notes), encourager (motivates group), organizer (leads and keeps time), reporter (reports to class). Each group is to write a story outline for a TV show which links the circled items on the grid in a single story. Anything goes!

■ When they are finished, have one person from each group tell their story outline to the rest of the class.

Hero	Heroine	Villain	Conflict	Setting	Ending

■ Have the students reflect on the use of the story grid:

- What struck you about this exercise? What was it like?

- What was fun? What was difficult? What was surprising? Why?

- What other ways could we use the story grid in our schoolwork?

- How could you use the story grid idea outside of school?

There are many obvious extensions possible for this lesson. Students could actually "flesh out" the full story they have outlined, either in the groups or as individuals. You could also have individuals use their own phone numbers and choose other items on the grid for an individual creative writing/thinking lesson. And of course, you could change the top categories so they are appropriate for different subject areas.

Reflection on the Story Grid Lesson

Along with various impromptu activities, this lesson is one of the best for improving creative writing and/or speaking skills. By forcing relationships between previously unrelated things and having to create a coherence among them, new patterns of thinking are introduced into the brain, and with them a flexibility and willingness to "take a sideways glance at life" emerges. Contemporary brain research in the area of creativity has destroyed the old myth that some people are born more creative than others. What the actual case seems to be is that creativity is a skill that can be learned, just like roller skating, cooking, driving a car, and playing a musical instrument. All it takes is continued practice!

Suggestions for other ways of working with the creative potentials of verbal/ linguistic intelligence in content-based lessons include:

☐ Have students individually start writing a story. Then have them stop and pass the story to the person sitting next to them. This person continues the story until you have them stop and pass the story to someone next to them.

☐ In history, when you are studying any situation in which there were two sides to an issue, such as the American and British perspectives on the struggle for independence, have students engage in cognitive debate taking both sides of the argument.

☐ Regularly involve students in impromptu speaking and writing activities related to different content areas that you teach, or to various aspects of a single content area.

☐ Have students write a sequel to a lesson they have just done, such as a sequel to a story in English, a sequel to a story problem in math, or have them write what things would have been like had the British won in 1776.

Transferring Verbal/ Linguistic Intelligence to Life

Some linguistic researchers today are suggesting that language is the vehicle of cultural transmission *par excellence*. Yet it is the primary mode of our communication with each other. However, language is not only a means of communication. Hidden within its structure (its grammar, semantics, syntax, phonetics, and pragmatic usage), are many layers of people's understanding about themselves and the world in which they live. Language also subtly embodies a culture's values, philosophy, social structure, and modalities of thinking. For example, the complexity of some Oriental languages involve completely different grammatical structures for saying the same thing to a child, someone who is your peer, your subordinate, or to someone who is your superior. Charles Laird comments on this in *The Miracle of Language*:

> Language is. . .the most important tool that man ever devised. Man is sometimes described as a tool-using animal; language is his basic tool. It is the tools more than any other with which he makes his living, makes his home, makes his life. As man becomes more and more a social community, communication grows ever more imperative. And language is the basis of communication. Language is also the instrument with which we think, and thinking is the rarest and most needed commodity in the world.[12]

The irony of language is that we create it, then it turns right around and creates us! It shapes our perception of self, others, and the world. It can offend, entertain, excite, and depress us. It can motivate us to great achievement. It can inspire spiritual commitment and national loyalty. It can express love for another person, bigotry, prejudice, hatred, and religious devotion or worship.

The following transfer strategy works with a practice called affirmation. It builds on the power of words to bring about profound change in our lives.

Transfer Strategy

Affirming Emerging Potentials

The power of verbal images in the mind for shaping the reality of our lives has fascinated humankind for many centuries. These images include beliefs, values, and attitudes we have about ourselves, others, and the world. Since the dawn of self-reflective consciousness, people have known that the content of their minds shapes the content of their lives and the world around them.

The focus of this exercise is taking charge of these images and, in a sense, self-programming your mind to be in alignment with what you want for yourself and your world.

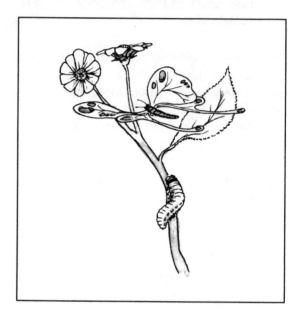

Contacting Your Latent Vision

- On a blank sheet of paper make a list of 5 to 10 things (including relationships, beliefs, possessions, events, attitudes, etc.) in your life at the present moment that you do not like, for whatever reasons.

- On a second sheet of blank paper make a list of 5 to 10 things (including relationships, beliefs, possessions, events, attitudes, etc.) in your life at the present moment that please you immensely, for whatever reasons.

- For each item on the second list, make a brief note to yourself on what pleases you about that item, or what is present in these that you like and want for your life.

- On a third sheet of blank paper, transform each item on the first list into something you would like to have in your life (i.e., if the item is something you don't want, then what do you want?).

- Now, in some very creative and satisfying manner, destroy the first list. *[NOTE: In doing this you are sending an important message to your unconscious regarding desired new directions in your life!]*

Creating Affirmations of the Possible

- Looking at your third sheet of paper where you transformed the "do-not-wants" into "wants," choose one item that you find particularly interesting or "on target" for you at this point in your life.

- Write this item at the top of a fourth sheet of paper and list several places in your life where you have even the slightest hint of movement happening in this new direction.

- Close your eyes for a moment and try to picture or imagine this newness you desire as completely as you can. See if you can get a sense of what it would be like to have exactly what you want.

- Now, create a statement which affirms this newness, or in some way claims its promise, as if it were already fully present in your life today. Keep working with this statement of affirmation until it feels right to you (i.e. until you could look at yourself in the mirror, say the affirmation, and not laugh).

Working with your Affirmation

- Begin to work with and use the affirmation you have created in the following way:

  - Close your eyes and repeat the affirmation several times, imagining the new reality to which it points as fully as you can.
  - Breathe deeply, experiencing with each breath this new reality coming into your cells, your brain and thought processes, into your actions, and into your style.
  - Keep repeating the affirmation, sensing it in every dimension of your life you can think of that seems appropriate to you at this time.

- As it seems right, create other ways of affirming (i.e. of giving positive encouragement and attention to what you want in your life). Here are some suggestions to help you get started:

  - Turn it into a "once upon a time. . ." story.
  - Find a trusted friend and verbalize it.
  - Try to dream about it.
  - Write a poem about it.
  - Write an essay about it.
  - Try writing the script for a very short play or drama about it.

For maximum benefit in this exercise, repeat the process with several different items on your list, beginning with the easier ones to affirm and moving to the more difficult when you're ready. Carefully watch what effect working with your affirmation has on you and record these observations.

Reflection on Emerging Potentials Strategy

Working with verbal affirmation sets in motion a very powerful process of communicating with unconscious parts of the mind. Part of the affirmation obviously occurs on the conscious level; namely, its creation and the decision to use it. However, as you experiment more and more with affirmations you may find subtle changes in perception, creative insights, feelings, behavior patterns, and a greater sense of freedom emerging. When we participate in actively and consciously affirming those things we want in our lives, giving them attention and positive energy, often the unconscious will release many of its old, familiar patterns and risk moving in new directions.

Answers to multiple intelligences crossword puzzle

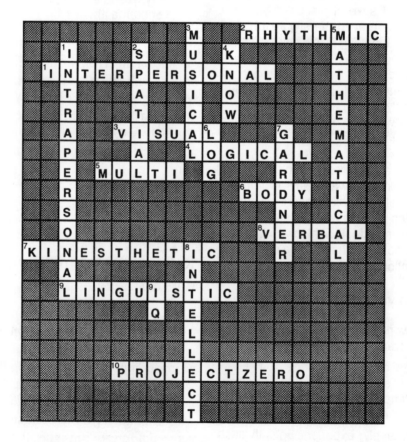

Personal Reflection Log
Verbal/Linguistic Intelligence

Observations made—what happened?

_____

_____

_____

Emotional/feeling states:

_____

_____

_____

Reflections, insights & discoveries:

_____

_____

_____

Self-evaluation (comfort zone/skill ability):

├ ─ ─ ─ ─ ─ ─ ─ ─ ─ ─ ─ ─ ─ ─ ─ ─ ─ ─ ─ ┤

Like a fish in water   Like landing on another planet

Practical strategies for fully activating/developing this intelligence within myself:

_____

_____

_____

Application ideas for my classroom, family, community, or organization:

_____

_____

_____

Chapter 2

As Easy as 1, 2, 3

Explorations of Logical/Mathematical Intelligence

Like a painter or a poet, a mathematician is a maker of patterns; but the special characteristics of mathematical patterns are that they are more likely to be permanent because they are made with ideas.

—Howard Gardner, *Frames of Mind*

Problem: How many angels can dance on the head of a pin?

Problem: Is the world really flat?

Problem: Which came first, the chicken or the egg?

Problem: If $x = y$ and $y = z$ what is x?

Problem: What are the origins of the universe?

Problem: Is there intelligent life beyond the earth?

The human mind is a natural problem-solver. All you have to do to see this in operation is to pose a problem which the mind grasps as a real problem needing to be solved. It will automatically "kick into gear," so to speak, almost like a high-tech computer and begin searching for answers. Whether it be a problem like balancing your checkbook, combining the right ingredients to bake a cake, finding a cure for cancer, or placing a human being on the moon, the love for solving problems and for making possible that which is impossible seems to be at the heart of "what makes us tick" as a species!

Fascination with our thinking patterns and problem-solving processes is at the center of the modern "thinking skills" movement in education. Dr. Barry Beyer, a key figure in this movement, advocates the explicit teaching of thinking skills and problem solving as the most important things a teacher can give students to prepare them for effective living in the future. In *Catch Them*

Thinking, James Bellanca and Robin Fogarty make the following statement about teaching thinking:

> As the research on cognition indicates, cognitive processing is one of the most important learning tools a student possesses. It is not enough to absorb information. The student must take time to make meaning from the facts and figures. In a hurry-up society full of mad hatters running around shouting 'I'm late, I'm late for a very important date,' students are more ready to adapt to the expectation for speed. How easy it is to get the message that a slow response is a dumb response![13]

At its most abstract level, problem solving can be reduced to the pure abstraction of the mathematician, the symbolic language of the philosophical logician, or the scientist's fascination for the universal patterns in nature. At its most practical and applied level, you find people counting their change at the supermarket checkout counter, measuring a piece of wood to make a bookshelf, or keeping score at a football game.

What are some of the dimensions and capacities related to our logical/ mathematical intelligence?

The following exercises provide a glimpse of some of the capacities connected with logical/ mathematical intelligence. They illustrate many of our patterns for thinking and problem solving. Give them a try and see if you can get a sense of this intelligence within yourself.

Abstract Pattern Recognition

There may be nothing that delights the mind more than seeking and discovering patterns and designs. This can range from visual patterns such as those in nature, patterns for thinking, mathematical patterns, word patterns in poetry, learning a foreign language, deciphering a code, and finding patterns in human-made objects.

This exercise provides an illustration of how the mind works with patterns. Give it a try. Then create several of your own that are more "in tune" with your own logical thinking/reasoning habits.

■ Look at the following number for 30 seconds and try to memorize it.

$$1,492,162,017,761,929,196,319,902,000$$

■ Now without looking at the number, see if you can accurately write it from memory.

■ Check yourself and try again if you didn't succeed.

■ If I reveal to you that the numbers are arranged in a special pattern of important dates in American history, can you improve your performance?

[1492-Columbus discovers the "New World," 1620-Mayflower Compact, 1776-Declaration of Independence, 1929-Stock Market crash , 1963-assassination of JFK, 1990-the present decade, 2000-the end of the 20th century]

Inductive Reasoning

Inductive thinking moves from particular examples to generalizations that include all of the particulars but is greater than any one of them. This is the way a TV detective works when trying to figure out who committed the murder or who stole the jewels (e.g. *Sherlock Holmes, Perry Mason*). It is a matter of finding the clues and then piecing them together to tell a larger, more complete story. This kind of thinking is most often used when you are trying to solve a problem for which you really do not have an answer, such as where to go for your summer vacation, how to afford a much-needed home improvement, or thinking through the qualifications necessary for a mate.

In this exercise see if you can figure out the answer to the problem using the clues in the following conversation and in the picture below.

■ The sales clerk, named Matilda, approached the nicely dressed customer and asked "May I help you find something?"

■ "Oh yes, I'd like to see today's special sale item," she replied, pointing to a sign by the cash register.

■ Matilda turned to look. "Oh, I'm sorry. The sign's all wrong now," she said with a smile. "The sale item you want was on sale three days ago. And what the sign says was on sale yesterday will actually be on sale tomorrow. Today's special sale item is shoes."

■ See if you can tell from this conversation and the picture on what day of the week the customer was in the shop (see end of chapter for answer).

Deductive Reasoning

Deductive thinking starts with a general rule and then tries to fit particular examples and situations into the general rule. This is the way TV

Special Daily Sales
only $24.95

Monday – Hand Bag
Tuesday – Shoes
Wednesday – Scarf & Gloves
Thursday – Jewelry
Friday – Beauty Aids

150,647

detective works when they know who committed the crime and is trying to prove it. They look for inconsistencies in behavior, alibi, personality patterns, etc. There is no question of "Who done it?" It is simply a matter of filling in the details. We most often use this kind of thinking when we get a bank statement informing us there is much less in our checking account than we thought and we go back through our checkbook to figure out what happened!

This exercise works with the thinking skill of applying a generalization to specific data. It also helps students learn how to classify using pre-set categories.

■ Brainstorm a list of at least 30 key changes that have happened during the 20th century. These can be from any area of life, both individual and social.

■ Now go through your list and mark each item with the symbol of the category in which it fits the best: 0—*economic changes*, X—*political changes*, Δ—*education changes*, √—*life style changes*, and *—*religious changes*.

■ Create a chart with five columns and label each with one of the categories. Relist the data under the appropriate column.

■ Write a summary statement for each column which starts "During the 20th century, the key *(category name)* changes that have happened are. . . ."

■ Read your statements and reflect on what you have learned by using these five categories. What are other general categories that you could apply to the list?

Exercise

Discerning Relationships and Connections

The mind is a natural pattern seeker. This capacity allows us to see relationships and connections between often disparate pieces of data or information. We can find strange and intriguing connections between things that normally would have no relationship, but when forced together they make perfect sense. This is a creative thinking process developed by Edward de Bono called "lateral thinking." Lateral thinking encourages the interaction of new and different ideas with old and familiar ones. Judgment is deferred and the thinker is asked to look at things in novel or unexpected ways. The following exercises present two adaptations of this lateral thinking approach.

The first exercise works with the thinking skill of "forcing relationships" (adapted from *Catch Them Thinking* by James Bellanca and Robin Fogarty). Making creative leaps in your thinking is the rule!

■ List at least three answers for each of the following questions:
- How is a TV like a snowflake?
- How is a table like a glove?
- How is a bird like a light bulb?
- How is a house like a flower?
- How is a book like a shoe?

The second exercise is a set of "mind-stretchers." Have fun and *sssstttttrrrrreeeettttcccchhhh* your thinking!

■ Each of the following diagrams represents a popular saying or phrase. Can you figure them out? Can you break the code? (See end of chapter for solutions.)

R|E|A|D|I|N|G	OHOLENE	<u>KNEE</u> LIGHT
R O ROAD D	**AGES**	Ø M.D. Ph.D. B.A.
DUMP DUMP DUMP DUMP DUMP DUMP GOOSE FEATHERS	<u>EZ</u> iiiiiiiiiii	TIME TIME

Exercise

Performing Complex Calculations

This capacity is at the heart of all problem-solving, be it numerical calculation or calculations using factors such as the environment, people, or situational variables. Generally, this capacity employs a series of small, relatively simple operations that are linked together in patterns to solve more complex problems. The ability to understand these smaller steps and bring them to bear on an appropriate problem is no mean feat! Strange as it may seem, this calculating, problem-solving process is "turned on" irrespective of the correct answer, simply by trying to tackle a problem that is presented to the mind.

This exercise includes a series of story problems. As you work on them notice the different smaller mathematical and thinking processes you bring to bear (answers at end of chapter).

- Sandra studied a Midwestern suburb in which 800 women lived. Three percent of them were wearing a watch. Of the other 97 percent, half were wearing both a watch and a bracelet and half were wearing neither a watch nor a bracelet. How many watches all together are being worn by the women?

- An amateur chemist discovered that a certain chemical reaction took 80 minutes when she wore a wool jacket. However, when she was not wearing the jacket, the same reaction always took an hour and 20 minutes. Explain.

- A man and woman were making a series of bets on what the weather would be on the weekend. On Monday morning the man counted up his winnings. At $1 per bet, the woman owed the man one times two times three times four times five times six times seven times eight times nine times zero dollars. How much did the man win?

- "I guarantee," said Jody to David, "that this mynah bird will repeat every word it hears." So David bought the bird from Jody, but found it would not speak a word. Nevertheless, Jody told the truth. Can you explain?

xercise

Scientific Reasoning

Of all of our logical thinking patterns, the so-called "scientific method" is the most empirically based. Its inferences, deductions, predictions, and sometimes wild ideas rely exclusively on the five senses. Some philosophers have even called it "gross knowledge" for it seems so obvious. However, the mystery of scientific reasoning is what happens in the space between objective observation and the interpretation of what has been observed, whether it be a sophisticated laboratory experiment or a simple observation of a natural phenomenon. Scientists themselves often talk about the "intuitive leap" that occurs between laboratory results and the "therefore what this means . . ." theories and hypotheses they create.

For the following exercise you will need at least two teams of two people each. You will be involved in a game of making inferences and drawing conclusions from a collection of objective facts. It is based on a lesson in *Catch Them Thinking* by James Bellanca and Robin Fogarty.

- Each team is to invent a new society, one that is quite different than our own. Brainstorm ideas for various things that every society must have to operate but adapt them to the society your team is inventing. Use the following to help you get started:

  - economic life (self-sustenance, means of production and distribution, means of exchange)
  - political life (organizing patterns such as laws, systems of justice, and ensuring the general welfare of the people)
  - cultural life (education, family life, the arts, social roles, religion, symbols)

- After you have finished your brainstorm, write a one-paragraph description of the society, mentioning its key distinguishing elements or features.

- After completing your brainstorm and paragraph, decide on six key artifacts from your society that you will put into a time capsule so that future generations can learn what your society was like. Take six index cards and *on each* explain and draw *one* artifact that in some way represents the society you have created. Make sure you include at least one economic, one political, and one cultural artifact.

- Now put these into the time capsule (envelope), seal it, and pass it to the other team.

- Pretend that you are living in a time many decades from today and that you have suddenly discovered a time capsule from the past. Open the envelope and look at the artifacts that have been left for you.

- Play detective now. Treat each artifact as a clue to the kind of society from which it came. Take notes on your intuitions and ideas about what the society must have been like.

- Look at your notes and write a one-paragraph description of the society you believe produced these kinds of artifacts.

- When you have finished, ask the other team for its description of the society it invented. Read the description and compare it with your team's conclusions.

LOGICAL/ MATHEMATICAL INTELLIGENCE AND THE BRAIN

The logical/mathematical capacities that you have just experienced represent an intriguing mix of *left- and right-brain* hemisphere processes. On the one hand, the ability to read and produce mathematical signs and symbols is a left-hemisphere processing mode, not unlike what happens when dealing with the phenomenon of language, including reading, writing, and speaking. On the other hand, the ability to understand numerical relationships, to discern abstract patterns, and to comprehend logical/ mathematical concepts and formulas is a right-hemisphere processing mode, not unlike what happens when an artist is in the midst of an act of creation.

So how do we begin to understand our logical/ mathematical intelligence? Let us first consider the kinds of knowing that are available to us through these capacities. In his book *Eye to Eye*, Ken Wilber discusses three classical ways of attaining knowledge in which we humans participate:

Men and women have at least three modes of attaining knowledge—three eyes. . . the *eye of flesh*, by which we perceive the external world of space, time, and objects; the *eye of reason*, by which we attain a knowledge of philosophy, logic, and the mind itself; and the *eye of contemplation*, by which we rise to the a knowledge of transcendent spiritual realities.[14]

Logical/mathematical intelligence is the knowing related to the "eye of flesh" and the "eye of reason." The "eye of contemplation" will be discussed when we look at intrapersonal intelligence. The eye of flesh is the world of shared sensory experience and is shared by all those possessing a similar way of sensing. As Wilber points out:

> Humans can even share this realm, to some degree, with other higher animals (especially mammals) because the eyes of flesh are quite similar. If a human holds a piece of meat in front of a dog, the dog will respond—a rock or plant will not . . .This is basic sensorimotor intelligence—object constancy—the eye of flesh. It is the *empirical eye*, the eye of sensory experience.[15]

The eye of flesh is therefore primarily the realm of science.

When we turn to the eye of reason we enter the world of ideas, logic, and concepts. The eye of reason (or the mental eye) cannot be reduced to the eye of flesh, for the eye of reason often transcends sensory experiences, thus Wilber calls it "transempirical."

This is often true in the realm of logic. The truth of a logical deduction is based on the internal consistency of the deduction, NOT on its relationship to external, sense objects. The eye of reason is, obviously, the realm of logic and mathematics.

On the one hand the **practice of science** is concerned with building models that will eventually explain the operation of the world in such areas as the physical world (physics and chemistry), the world of living things (biology), human beings (sociology and psychology), and the world of the mind and how it functions (the cognitive sciences). On the other hand, the **practice of logic and mathematics** is interested in the exploration of abstract systems, such as the investigation of patterns of order, harmony, balance, and finding or creating abstract and symbolic relationships between things. As the quote at the beginning of the chapter suggests, the pure mathematician is a maker of patterns. As such, both the mathematician and logician love the sheer beauty of pattern for its own sake, whether or not there is any practical use for it!

In *Frames of Mind*, Howard Gardner describes the friendly tension that exists between scientists and mathematicians:

> The desire to explain nature, rather than to create a consistent, abstract world, engenders an instructive tension between pure scientists and pure mathematicians. The mathematician may peer down his nose at scientists for being practical, applied, insufficiently interested in the pursuit of ideas for their own sake. The scientist, in turn, may feel that the mathematician is out of touch with reality and tends to pursue ideas forever even when

(or perhaps especially when) they do not lead anywhere and may not be of practical consequence.[16]

In spite of these comments, scientists often rely heavily on the work of logic and mathematics as a tool to help order the chaos that results from trying to figure out how the whole universe works. Therefore, the sections that follow will deal with these capabilities as a whole. Let us now turn to the task of awakening, amplifying, and teaching logical/mathematical intelligence.

Awakening Logical/ Mathematical Intelligence

The exercises at the beginning of the chapter provide a point of reference for getting in touch with your logical/mathematical intelligence. In general, logical/mathematical intelligence is awakened when the mind is presented with a problem that it feels needs to be solved. Problems can range from fixing a piece of machinery that is broken, to baking a cake for someone's birthday, to an algebra worksheet assigned by a teacher, to conducting a scientific experiment, to understanding the natural laws of the universe! The impact of this problem-solving intelligence on the 20th-century world is astonishing. There is no part of the world that has not been radically altered by the scientific/technological revolution, which represents logical/mathematical intelligence applied to the "nth" degree. However, these very changes then double back on logical/ mathematical intelligence and shape its further development. In *The Global Mind Change*, Willis Harman comments on this as follows:

> Every knowledge system is shaped by the characteristics of the society that produces it. We are accustomed to considering the flow in the opposite direction, seeing how scientific and technological advances have shaped modern society. But it is of critical importance

to recognize both flows. We have the kind of society we have in part because of the fruits of science and technology. But the converse is also true: We have the kind of science we have in part because of the particular nature of the society in which it was developed.[17]

Amplifying Logical/ Mathematical Intelligence

Once you have awakened this problem-solving, pattern-seeking intelligence as a way of knowing, you can start working to further expand and strengthen it, and to develop and/or refine its "knowing skills," along with your own ability to trust and understand its wisdom.

According to Howard Gardner, logical/mathematical intelligence can be traced to our early experiences with the physical world of objects and things. However, a great mystery unfolds from this point onward with the development of our capacities for high-level abstraction and symbolism. Gardner explains this as follows:

> It is in confronting objects, in ordering and reordering them, and in assessing their quantity, that the young child gains his or her initial and most fundamental knowledge about the logical-mathematical realm. From this preliminary point, logical-mathematical intelligence rapidly becomes remote from the world of material objects. . . .Over the course of development, one proceeds from the realm of the sensori-motor to the realm of pure abstraction—ultimately, to the heights of logic and science.[18]

Logical/mathematical intelligence was the primary focus of much of Jean Piaget's important research on human development. He suggests that the first encounter we have with logical/ mathematical intelligence is through manipulation of objects in the nursery. Very quickly the first abstraction emerges, namely numbers. From that point on, logical/mathematical intelligence moves to greater and greater levels of abstraction, and it becomes more and more interiorized, separated from its original contact with the physical world.

Following are three practices you can use to nurture and strengthen logical/mathematical skills. They deal with different aspects of this intelligence including arranging and discerning patterns, and developing both inductive and deductive patterns for thinking. We can train ourselves to be more skillful in using this way of knowing.

BET What Will Happen Next

The first practice is primarily an inductive reasoning exercise that works with strengthening predicting skills based on available pieces of information. It is an adaptation of a predicting exercise from *Patterns for Thinking—Patterns for Transfer*, by Robin Fogarty and James Bellanca. Predicting is the skill of anticipating what will occur with high degrees of success. Ready? OK, look into your crystal ball!

■ Select a short story with which students are not familiar and one which has some genuine human interest to it. Divide it into four parts. At the end of each part, insert phrases similar to the following:

"BET what will happen next. Why do you think so? Find data to support. Read to verify."

■ Photocopy the divided story for the students. Cut it apart into four sections.

■ Present the following "mental menu" for helping students learn a thinking pattern for their predicting:

*B*ase on facts.
*E*xamine clues for probabilities and possibilities.
*T*ender your bet and make a guess.

■ Distribute the first section of the story. Have them read the story and BET what will happen next. After all have had time to BET, distribute the second section of the story, and continue as above until the entire story is finished.

■ After reading all four parts of the story have them go back and evaluate their predicting: How did you do? Go back to the story and look for facts and/or clues in the early part of the story that you missed.

■ Have students make a list of five situations in which they might use BET, both in and out of school.

[NOTE: See a sample story blackline of "The Captive" at the end of this chapter (see answer to "The Captive" at end of the chapter text).[19]

Reflection on BET Practice

Our patterns for thinking can be compared to habit patterns we have developed in other parts of our lives. Some of these are helpful to us, while others are not. In our cognitive life, we have frequently developed sloppy, lazy, and imprecise thinking patterns. That is, patterns that do not get us the results we desire. They can change, however, once we are aware of them. The use of "mental menus" like **BET** can help us learn new, effective patterns for thinking which can replace old ineffective ones, such as wild guessing, when doing predicting. An excellent resource for more mental menus is *Teach Them Thinking* by Robin Fogarty and James Bellanca.

Ideas for other inductive activities you can incorporate into your daily routine could include:

☐ When you arrive at work, observe such things as people's moods, how they are dressed, the weather, the schedule of the day, the work load, etc. and then make some predictions on what kind of day you think it will be. Evaluate your accuracy at its conclusion.

☐ When sitting in a meeting, carefully watch others' behavior and reactions to what is happening in the meeting. See if you can predict its outcome.

☐ In the midst of a discussion with another person or persons, practice listening to all of the pieces of the conversation/discussion and then make statements which paraphrase, summarize, and honor all of the specifics of the discussion.

ractice

Comprehensiveness Screen

Inductive thinking/reasoning patterns tend to start with observing various factors in a given situation and then making generalizations based on things that have been observed time and time again (as in the previous exercise). Deductive thinking/reasoning patterns, on the other hand, start with generalizations and then seek ways to apply them to specific factors or particular situations.

Following is a deductive thinking practice to help you get a rational picture of some of the issues/concerns that shape your life. It's called a "Comprehensiveness Screen." It is a way to classify or analyze some of your concerns. Give it a try and see what happens!

■ Begin by brainstorming two to three answers to each of the following questions. Jot down the first things that come into your mind.

- What are your biggest concerns about the future?
- What concerns/issues keep you awake at night?
- About what issues do you tend to "get on a soap box"?
- What do you feel we must solve before the turn of the century?
- What concerns/issues do you think about when there's nothing else on your mind?
- What *specific* topics do you like to read about in books, magazines, and newspapers?
- What confuses you most these days?

■ The comprehensiveness screen is a way to help you see and keep the "big picture" before you. Using the categories on the screen below, reorganize the items on your brainstorm into the various boxes. Move rapidly and trust your first impressions on where something should go.

Inclusive concerns— historical concerns; not something new every day.	**Intellectual reflections—** things you're trying to figure out, searching for clues.
Concrete planning— models you feel must be created as soon as possible.	**Intruding issues—** unavoidable concerns, like a rock through the window.
Low-key ponderings— things you're undecided about but you're watching and waiting.	**Internal broodings—** areas in which you're preparing for the future like a hen sitting on her eggs.

Reflection on Comprehensiveness Screen Practice

The practice is an example of comparing something against a standard, namely the categories of the comprehensiveness screen. This pattern of thinking is very prevalent in our society. All around us pre-established standards or generalizations measure degrees of success; for example, performance standards in the workplace, achievement standards in the classroom, safety standards which must be met when constructing a new building, and standards of health, cleanli-

ness, and quality in the food industry. One important thing to remember in this area is that the standards or generalizations themselves were created by human beings just like you. Therefore, they can be changed as needed! However, skill in applying pre-established standards and generalizations to specific information, data, and situations is a key skill for effective living in these times.

Following are some ideas for continuing to work with and develop the more deductive thinking patterns in your everyday life.

□ Read the newspaper or a magazine and mentally sort what is there into different general categories such as economics, politics, education, lifestyle, and religion.

□ Think of the different personality types that people often manifest. Then during the day see if you can "peg" another's personality type as you encounter them in different situations, for example, intuitive, aggressive, concrete/rational, creative.

□ Make a list of your favorite sayings, quotes, or adages. Choose one of them and see how many examples of its truth you can find throughout the day. Try a different one each day for a week.

Time Line of the Day

The final practice in this section employs a technique for discerning patterns in ordinary experience and beginning to interpret their meaning and significance. Very often we fail to come up with creative ideas simply because we don't look at things from enough differing perspectives. When we are forced to look for and make interpretations of things, we often see things we have never seen before and find new solutions to problems we are facing.

This practice is excellent for reflecting on and bringing closure to a day or a week. It can help you gain new understandings about the patterns of your daily life. Try it daily for at least two weeks and see what happens.

■ Think back over the day you have just completed. Below the time line on the following page, list as many things as you can remember that happened to you during the day. Include such things as conversations with people, important thoughts, things that caused you happiness, sadness, frustration, etc., and things you read and ate. Try to write them at the approximate time they occurred along the time line.

■ Now, look at all of the things you have written and see what patterns you notice. Divide the day into two to three parts by drawing vertical lines from the chart at the appropriate places through the area called *Sections*.

■ In the Sections area, make up a title or name for each section of your day represented by these divisions. [*NOTE: Use the information under the line to help you come up with titles for the divisions.*]

■ Now in the top part of the chart, create a title for the whole day. This was "*The great day of . . . .*"

Reflection on Time Line of the Day Practice

One participant in a workshop, after doing this practice, commented that she did not realize that her life was the "stuff from which epic stories could be written." When we approach our lives from the perspective that "there are no coincidences" or that "everything is meaningful," we suddenly rediscover a profound significance in the ordinary, mundane aspects of our lives. However, once again, the ability to do this is a thinking pattern that must be learned and developed—especially in light of the fact that most of us are trapped in the syndromes of, "If only . . ." or "Wouldn't it be nice if . . . ?" What might be possible and what could happen if we found ways to appropriate and celebrate the significance of now?

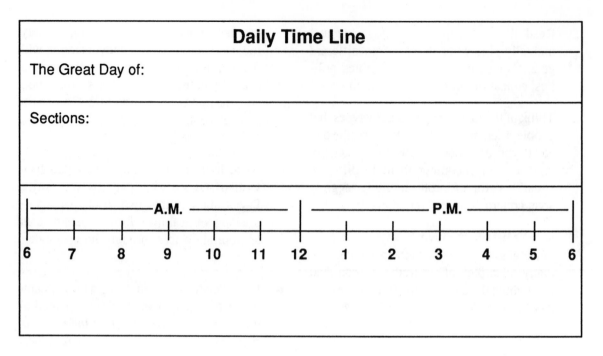

Daily Time Line

The Great Day of:

Sections:

| 6 7 8 9 10 11 12 — A.M. | 1 2 3 4 5 6 — P.M. |

Other ways you could use the charting method in your everyday life might include such things as:

- Try charting a short article you've read. Number the paragraphs. Look for key words or phrases in each paragraph. Group paragraphs together that are dealing with similar topics or ideas then give these groupings a name. Finally, make up your own title for the article.

- If you have charted each day in the week, create a chart of the week. Make seven divisions and write the name you created for each day in its appropriate place. Then list the most important events from the week and divide the week into two parts. Name each part and create a title for the week.

- Create a chart which shows the stages and/or steps of a project that you are about to undertake, such as building a bookcase for your home, preparing an elegant dinner for friends, or getting ready to go on a vacation.

Teaching and Learning with Logical/Mathematical Intelligence

In the first stage of experimenting with logical/ mathematical intelligence we have attempted to "trigger" this intelligence in the brain, thus awakening it from a state of dormancy. Second, we have tried exercises and practices for making ourselves more familiar with this intelligence as well as improving and strengthening our skill in using it. We now move to the active use of logical/mathematical capacities for learning and teaching content-based information. The lesson will focus on teaching several thinking skills through a reading lesson. In *Patterns for Thinking—Patterns for Transfer*, Robin Fogarty and James Bellanca make the following statement about teaching thinking:

> A thinking skill is just that—a skill— and like any skill it requires explicit instruction to fully develop the inherent intellectual talent. To introduce an explicit thinking skill, the skill itself becomes the focus of the lesson. The content used to develop the lesson is

merely a vehicle to present the skill. That content should be familiar to the students. **Once the skill has been taught explicitly, it can be applied with new content as students interact to process the material.**[20] (emphasis mine)

The most effective way to teach students the conscious use of their logical/ mathematical intelligence in the classroom is through cognitive (or graphic) organizers. **Cognitive organizers** are visual aids that help students order and pattern their thinking in ways that are both logical and that promote higher-order reasoning in daily classroom lessons. Cognitive organizers employ an intriguing blend of inductive and deductive thinking modes, while at the same time teaching students a specific thinking skill. When applied to a variety of content areas to various thinking skills, connected to a given cognitive organizer are, can be easily internalized by students. Most teachers have found that it is generally best to teach the students how to use a particular cognitive organizer in a non-academic or "familiar content" lesson before applying it to a "new content" lesson.

The following lesson utilizes four different cognitive organizers. In using the lesson with your students, depending on the thinking skills already present and the amount of time you have, you will most likely want to use just one organizer at a time.

Lesson

Reading Comprehension Using Cognitive Organizers

This is a language arts lesson in reading comprehension and thinking. It utilizes cognitive organizers to help students understand and think about the story they have read. Each organizer can be a separate lesson as you choose.

SUPPLIES: Newsprint, marking pens, copy of the story, and cognitive organizers. *[NOTE: Copy blacklines "Through the Looking Glass" and "Cognitive Organizers" which are at end of chapter].*

■ Place the students into groups of three or four.

■ Begin the lesson by reading the passage from *Through the Looking Glass*, by Lewis Carroll, to the students.

■ Pass out one copy of the story and the cognitive organizers sheet to each team and briefly explain how they are to use the organizers as follows:

New Title:										
Section Divisions:										
1	2	3	4	5	6	7	8	9	10	11

Charting format (comprehension, pattern, and meaning). Begin by numbering the paragraphs of the passage. Then on a piece of newsprint turned sideways, draw a line one-third of the way down and divide it into the same number of sections as paragraphs (in this case 11). In each paragraph section on the chart write key words which remind you of what the paragraph is about. Look at the chart and decide where to divide the chart into two parts. Draw a vertical line on the chart at that point. Make up a title that tells what is happening in these two parts of the story and write it in the area called "Section Divisions." Finally, create a title for the whole story. If you had written it, what would you call it?

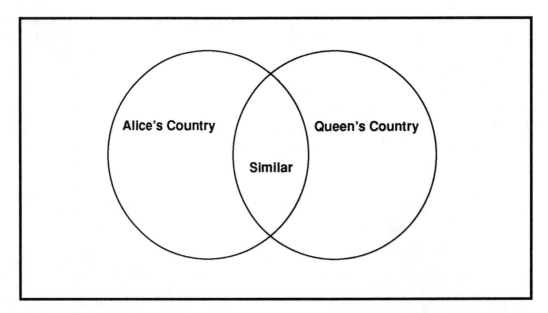

Venn diagram (compare and contrast). Draw the Venn diagram on a piece of newsprint with a marking pen. Label the two over-lapping circles, calling one Alice's Country and the other the Queen's Country. Label the parts of the circles which overlap Similar. Go back through the story and write down things that describe how Alice's country is different from the Queen's and how the Queen's country is different from Alice's. In the center, write down things that are similar or the same in both countries. *[NOTE: You may have to do some inferring based on what the passage tells you.]*

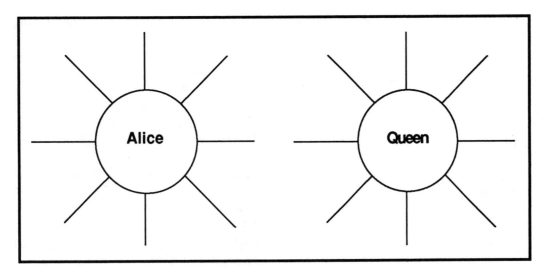

Attribute web (*defining key character attributes*). Draw two webs on a piece of newsprint. Go through the story and list key character qualities of Alice on one web and of the Queen on the other. [*NOTE: You may have to do some inferring based on what the passage tells you.*]

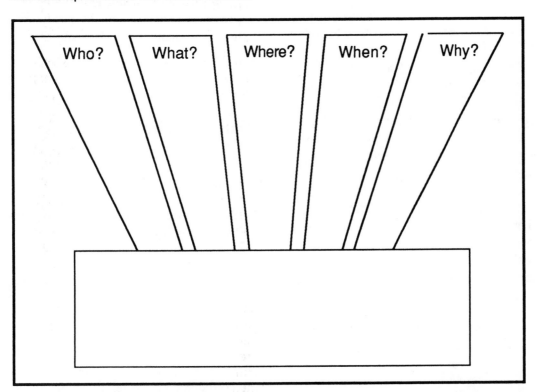

Who? What? Where? When? Why?

The 5 Ws (*predicting outcomes*). Draw the 5 Ws format on a piece of newsprint. Your task is to write the next part of the story. What do you think will happen next? For each question discuss and agree with your team on WHO are the characters in the next part, WHAT action happens, WHERE it takes place, WHEN it occurs, and WHY whatever action occurs. In the box under the 5Ws write the new story.

■ After students have completed working with each cognitive organizer, discuss and evaluate their work in the following manner:

- What did you notice about working with these different formats?
- What did you like? Why? What did you not like? Why?
- What did you learn about your own thinking?
- How could you make it better?
- Where else in our classroom work could we use these?
- Where could you use these outside the classroom?

Reflection on Reading Comprehension Lesson

This lesson, as presented here, is obviously one that should be used over several days. Nevertheless, it is instructive to see how one piece of content can be used to teach so much. In fact, the lesson only scratches the surface of what is possible with this story. It could also have been used to teach a wide range of other logical/mathematical thinking skills such as classifying, prioritizing, problem-solving, sequencing, etc. In some ways, all thinking skills are parasites. That is, they need a content-base to operate. In and of themselves they are contentless and process-based. Given the temporality of all knowledge today, it may be that the most important things we can teach students are how to learn, how to think, and how to process information, regardless of specific content.

Here are some suggestions for continued use of logical/mathematical capacities in and through daily lessons:

☐ Teach students a variety of note-taking techniques such as outlining, diagraming (like diagraming a sentence), or concept-mapping.

☐ Give students a pre-set screen of things to look for or listen to when watching a film, reading material from a book, or listening to a lecture.

☐ Have students gather articles from newspapers and magazines which fit into specific categories related to a particular unit.

☐ Conduct creative thinking activities where there is no "right answer," such as brainstorming, inventing, transforming one thing into another, forcing relationships, etc. After any of these, stop and look for the logical thinking patterns that were present.

☐ Consciously work with different approaches to problem-solving. First of all, teach them a "skillful problem-solving" model. Then apply it to an academic lesson, something in the classroom or school that needs problem-solving attention, or to a situation in the larger society.

Transferring Logical/ Mathematical Intelligence to Life

Let me share two further comments from Howard Gardner regarding the nature and dynamics of logical/mathematical intelligence. With these comments we return to the realm of the mathematician and the realm of the scientist. First the mathematician:

What excites mathematicians? One obvious source of delight attends the solution of a problem that has long been considered insoluble. Inventing a new field of mathematics, discovering an element in the foundation of mathematics, or finding links between otherwise alien fields of mathematics are certainly other rewards.

In fact, the ability not merely to discover an analogy, but to find an analogy between kinds of analogies, has been singled out as an especial mathematical delight.[21]

And now for the scientist:

Just what is the nature of the intuitions that characterize outstanding scientists, ones the caliber of a Newton and an Einstein? Beginning with an absorbing interest in the objects of the world and how they operate, these individuals eventually enter into a search for a limited set of rules or principles which can help to explain the behavior of objects. The greatest progress is made when disparate elements are linked and a few simple rules can explain observed interactions.[22]

In the final exercise you will have an opportunity to be both mathematician and scientist. You will be asked to think about your life's journey to the present moment and to briefly anticipate the future. You will have a chance to utilize several of the techniques in the previous exercises in a more complex, integrated fashion.

Transfer Strategy

Exploring the Stages of Your Life

Each of our lives has been a fascinating mosaic of events, struggles, periods we've gone through, etc. In fact, the real-life dramas that we have lived and continue to live, make television soap operas look odorless and pale (once you strip away all the contrived sensationalism). And yet,

how in touch are we with the fantastic voyages we have taken? How aware are we of the epic and cosmic proportions of our existence? Do we really believe that our lives contain material for novels every bit as compelling as the lives about which Clavell and Mitchner write? The final exercise in this chapter helps you begin to consider your life from this perspective.

■ Turn to the blackline titled "Life Events Brainstorm/Journey Stages" at the end of this chapter. In the first column, begin listing the key events, happenings, and turning points you can remember in your life up until the present moment. List them in a purely random fashion. Work quickly, writing down whatever pops into your mind. Don't screen out anything. Try to think of a minimum of 25 events. Consider things related to such areas as:

- pets that have been in your life
- movies you have seen/books you have read that have influenced you
- best friends, favorite foods, plants, toys, family vacations
- music and songs that have been important in your life
- favorite colors, smells, and tastes and your associations with them
- powerful encounters with nature or natural events like death, illness, and birth
- humorous happenings and moments of great joy and ecstasy
- school teachers and important educational events

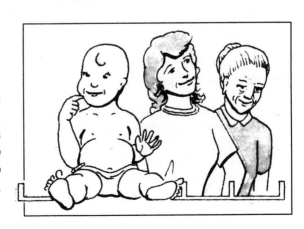

- Now go through your list noting the approximate year and/or age you were for each event. If there are some that occurred over a number of years, note this as well.

- Decide into how many time periods or stages you could divide your life. In the second column relist the events of your life from the first column as clusters under the various symbols in this column, using one symbol for each period or stage upon which you've decided. Don't worry about being too precise here. Let your intuitions be your guide. Assign each item on your list to a stage or period based on the approximate year(s) when it occurred. For each of the symbols in this column, note the years it encompasses. [*Note: You may not need to use all of the symbols in the second column.*]

- Turn to the blackline titled "Story of My Life's Journey" at the end of this chapter. Begin by dividing the line called *Years* into sections which correspond to the number of Life Journey Stages you had in the second column of the "Life's Events Brainstorm/Journey Stages" blackline. Draw these divisions as vertical lines from the Years line to the bottom of the page. Write the encompassing years for each division on the time line.

- Now, for each stage, work with the side categories of the time line:

  - *Section Title.* Create a name for each stage of your life's journey.
  - *External Situation.* Relist the most important factors from your brainstormed list of life journey stages.
  - *Inner Experience.* Describe the emotions and feelings of each stage.
  - *Motivating Factors.* What was the "driving force" of each period?

- After you have completed your work below the Years line, move to the space immediately above it. If you were going to divide your life into two parts, where would you make the division? Draw it on the chart

and create a title for each part that summarizes what that time of your life's journey was for you.

- Finally, on the top line, create an overall title for your life up to the present moment.

- Now, considering the time line of the stages of your life's journey, create the table of contents for the epic story that this chart represents. Be creative. Make chapter titles that have a certain grand marquee nature to them—like titles of movies, TV shows, or novels—something that you think would make others really want to see the show or read the book about this life!

- Pause for a few minutes of reflection on what has happened as you did this:

  - What really catches your attention as you look at the chart?
  - What was surprising? exciting? challenging? fun? difficult?
  - What did you learn about yourself from the exercise?
  - Looking at your life's journey to date, what do you anticipate is in store for you in the next stage(s) of your journey?
  - What other things would you like to do with this exercise?

Reflection on the Stages of Life Strategy

An old adage comes to mind at this point: "The unexamined life is not worth living." Many people, who have done this exercise in workshop situations, talk about its healing impact in giving them a new story about the past and a "new set of eyes" through which to approach the future. From the perspective of this exercise, there are no mistakes in our past journey, for **everything** that happened to us (both positive and negative) has brought us to the present moment of opportunity. The exercise presupposes that the present is good. It also asks us to face the future with the knowledge that it is a chapter yet to be written and what is more, we are its primary author!

Answer to "Today's Special Sale" exercise: Thursday.

Some possible answers to "Mind Stretchers": (from upper left to right)

reading between the lines
hole in one
neon light
crossroads
dark ages
three degrees below zero
down in the dumps
easy on the eyes
time after time

Answers to "story problems":

412
1 hour and 20 minutes = 80 minutes
nothing
David can't talk **or** the bird can't hear

Answer to "Bet What Will Happen Next" exercise with "The Captive": the prisoner is a lion; the prison is a zoo.

The Captive

I haven't slept in days, maybe in weeks. My waking hours are spent pacing up and down this 12-by-12-foot chamber of horrors. Why couldn't they have just killed me, put a bullet in my head? But no, for the rest of my life I have nothing but four walls and barred windows to look forward to.

It's a nightmare. I've tried to understand it, but I can't. What have I done, what laws have I broken to warrant this solitary confinement?

It seems so very long ago that I was happy. Certainly we had problems, maybe more than most, but she stood by me all the way. Then came the baby and more problems, but we were in love and would have overcome all obstacles.

BET: What will happen next? Who is this? Where is he? Explain and tell why.

Then it happened, I was out for a walk as was my custom after dinner. The sun was shining on my face and the wind was blowing through my hair. I was tired. I'd had a long, hard day and shortly would return home for a leisurely evening with my family. The events that followed are even now vague in my memory.

Suddenly I felt a piercing pain in my side, and I began to run. I didn't know why I was so afraid, but I knew that I was running for my life. Finally, I could run no more. I fell on my face and lay there. Soon there were men holding guns all around me. They were looking down at me. Everything went black.

BET: What will happen next? Who is this? What happened? Explain and tell why.

The next month was spent moving from place to place. People were yelling at me, pointing at me, accusing me. There were times I thought I was completely insane, that everything happening around me was a nightmare.

I have murdered no one, so why am I here? I have stolen nothing. To the best of my ability I have obeyed the laws, yet for reasons I do not understand, I am to spend the rest of my life in a prison. What have I done?

When I was young I heard about places like this—stories told late at night in whispered voices about the cold, damp dungeons and whip-wielding monsters that inhabit them.

It was common knowledge, the older ones said, that maggot-infested horse meat was the only food given to the captives—and that, only once a week—and dry bread soaked in sewer water. For the crime of even making a sound, one could be stabbed through the bars with long spears, leaving not fatal wounds, but deep slashes of painfully exposed flesh. If only I had known the truth, which is so much worse.

BET: What will happen next? Who is this? Where is he? Explain.

I am never allowed to leave this room and can communicate with no one. I can hear my fellow prisoners on both sides, but I cannot talk to them. They both speak different languages. The guards ignore me and what little communication they have between themselves is also in a foreign tongue.

All day long people are coming and going past my cell. They do not come in. They just stand outside, look at me, then leave. They speak the same language as the guards. In the beginning, I tried to get them to understand me, but like those whom I first came in contact with, they were deaf to my pleas. So now I am quiet. Somehow I know that I have been sentenced to remain here for the rest of my life, and I don't know why.

They have even robbed me of my name. All my life I have been known as Iflan. Even though I can't understand their language, I have picked up two rather unimportant facts. Through the repeated use by my guards and the constant daily spectators, I have learned the name of my prison and the new name I have been given.

BET: What is the name of the prisoner? What is the name of the prison? Explain your ideas.

[*Patterns for Thinking—Patterns for Transfer*, (1989). Fogarty & Bellanca.]

SKYLIGHT PUBLISHING, INC.

SEVEN WAYS OF KNOWING

EXCERPT FROM

THROUGH THE LOOKING GLASS

by Lewis Carroll

Alice never could quite make out, in thinking it over afterward, how it was that they began: all she remembers is that they were running hand in hand, and the Queen went so fast that it was all she could do to keep up with her: and still the Queen kept crying "Faster! Faster!" but Alice felt she could not go faster, though she had no breath left to say so.

The most curious part of the thing was that the trees and the other things around them never changed their places at all; however fast they went, they never seemed to pass anything. "I wonder if all the things move along with us?" thought poor puzzled Alice. And the Queen seemed to guess her thoughts, for she cried, "Faster! Don't try to talk!"

Not that Alice had any idea of doing that. She felt as if she would never be able to talk again, she was getting so much out of breath; and still the Queen cried "Faster! Faster!" and dragged her along. "Are we nearly there?" Alice managed to pant out at last.

"Nearly there!" the Queen repeated. "Why, we passed it ten minutes ago! Faster!" And they ran on for a time in silence, with the wind whistling in Alice's ears, and almost blowing her hair off her head, she fancied.

"Now! Now!" cried the Queen. "Faster! Faster!" And they went so fast that at last they seemed to skim through the air, hardly touching the ground with their feet, till suddenly, just as Alice was getting quite exhausted, they stopped, and she found herself sitting on the ground breathless and giddy.

The Queen propped her up against a tree, and said kindly, "You may rest a little now."

Alice looked around her in great surprise. "Why do I believe we've been under this tree the whole time? Everything's just as it was!"

"Of course it is," said the Queen. "What would you have it?"

"Well, in our country," said Alice, still panting a little, "you'd generally get to somewhere else—if you ran very fast for a long time, as we've been doing."

"A slow sort of country!" said the Queen. "Now here, you see, it takes all the running you can do, to keep in the same place. If you want to get somewhere else, you must run at least twice as fast as that!"

"I'd rather not try, please!" said Alice. "I'm quite content to stay here."

SKYLIGHT
PUBLISHING, INC.

Cognitive Organizers

Learning Patterns for Thinking

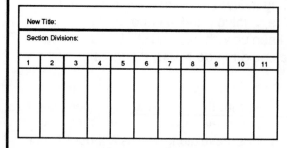

Article Chart
discerning relationships/
understanding content

Attribute Web
describing characteristics
or attributes of something

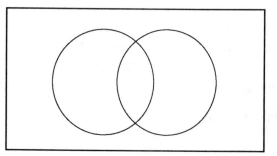

VENN Diagram
comparing likeness and
contrasting differences

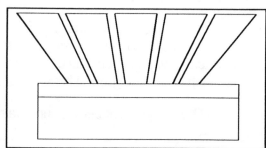

5W Model
analyzing who, what, when,
where, and why

[*Patterns for Thinking—Patterns for Transfer*, (1989). Fogarty & Bellanca.]

SKYLIGHT
PUBLISHING, INC.

Life Events Brainstorm	Life Journey Stages
	● (years:)
	✖ (years:)
	▲ (years:)
	❖ (years:)
	☆ (years:)

SKYLIGHT PUBLISHING, INC.

Story of My Life's Journey

MAJOR JOURNEY THEMES

Title

Years	Birth			Present
Section Title Make up a title that names/summarizes this period of your life journey.				
External Situation List things that happened, people who influenced you, events that had an impact, ideas, books, movies, etc.				
Inner Experience Describe feelings, thoughts, struggles, breakthroughs, anxieties symbols, key decisions you made, etc.				
Motivating Factors What were the major inner forces motivating you? What was really important/ meaningful to you?				

SKYLIGHT PUBLISHING, INC.

Personal Reflection Log
Logical/Mathematical Intelligence

Observations made—what happened?

_____

_____

_____

Emotional/feeling states:

_____

_____

_____

Reflections, insights & discoveries:

_____

_____

_____

Self-evaluation (comfort zone/skill ability):

|——————————————————————————————|

Like a fish in water   Like landing on another planet

Practical strategies for fully activating/developing this intelligence within myself:

_____

_____

_____

Application ideas for my classroom, family, community, or organization:

_____

_____

_____

Chapter 3

Seeing Is Believing... and Knowing!

Explorations of Visual/Spatial Intelligence

The image is. . . a way of knowing about the world that is older and more global than language and verbal symbolism.—Willis Harman & Howard Rheingold, *Higher Creativity*

 In the beginning—before words, language, abstract reasoning, cognitive patterning, and conceptual thinking—were images. The human brain naturally thinks in images. In fact, its capacity to form images or to visualize is one of its most basic mental processes. In the Preface of the classic on visualization, *Seeing with the Mind's Eye* by Nancy and Mike Samuels the following statement is made:

> The human mind is a slide projector with an infinite number of slides in its library, an instant retrieval system and an endlessly cross-referenced subject catalogue . . . Visualization is the way

we think . . . The human brain programs and self-programs through its images. Riding a bicycle, driving a car, learning to read, baking a cake, playing golf—all skills are acquired through the image-making process.[23]

Just what are images, and how do they function in our lives?

☐ Images are interior road maps that help us make sense out of life.

☐ They are often unconscious but they control our conscious behavior.

☐ They comprise our pictures of ourself and our world.

□ They are an inner guidance system that tells us who we are.

□ And they give us direction in deciding what to do with our lives.

Images are formed and shaped by every experience we have had. And these images in turn shape both our present and future experience!

What are some of the dimensions and capacities related to our visual/spatial intelligence?

Following are a series of exercises that illustrate the capacities with which researchers work when trying to understand visual/spatial intelligence. Choose several and give them a try with students. See if you and they can get a sense of this intelligence within yourselves.

Active Imagination

The ability to discover pictures, shapes, and designs is something we used to do as children when we would lie on our backs, look at the clouds and find people, fantastic creatures, and magical places to visit. The mind loves patterns, colors, and designs for their own sake. It can also create visual relationships and intuitive connections which transform apparent chaos and confusion into a place of creativity and imagination.

Following is another version of "finding things in the clouds." Give it a try and see what you can find.

■ Take a blank sheet of paper and a pen or pencil. Create a scribble that covers the whole page.

■ Now, looking at the scribble, see what pictures, shapes, and designs you can find (just like you used to when looking at the clouds).

■ Using colored pens, crayons, or markers outline and/or color the pictures, shapes, and designs that are most interesting to you.

■ Pause for a moment and reflect on what happened to you as you did this. How do you feel? What are your observations?

Forming Mental Images

One of the capacities involved in our visual/spatial knowing is being able to form mental images/pictures of experiences and to manipulate or transform those pictures, even when the so-called "external" and "objective" stimuli are no longer present. Our active imagination is so powerful that we can even create images that have no corresponding reference in the so-called "real world." It is said that Albert Einstein first

grasped the theory of relativity while imagining he was riding a sunbeam, traveling the speed of light!

Let your imagination play for a few minutes and try the following:

- In your mind's eye, as vividly as you can, imagine a red balloon.

- Now put the balloon on the ceiling. Put it on the floor. Bounce it off the wall.

- Change the size of the balloon so it is much larger than before. Now make it much smaller.

- Change the color of the balloon to green, then yellow, then blue. Now make it black and white striped. Now make the balloon your favorite color.

- Change its size so that it can take you for a ride. Now get on the balloon. Where is it taking you? What are you seeing? What are your feelings?

- Now return, put the balloon away and get back to serious work.

- Reflect upon your experience.
    - What was this like?
    - What happened?
    - What surprised you?

Finding Your Way in Space

Visual/spatial intelligence capacities also involve the ability to find your way around a given location, including being able to get from one place to another. This spatial potential, which we all have, can be seen most vividly in persons who have lost their sight and yet are able to find their way around, sometimes with greater accuracy, confidence, and skill than sighted people! Likewise, one cannot help but marvel at the Pulwat peoples in the Caroline Islands who are able to sail boats on the open ocean with no compasses, maps, or electronic guidance systems. They rely on the stars and the patterns of the waves in the ocean to tell them where they are.

This exercise is excellent for exercising the spatial part of visual/spatial intelligence. Go ahead and try it!

- Sometime, when you are away from your home, see if you can draw a map of your house that includes the positioning of all furniture and appliances. Check your spatial accuracy when you get home and make corrections on your map as needed.

■ Now blindfold yourself. Visualize your map in your mind's eye and begin walking around your house. See how well you can find your way around and how well you can sense where different objects are. Try this for at least 15 minutes.

■ As further extension of the above, have a trusted friend lead you around outside with your eyes closed. See if you can tell where you are. Notice what happens to your other senses when you inhibit the sense of sight.

■ Pause and note your observations and reflections.

Image Manipulations

What we see is often determined by how we look at it. In the first two pictures below, the ability to see two things in one picture and to shift back and forth between them at will illustrates one of the most intriguing perceptual capacities we have. In the third picture, we can experience the ability to create visual illusions of perspective, depth, and movement on a one-plane, static surface.

The objects below represent several "gestalt shift" visual illusions. Work with each until you can easily make them visually shift back and forth.

■ Look at the following box and see if you can make the "front" of the box change places with it's "back" side so the back becomes the front.

Can you make the "back" change places with the "front?" Now shift them back and forth at will.

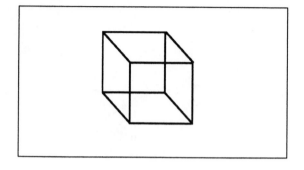

■ Look at the ink smear below. What do you see?

See if you can find the face of a man in the ink smear. Now try to make it only an ink smear again. Then back to the face.

■ Gaze intently at the following spiral and see if you can create a visual sense of movement in the pattern.

Now make it stand still. And then make it move once again.

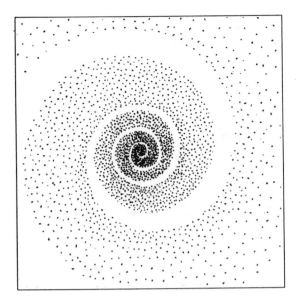

■ On a blank piece of paper, draw a likeness of yourself. Make it a full-body, front-view picture sketching in as much detail as you can. [NOTE: It's OK to do this in front of a mirror if that will help!]

■ On a second sheet of paper draw yourself from a side view, again full-body, including as many details as possible.

■ Now, imagine that you can look down on yourself from the ceiling. You are directly above yourself looking down. Try drawing yourself from this "bird's eye" perspective.

■ Finally, pretend that you are standing on a clear glass floor and that you can look up at yourself from under the floor. You are directly under your feet looking up. Now draw yourself from this "down under" view.

■ Place all four pictures side by side and see what strikes you.
  - What similarities do you see?
  - What are the major differences?

■ Reflect on what happened as you did this exercise.
  - What were your feelings?
  - What did you learn?

■ Reflect on your experience of experimenting with these optical illusions:
  - What did you notice? What was it like?
  - What did you learn about your visual/spatial capacities?

xercise

Graphic Representation

It has been said that a picture is worth a thousand words. So many things can only be expressed in graphic images. Have you ever tried to capture the beauty, power, and intensity of a sunset in words? Inner feelings and emotions are likewise often expressed best in symbolic form such as drawing, painting, or sculpture.

This exercise involves drawing. Its point is NOT whether you draw well or not. Its point IS to give you a chance to play with your visual/pictorial/graphic sensibilities. Come on, risk a bit!

xercise

Recognizing Relationships of Objects in Space

This capacity is generally highly developed in people who play any kind of sports. Being able to put a physical object precisely where you want it (such as a basketball through a hoop, a football through the goal posts, or a hockey puck into the net), and being able to strike a physical object in motion through space (such as hitting a baseball, making connection between a tennis racket and a tennis ball, or bouncing a soccer ball off your head) are at the heart of success in sports. However, less physical games such as chess, checkers, backgammon, and the old "pea and shell" game require acute spatial intelligence as well.

See if you can solve the following "spatial puzzles" (answers at end of chapter). Each requires skill in seeing relationships between objects in space. Give them a try (but don't get too frustrated—enjoy)!

■ This diagram is called "The Devil's Tuning Fork." Study it and see if you understand it. Can you explain it to someone else? Can you draw it?

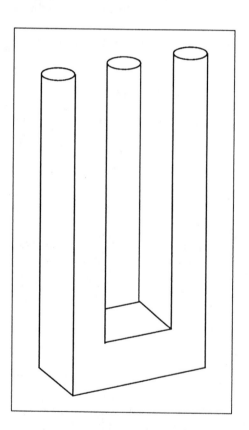

■ For the second puzzle, look at the design below and find a perfect star.

■ Begin this puzzle at either point "A" or "B." Try to trace the pathway to the opposite point.

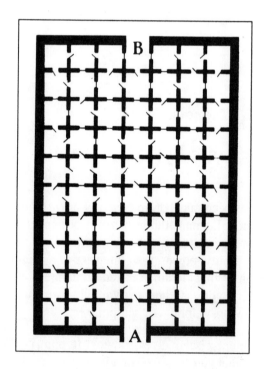

■ Pause for a moment now and reflect on what these were like for you. What are your observations about working with this dimension of your visual/spatial intelligence?

Accurate Perception from Different Angles

We take for granted the ability to recognize similarities and differences between objects, but an immensely complex process occurs in the brain when doing simple tasks. Likewise, when we are asked to view an object from different perspectives, we tap the power of our mind to form mental images. We are able to recognize an object or place as the same, even though the vantage point has totally changed.

Following are three visual/spatial tasks. See how quickly you can see what you're asked to see.

■ From the four objects on the right, choose the one that is identical to the target object (answers at end of chapter).

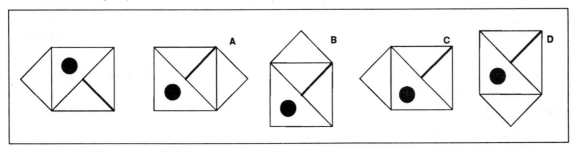

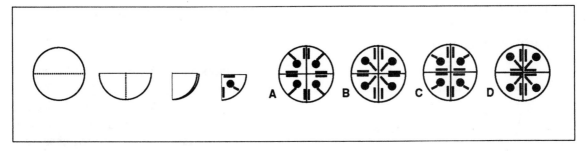

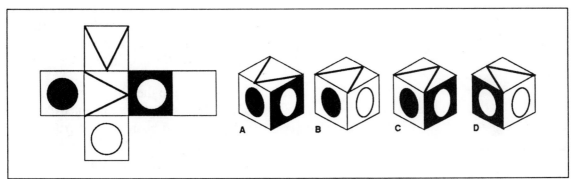

■ Spend a couple of minutes reflecting on what this was like for you. What did you notice happening to you? Was it easy? Hard? Why?

VISUAL/SPATIAL INTELLIGENCE AND THE BRAIN

Our visual/spatial capacities are mostly located in the right hemisphere of the brain in what is known as the "parietal lobes" (see illustration). When we were children our visual/spatial capacities were very acute. Such things as vivid daydreaming and the ability to pretend and imagine were second nature to us. Do you remember a time when you could make yourself invisible? What were some of the special magical powers you used to possess? Can you still remember when you were the hero/heroine in fabulous adventure stories of your own making? Too bad we are later taught that this kind of active imagination is "only for children!" In his book *Creative Visualization*, Ronald Shone says:

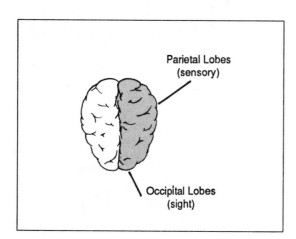

Parietal Lobes
(sensory)

Occipital Lobes
(sight)

Western dependence on reason has meant that we frown on such things as the imagination. Schooling develops reasoning powers and implicitly, if not explicitly, treats the imagination as unimportant. It is not surprising, therefore, that children very soon give up being imaginative. As this process continues the growing person finds it more and more difficult to form mental images, simply because this particular faculty goes unused. . . But remember, **imagination is inherent in the nervous system and as such it can be relearned.** [24] (emphasis mine)

This means that you can improve your visual/ spatial capacities for knowing. As with each of the intelligences, it involves a process of first awakening the intelligence, amplifying and strengthening it, training it to work for you in the process of learning and thinking, and finally transferring it into daily life as a regularly used tool for knowing and understanding your life and your world.

Awakening Visual/Spatial Intelligence

The exercises you tried above are excellent for awakening visual/spatial intelligence. In general visual/spatial intelligence is awakened and activated through the presentation of intriguing pattern, design, color, and texture to our sense of sight and touch. These can be presented externally to "the eye of the flesh" or internally to "the mind's eye." In *Seeing with the Mind's Eye*, Nancy and Mike Samuels state:

From the eye to the visual area [of the brain], the system functions much like a complex switch-board or a computer. . . It follows from this that all people need to experience is an image for the right neuronal pathways to fire. It does not matter whether they fire because of stimulation to the retina or other sense organs, or because of an internal stimulus.[25]

Researchers have found that many of the same physical aspects are present in mental imagery and seeing as with open-eye, "normal" perception. For example, a person's eye movements when dreaming correspond to the eye movements that would be present if the person were physically seeing what is in the dream. Also, when working with visualization or guided imagery exercises in which a person is imagining examining an object, the eye movements represent those that would be present if the object were physically present.

Amplifying Visual/Spatial Intelligence

In *Higher Creativity*, Dr. Willis Harman and Howard Rheingold discuss the relationship between visual/spatial capacities and creativity. They believe that if we learn how to more fully activate and use these capacities, we take a major step toward becoming more creative:

> Since the mind also operates by the process of inference, the mere creation of a mental image, similar to the real object, will cause it to react as if faced by the actuality.

> The image of an imagined object has mental effects that are in some ways very similar to the image of an object that is actually perceived. . . .If one is able to imagine something to be true, part of the mind appears to accept that imagined outcome as reality.[26]

Notice what happens if you actively and vividly imagine your favorite food sitting in front of you

instead of this book! Chances are saliva begins to flow, subtle swallowing movements begin in your esophagus, and your stomach starts churning getting ready to digest what you're imagining!

Once you have called your visual/spatial intelligence out of its state of sleep, the next task is strengthening, expanding, amplifying, and nurturing it. Below are several practices that you can use to begin this task. If you use them in a disciplined and consistent manner, new neurological connections will be made in your brain, and old memory connections related to this intelligence will be strengthened. Your visual/spatial capacities will get stronger and will work for you much more in your everyday life.

Thinking in images is very easy for some people and quite difficult or almost impossible for others. However, we can relearn this skill that was the dominant mode of thinking and knowing in our childhood. In *The Possible Human*, Jean Houston of the Foundation for Mind Research says:

> Imagery can be developed, however, in most non-imagizers, although this gets more difficult with age. It takes regular and devoted practice since **it literally involves an activation of latent electrochemical circuitry in the brain.**[27] (emphasis mine)

We can improve our ability to do internal visualization/imagining. This involves working with what researchers call "eidetic" images. These are the images/ pictures that remain in the brain immediately after looking at something.

Practice

Eidetic After-Images

The following practice is one of the best to help students improve their visualizing/imagining capacities. As they work with the practice over time, they will discover that it becomes easier and that they are having a much stronger "inner sense" of the images suggested.

■ Begin by staring at a burning candle or light bulb for a minute or so. Then close your eyes and try to continue to see the flame or the bright "after-images" of the light.

■ When you can no longer see it, open your eyes and stare at it again for another minute, then close your eyes again and see how long you can see the after-image. Try to increase the length of time you see the after-image each time.

■ Now try a variation on the above. Look at a small table, staring at it the same way you did with the candle or light bulb. Close your eyes, continuing to see the after-image of the table, but imagine that there is a polar bear sitting on it!

■ Keep working on this placing different things in the chair when you close your eyes. *[Note: It is often easier to elicit outrageous and unexpected imagery in the beginning, so remember this when placing things on the table.]*

■ Take a few moments and note your observations and reflections. Think about how you can integrate this practice into your life so you keep improving your imagination capacities each day.

Reflection on Eidetic After-Images Practice

Through regular and devoted practice you can improve your internal imagination capacities. As Jean Houston pointed out above, neurologically latent electro-chemical circuitry in the brain is being activated with these kinds of practices. The outrageous imagery helps the brain stay more engaged, plus it more fully charges the parietal lobes of the right brain.

Examples of how to use this daily could include such things as:

☐ Look at a blank computer screen, then close your eyes for a moment and see the after-image. Then imagine your favorite TV or movie star on the "inner screen."

☐ Look at a picture of someone you know well. Close your eyes and see the afterimage. Now imagine them as a very old person, as an infant, as a plant, and as an animal.

☐ Look at a picture from nature, such as a mountain scene, a beach, or a woods. Close your eyes and see the afterimage. Now place yourself in the picture doing something you would love to do.

Drawing a Concern for the Future

The following practice uses the ability to produce concrete/graphic representations of thoughts, feelings, ideas, and experiences that happen to us. These capacities are generally highly developed in such persons as artists, painters, sculptures, graphic designers, and photographers.

In this practice students have an opportunity to explore aspects of their life primarily through the visual/spatial mode. At first it may be difficult, but encourage them to stick with it, and try it several times. We can improve our visual/spatial intelligence simply by using it!

■ Begin by making a list of 5-10 concerns you have for the future (include concerns for your family, friends, school, church, and for a club or organization of which you're part).

■ Choose one of the concerns that you would like to explore and work with in this exercise. For the concern you have chosen, list several things that are of concern to you. What about this is concerning you? What are the questions it poses for you?

■ Now, with your eyes closed, consider the following images as they relate to your concern:
  - What is its color? its texture? its smell? its taste?
  - If the concern was a weather condition, what would it be?
  - What kind of background music does this concern need?
  - If the concern was an animal, what animal would it be?

■ Keeping your eyes closed, take a few deep breaths and relax for a minute.

■ Begin to visualize the concern in your mind's eye. Notice shapes, colors, objects, people, etc. that are associated with it.

■ When you are ready, and you feel you have a good visual sense of the concern, open your eyes and draw what you have seen and visualized internally. Work with colors. Allow things to naturally and intuitively happen. Don't try to plan your drawing. Just draw whatever comes to you in the moment.

■ When you have had ample time to complete your drawing, place it in front of you and study it intently for a few minutes. Ask yourself questions such as:
  - What objects, shapes, colors, and designs immediately grab my attention?
  - What surprises me? delights me? intrigues me?
  - As you gaze at the drawing, look for clues to help you deal with the concern that may be hidden in the picture.
  - What name/title would you give the drawing?

■ Find an appropriate place to post your drawing—some place where you will see it often. Continue to dialogue with the drawing and see what else it may reveal to you.

■ Finally, spend a few minutes reflecting on the exercise. Especially reflect on what you learned about using your visual/spatial intelligence as a way of knowing.

Reflection on Drawing Concerns Practice

Force yourself to work and express yourself using images, shapes, and designs is a key to strengthening the visual/spatial way of knowing. This can also be done using media like paints, clay, and collage (pictures/images cut from a magazine) such as in the "Transfer Strategy" at the end of this chapter. This is one of the quickest ways to access visual/spatial intelligence, even when it seems a little strange and isn't your normal mode. Remember you may not see interiorly with the same clarity that is present when you're watching TV. Many people only get an "inner sense" of what is being suggested. No problem! Go with it and see if you can make it stronger. An excellent ongoing practice would be to find a visual/spatial component to each day's work, learning, and knowing.

Examples of this could include such things as:

☐ Each time you have an insight or new thought during the day, create a visual symbol or picture which will somehow remind you of the insight.

☐ Imagine the colors and design patterns of your different feelings/moods during the day.

☐ Draw a picture of a problem you're facing. Then look at it and draw things that would solve the problem as it is represented in the picture. Does this give you any clues to solving the problem in real life?

A Visualization Practice

The following practice utilizes the mind's natural imagination/visualization process as well as its tendency to think in pictures that are more or less concrete. It builds on the previous practice of strengthening internal visualization skills and is a more complex active-imagination exercise.

This is a guided imagery/visualization practice in which students imagine that they are talking to a wise inner guide or teacher. *[NOTE: If you want to try this for yourself, you may want to record the instructions on an audio-cassette tape so that you can simply turn it on and be led in the process. If you do this, make sure you pause between each step so that you have time to imagine what is suggested.]*

■ Think about an issue or challenge you are now facing, one for which you need some answers. On a piece of paper, list several related questions on which you need some help.

■ Sit in a comfortable position so you can completely relax and focus your attention on the flow of your breath. Relax more and more with each breath.

■ When you feel ready, as vividly as you can, imagine that you are standing at the edge of a beautiful wooded area. Notice the colors, sounds, smells, and the feel of the breeze. (PAUSE)

■ Suddenly you notice a pathway into the woods. It looks inviting so you decide to follow it. (PAUSE)

■ As you walk deeper and deeper into the heart of the woods you come upon a clearing where there is an old one-room school house. You decide to enter it. What is it like? (PAUSE)

■ At the front of the classroom there is a person. You instinctively know this is one of your inner guides or teachers. The person invites you to the front to be seated. (PAUSE)

■ Now spend several moments imagining that you are talking with this teacher/guide, getting to know them. As you talk you realize this person knows a great deal about you. You realize this person has great wisdom and insight to share. (PAUSE)

■ Ask this wise teacher/guide one of the questions you listed earlier. Wait for an answer. Receive whatever he or she has to offer, knowing that there may be non-verbal communication as well—symbols, gestures, emotions, or feelings. (Jot brief notes to yourself if you wish.)

■ When you sense you have received what the teacher/guide has to offer on one question, ask another if it seems appropriate, again waiting and listening for whatever is given and jotting down notes on what he/she says if you want to.

■ After asking all of your questions, thank your teacher/guide and promise to visit again. (PAUSE)

■ When you are ready, leave the school room making your way back through the woods. (PAUSE)

■ As you reach the edge of the woods, where you began, stop and reflect for a moment on the journey. Then slowly return to the present space and time. Open your eyes and stretch.

■ Spend a few minutes debriefing yourself, writing down anything you remember from your journey—even if it doesn't make sense to you right now!

Reflection on Visualization Practice

Each person has their own way of imagining when doing an exercise like this. Some will imagine in full-blown technicolor and stereophonic sound, as vividly as if watching a movie or TV. Some may not "see" clear images at all, but have only a sense of shape, pattern, color, texture, or movement. Others may not even sense images, but simply have an inner feeling for what is suggested to the imagination. In any visualization practice the key to success is **whatever works for you.** There is no right way! If images suggested aren't working, **then cheat** and pretend they are working. Sooner or later they will. This kind of practice strengthens our capacity for creating complex mental images and for active imagination. We can teach ourselves to get better at this "inner seeing" if we keep practicing.

To continue practicing this way of knowing in everyday life:

☐ Imagine yourself giving a presentation before you do it, noticing such things as audience response, how you present yourself, questions they ask, and how you answer them.

☐ Visualize yourself handling a variety of difficult situations with great ease and success, such as a family issue or a problem in the workplace.

☐ Repeat the exercise above regularly with different kinds of teachers/guides, such as persons from the distant past or future, male and female teachers/guides, animals, and even mythological or fictional characters.

Teaching and Learning with Visual/Spatial Intelligence

In the first two stages of working with visual/spatial intelligence we have attempted to "trigger" this intelligence in the brain, thus awakening it from a state of dormancy. Second we have done various kinds of exercises and practices for making ourselves more familiar with this intelligence, as well as improving and strengthening our skill in using it. We now move to the active use of visual/spatial capacities for learning and teaching content-based information. This, however, is not something new or strange. Let us expand on the quote at the beginning of this chapter from Harman and Rheingold's *Higher Creativity*:

The image is also a way of knowing about the world that is older and more global than language and verbal symbolism. The oldest cave paintings are thought to date from the very period when *Homo sapiens* began to emerge as a distinct species. Examination of the fossil record indicates that long before the anatomical apparatus for spoken language evolved, the organs of vision were already highly developed, and visual communication was an important tool of the evolving human species.[28]

The practice known as "mind-mapping" is a powerful, practical tool for beginning to employ visual/spatial capacities in daily lessons. Mind-mapping is a style of note-taking invented by Tony Buzan in his book *Using Both Sides of the Brain*. In an article by Ian Graham, "Mind-mapping: An Aid to Memory" from the journal *Planetary Edges*, the basic process is described as follows:

> Mind-mapping is like building a jigsaw puzzle; you start where you can by putting the largest, most central idea in the middle of the page. Then start linking the pieces that you recognize. If you don't recognize the connection, you may instead start a smaller cluster off to one side and hook it in later.[29]

There are fourteen steps to mind-mapping. These have been developed by Peter Russell in *The Brain Book* and are based on Buzan's original work (see list below).[30]

On the next page is an example mind-map of the mind-mapping instructions below. It cannot, obviously, illustrate the use of color, but it does demonstrate the other principles.

Mind-Mapping

1. Start in the center of the page with the topic idea.

2. Work outward in all directions producing a unique pattern that reflects your mind's unique habits.

3. Have well-defined clusters and sub-clusters, keeping to between five and seven groupings.

4. Use keywords and images.

5. Use color imagery and 3-D perspectives in your symbols.

6. Print the words rather than write them for more distinct and memorable images.

7. Put the words on the lines, not at the end of the lines.

8. Use one word per line. It is more concise.

9. Make the pattern noteworthy, even odd. The mind remembers things that stand out.

10. Use arrows, colors, designs, etc. to show connections.

11. Use personal short-forms, codes for fun and effectiveness.

12. Build at a fast pace. It's more spontaneous and you capture more associations as they occur to you.

13. Be creative and original.

14. Have fun.

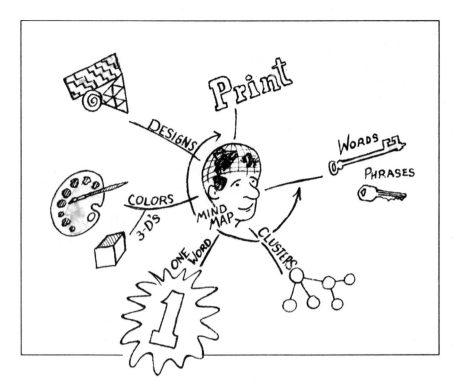

Why do mind-maps work so well? Ian Graham explains:

> The brain works by engaging the attention of the decision-maker through prioritizing the level of importance it attaches to ideas; it associates ideas and groups and links them in short-term memory; it engages the pattern-building process in long-term memory and uses primarily visual imagery.
>
> The mind is not a basin to be filled up; it is more like a tree, growing outwards in all directions. The more branches it has, the more room there is for leaves to grow. So too with the mind. More knowledge means more hooks on which to hang new concepts, facts, ideas, etc.[31]

esson

Creating a Mind-Map

Now let's try creating a mind-map to learn the method, then we will use this method in a content-based lesson. This exercise gives students a chance to practice making their own mind-maps. In the sample lesson that follows they will then use the mind-mapping process.

SUPPLIES: paper and a variety of colors of markers or crayons for each student.

■ Following the mind-mapping guidelines above, write the word "BEND" in the center of a blank piece of paper.

■ As you think about the word, watch the movements of your mind, or the directions it takes in relation to BEND. For each new thought or idea, create a branch off of the central word.

- You may notice that some thoughts are branches off a branch. Draw these on the map. You may even have branches off a branch off a branch!

- Your mind may start to go on what seems like a tangent. That's OK. Just include it as a part of the map—follow it until it dead ends or leads to something else.

- After you have been working for a while, start looking for connections between different branches. Draw these connections and relationships using arrows, spirals, stair steps, etc.

- When you are finished, stop and reflect on your mind-map for a few minutes. Turn to a person nearby and compare your mind-maps noticing differences and similarities.

- Reflect with the whole group:
  - What was this like? What happened in the exercise?
  - What are some of the uses for the mind-mapping process in the classroom?
  - What did you learn about how your mind operates?

Reflection on Mind-Map Lesson

Mind-mapping trains the mind in non-linear or divergent thinking and perception. It helps us learn to see and appreciate unusual or complex relationships. Images help the mind remember. The mind will "store" the map in its "library" for use at a later time. And what is more, it can retrieve all of the information contained on the map simply by visualizing it in the mind's eye! In *The Brain Book*, Peter Russell says:

> Paradoxically one of the greatest advantages of mind maps is that they are seldom needed again. The very act of constructing a map is itself so effective in fixing ideas in memory that very often a whole map can be recalled without going back to it at all. A mind map is so

strongly visual and uses so many of the natural functions of memory that frequently it can be simply read off in the 'mind's eye.'[32]

Learning the Metric System Through Mind-Mapping

The following sample lesson is a content application of mind-mapping. This is a math concepts lesson dealing with the metric system. The lesson presupposes that students know how to mind-map.

SUPPLIES: paper, a variety of colors of markers for each student, an explanation of the metric system and several objects for which *you* know the metric measure *[NOTE: Copy the two blacklines, "The Metric System" and "Metric Measurements at the end of this chapter.]*

- Have students work in teams of three. Assign one to be the recorder/materials person, one to be group organizer/time keeper, and one to be the group encourager/checker. Have the recorder/materials person get the supplies for the group.

- The assignment is to create a mind-map of the article about the metric system on a piece of newsprint.

- Review the mind-mapping guidelines using the mind-map of the mind-mapping procedures.

- Now create a mind-map of the article on the metric system.

- After the teams have completed their mind-maps, the checker is to make sure that each member of the team knows the material on

EXAMPLE QUIZ: The Metric System

1 Length of the classroom	2 Mass of the math textbook
3 Capacity of a pitcher	4 Area of a piece of newsprint
5 Mass of a large paper clip	6 Volume of a cardboard box
7 Temperature outside	8 Capacity of a coffee cup

the mind-map in preparation for a quiz that will test their ability to do metric measuring.

■ Give the teams 20 minutes to create their mind-maps. At the end of this time have them put away both the article and their mind-maps.

■ Have each team get ready for the quiz by taking out a blank sheet of regular paper. Have them divide it into two columns, and each column into four boxes (for a total of eight). Ask them to number the boxes. *[NOTE: You should also draw this form on the board or a piece of newsprint.]*

■ The quiz not only tests their understanding of the article but allows them to use their visual/spatial intelligence to do some estimating. In each box have them write the name of one object you want them to measure using what they have learned about the metric system.

[NOTE: Have the objects present in the room so they can handle them. Also make sure you have figured out the right answer ahead of time!]

■ Each team is to estimate "how much" or "how many" based on what they have learned in their study of the article. They must use the correct unit of measure and be reasonably accurate on their estimations. *[NOTE: Instruct them to visualize their mind-map to help remember the different units of measure as well as the "how much/how many" clues the article gave.]*

■ After about 10 minutes, call the class back together and have each team tell you their estimates for each box. Then you tell the correct answers.

■ Have the students turn back to their teams and talk about how they did with the lesson— both with the mind map and the estimating quiz. They should ask: "What did we do well? If we were to repeat this lesson, what could we do better?"

■ After about 3 minutes, have the class come together as a whole group and lead the following reflection:
 - What happened in this lesson? What things did you notice?
 - What surprised you? What was exciting? What was hard?

- What have we learned about the metric system in this lesson? About mind mapping?
- What have we learned about our visual/spatial intelligence?

Reflection on the Metric System Lesson

This lesson illustrates some of the possibilities of visual/spatial intelligence in the teaching/learning situation. Extensions of the lesson could involve: using different media such as watercolors and clay (where students paint or sculpt the article rather than draw it); using construction paper, scissors, and glue; or having students work in cooperative groups and create metric murals. You could have students mind-map a history or social studies lesson then create a visualization journey, modeled after the "inner teacher/guide" visualization, which takes students into the past to talk with forefathers and mothers, or to another culture to learn about it by talking with the people from the culture. Visual/spatial intelligence can take us to realms of knowing and understanding whose only limits are the limits of our imagination!

Other ways to work with mind-mapping in content-based lessons include:

☐ Use it as a note-taking exercise during a lecture, film, or other presentation.

☐ Mind-map a story, a history lesson, or a social studies unit.

☐ Mind-map abstract ideas such as mathematical concepts and terms, or parts of speech and their role in a sentence.

☐ Map your inner feelings about some external event.

☐ Mind-map an assigned topic or theme prior to a creative writing exercise or to writing a report.

☐ Mind-map to review a unit or prepare for a test. Have students create their own mental maps of the relevant information.

Transferring Visual/Spatial Intelligence to Life

We live and move through a wide variety of both conscious and unconscious images of ourselves, others, and the world around us. These images help us cope with and understand our universe. They give us a point of stability in the midst of the ambiguity and chaos of the world.

At the same time, this rich inner world of images deep within our psyche is a montage of inner maps and screens which hold us before the mystery, depth, and greatness of our existence. This inner world of images represents a richness and complexity that is literally "beyond what words can utter." In Dr. Kenneth Boulding's classic on this topic, *The Image*, he presents a classification of various aspects of our images as they show up in daily living:

> We have first the *spatial image*, the picture of the individual's location in the space around him. We have next the *temporal image*, his picture of the stream of time and his place in it. Third, we have the *relational image*, the picture of the universe around him as a system of regularities. Perhaps as a part of this we have, fourth, the *personal image*, the picture of the individual in the midst of the universe of persons, roles, and organizations around him. Fifth, we have the *value image* which consists of the ordering on the scale of better or worse of the various parts of the whole image. Sixth we have the *affectional image*, or *emotional image*, by which various items in the rest of the image are imbued with feeling or affect. Seventh, we have the

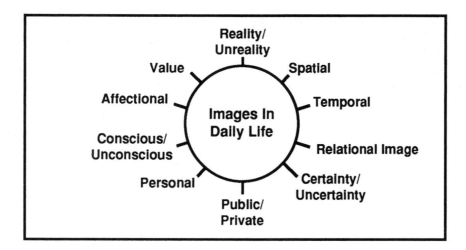

division of the image into *conscious and unconscious areas*. Eighth, we have a dimension of *certainty or uncertainty, clarity or vagueness*. Ninth, we have *reality or unreality*, that is, an image of the correspondence of the image itself with some "outside" reality. Tenth, closely related to this but not identical with it, we have a *public, private scale* according to whether the image is shared by others or is peculiar to the individual.[33]

These images shape and control our behavior. Nevertheless, we are in charge of the content and the role we allow them to play in our lives. The following exercise can help you become aware of this inner world of images within your own psyche. These are the images that make you who you are! In the final exercise you will hopefully rediscover deep sources of empowerment and transformation that are possible through working with visual/spatial intelligence. The exercise begins with a visualization process and then moves to the creation of a montage of what you have seen and sensed in the inner world.

Transfer Strategy

Creating a Montage

SUPPLIES: Four or five magazines with lots of pictures (National Geographic is excellent), a cardboard or poster board backing sheet for the montage (8 1/2 x 5 1/2 is a good size), scissors, rubber cement, an audio-cassette tape player, and a tape of some relaxing, instrumental music (preferably classical or non-specific music). Put these supplies in some special place where you want to work later in the exercise.

Accessing the Inner World of Images

■ Play some relaxing instrumental music in the background as you begin. Lie down on the floor or sit where you can completely relax. Close your eyes and breathe deeply from your abdomen. Be aware of your breathing for a few minutes, allowing yourself to relax more and more with each breath. (PAUSE)

■ Now as vividly as you can, imagine or picture our planet, the Earth, letting yourself become aware of the beauty, the variety of colors and shapes, and the simplicity of form. (PAUSE)

- Imagine that the Earth is a single living organism in its own right. Spend a few moments sensing and experiencing this image in any and all ways that you can, thinking about its power to sustain life, plants, animals, humans; aware of oceans, rivers, mountains, plains, lakes, forests, deserts; and consider the many varied weather conditions. (PAUSE)

- Imagine the Earth as a living being. Allow yourself to become aware of its desire for wholeness and for harmony and let this desire become your desire. (PAUSE)

- Now, imagine a stream of healing white light encircling the Earth. In your mind's eye, allow this light to completely envelope and surround the Earth. (PAUSE)

- Visualize situations in our world that are in need of healing and wholing. Focus this stream of light so that it bathes these situations and allows for the needed healing and wholing to take place. (PAUSE)

- And now finally, focus this stream of light on yourself and consider situations in your own life that need this healing, empowering, transforming energy. What old habit patterns do you sense dying (or needing to die)? What new potentials do you sense being actualized? (PAUSE)

- When you feel that this process of healing, empowerment and transformation has completed itself within you, open your eyes, stretch, and move to the space where you placed your montage-creation supplies earlier.

Montage Creation

The montage you create may directly or indirectly reflect things you have seen, insights that have been revealed to you, and profound knowings you have sensed in the inner world of images during the visualization. Think of a theme for the montage that is related to what you saw and experienced in the visualization.

- Continuing to play the same music you used during the visualization, start looking through the magazines allowing your attention to be naturally drawn where it will. When you find a picture, image, pattern, or color that is related to the theme you have chosen for the montage quickly tear it out of the magazine (not bothering to carefully cut it out at this point). Then continue searching until another one "reaches out and touches you," so to speak.

[NOTE: If you find yourself loosing contact with what happened and things you saw in the visualization, simply stop for a moment, close your eyes and breathe deeply, let yourself be re-connected with images, feelings, colors, patterns, etc. that you experienced in the visualization earlier.]

- After collecting 10-15 pictures, begin cutting out the pictures. When you have cut out about three fourths of the pictures, start arranging them on the backing card. (Remember, you don't have to use them all, and you can always return to the magazines if you need more or different pictures as the montage begins to take shape.) As much as is possible, allow this to be an intuitive process, almost as if the pictures were arranging themselves.

- Do not glue anything in place yet, but play with the pictures noting the impact they have in different arrangements. Which arrangement is most appropriate to the experience you want to embody or symbolize in the montage?

- Suggestions and guidelines for creating a powerful montage include:

  - The montage should be all visual—no words—in order to embody the non-verbal dimension of your experience in the visualization.
  - Let the pictures/images completely fill the backing card so there is no blank space.
  - Try to make the color scheme consistent; i.e. either all black and white or all colored pictures. Colors help express moods and feelings more dramatically.
  - Don't allow any overlapping of pictures on the edges of your backing card. This will help frame the montage.
  - If it seems appropriate to what you have seen and sensed within, try to create a

montage that has a single impact or that embodies a single message/theme through its many images and patterns.

- When you feel good or have an "Aha" experience (i.e. a spontaneous inner experience of rightness) about the choice and arrangement of pictures, glue them in place.
- If you discover you need additional pictures and/or background colors, go back to your magazines and look more specifically for what you need.

Reflection and Dialogue

■ When you have completed your montage, place it in front of you. Close your eyes for a few minutes and get in touch once again with the inner reality from whence this creation has come. (PAUSE)

■ Now open your eyes. Gaze intently at the montage for several minutes asking yourself these questions (and others that may occur to you):
  - What particular images, pictures, patterns, colors immediately grab my attention?
  - What surprises me? Shocks me? Delights me? Intrigues me?
  - Into what realms of my everyday life experience does this take me?
  - What is disclosed or revealed to me about myself and my potentials as I look at the montage?
  - What title(s) would I give the montage?

■ Choose a place in your home to post your creation—a place where you will encounter it often. Allow your montage to continue to "speak" to you, evoking you to be all that you can be, and its message of transformation to grow and mature within you!

Reflection on Montage Strategy

Becoming aware of the pictures/images that inhabit our mind is the first step to taking responsibility for them and for changing the images that are not helpful in our lives. The practice of montage creation is a powerful tool both to catalyze this awareness and for becoming proactive in deciding which images we want. Remember, we are (or can be) in control of our images and thus in control of our lives!

Answers to "Recognizing Relationships of Objects in Space" exercise:

 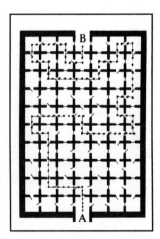

Answers to "Accurate Perceptions at Different Angles" exercise:

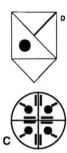

The Metric System

Prefixes and Symbols
This table shows the most common prefixes in the metric system, as well as their symbols and meanings.

Prefix	Symbol	Meaning
mega-	M	million
kilo-	k	thousand
hecto-	h	hundred
deka-	da	ten
deci-	d	tenth
centi-	c	hundredth
milli-	m	thousandth
micro-	M	millionth

Here are official symbols for some common metric measures. They do not need periods. You need not add an -s for the plural form.

meter	m
kilometer	km
centimeter	cm
millimeter	mm
liter	L
milliliter	ml
kilogram	kg
gram	g
square meter	m^2
square centimeter	cm^2
cubic meter	m^3
cubic centimeter	cm^3

 **SKYLIGHT**
PUBLISHING, INC.

Metric Measurements

Length
The basic unit of length is the meter. The distance from a door knob to the floor is about 1 meter.

Millimeter, centimeter, and kilometer are other commonly used units of length.
The thickness of a dime is about 1 millimeter.
The distance across a fingernail is about 1 centimeter.
The length of ten football fields placed end to end is about 1 kilometer.

Mass (weight)
The basic unit of mass is the kilogram. The mass of a football is about 1 kilogram.

Gram and milligram are other commonly used units of mass. The mass of a dollar bill is about 1 gram. The mass of a grain of sand is about 1 milligram.

Capacity
The basic unit of capacity is the liter. A milk carton holds about 1 liter.

Milliliter is another commonly used unit of capacity. An eyedropper holds about 1 milliliter of liquid.

Area
Square centimeter and square meter are commonly used units of area in the metric system. A square centimeter measures one centimeter on each side of the square. A square meter measures one meter per side.

Volume
The cubic centimeter is a commonly used unit of volume. If a cube, measuring one centimeter per side, was filled with water, the amount of water would be 1 milliliter. The mass of water would be 1 gram. A cube with a volume of 1 cubic decimeter measures 1 decimeter, or 10 centimeters, on each edge.

If a cubic decimeter was filled with water, the amount of water would be 1 liter. The mass of the water would be 1 kilogram.

Temperature
The Celsius scale is commonly used in countries employing the metric system. Water boils at 100 degrees Celsius. Body temperature is 37 degrees Celsius. Water freezes at 0 degrees Celsius.

Personal Reflection Log
Visual/Spatial Intelligence

Observations made—what happened?

_____

_____

Emotional/feeling states:

_____

_____

Reflections, insights & discoveries:

_____

_____

Self-evaluation (comfort zone/skill ability):

├─ ┤

Like a fish in water   Like landing on another planet

Practical strategies for fully activating/developing this intelligence within myself:

_____

_____

Application ideas for my classroom, family, community, or organization:

_____

_____

_____

Chapter 4

Actions Speak Louder Than Words

Explorations of Body/Kinesthetic Intelligence

The unity of the perceptual field. . . must be a unity of bodily experience. Your perception takes place where you are and is entirely dependent on how your body is functioning.—Alfred North Whitehead, *Modes of Thought*

Through our bodies we experience the external world and come to know it. The body is like a very complex receptor through which we receive and interpret thousands of bits of information every second—information about the weather so we know what clothes to wear; information that allows us to move from one place to another without bumping into things; information that enables us to protect ourselves from physical harm; and information by which we can participate in a wide variety of complex motor activities such as sports, ice skating, driving a car, and walking without toppling over.

One of the most important findings of contemporary brain research is the discovery of the deep connection between the body and the mind. In fact, some researchers no longer talk simply about the body, but of the "body-mind." In *The Possible Human,* Jean Houston describes this as follows:

Each of us can bring awareness to body functions and to movements that we had, in the mainstream of Western thought, only recently assumed to be totally autonomous. Indeed, it has been shown that it is possible, through conscious directed thought, to control the firing of a single motor neuron [in the brain]. With subtly developed body awareness, it is possible for the individual to become the conscious orchestrator of health. We can no longer escape the understanding that *psyche* [mind] and *soma* [body] are inextricably woven together.[34]

Modern biofeedback research and training is teaching thousands of people how to consciously control what were once thought to be "automatic" physiological process by learning to shift attention to those processes. For example:

□ We can learn to control the temperature in our hand and other body parts.

□ We can learn how to slow down or speed up our heart rate, including lowering or raising overall blood pressure.

□ We can be taught "mind-control" techniques for cooling ourselves down when too hot and warming ourselves up when too cold.

□ We can learn how to consciously alter or modulate the electrical frequencies (brain wave patterns) of our own brains, thus creating optimal states of mind for various situations we must deal with daily.

Unconsciously we know how to control these things and much more. The sensitive electronic equipment used in biofeedback training simply helps us to know consciously what we already know unconsciously. And once we have learned to pay attention to our bodies in this way, the knowledge and wisdom of the body is available to us in our everyday lives. What is more, the abilities mentioned above are just the "tip of the iceberg" of the potentials we all possess in this amazing body-mind connection.

What are some of the dimensions and capacities related to our body/ kinesthetic intelligence?

The following exercises illustrate capacities connected with the body and physical motion. Give some of them a try with yourself and students and see if you and they can get a sense of this intelligence.

xercise

Control of Body "Voluntary" Movements

The ability to consciously make the body respond to or do what the mind expressly wants is itself no small feat. There are whole ranges of so-called "voluntary" movements we make where the mind is more or less consciously directing the body's performance, such as in dancing, hitting a ball with a bat, riding a bike, knitting a sweater, or learning to drive a car. With conscious and disciplined practice, all of these things improve and become internalized until they are almost "second nature" to us.

This is a version of the childhood game of patting your head and rubbing your stomach at the same time. I have created the following short exercise based on a much larger, more involved exercise called "Multitracking" by Jean Houston. You may be surprised at how many things you can train yourself do at the same time!

■ Start by slowly jogging in place. As you jog, move your head back and forth from left to right and right to left. Start swinging your arms with your head from left to right.

■ Keep the jogging going, but now move your head and arms in opposite directions from each other. Now move them together again. Now apart. Now together.

■ Continue the jogging while moving your head and arms in opposite directions. Add to this the snapping of your fingers and looking with your eyes in the opposite direction your head is moving. (Keep working on this sequence until it gets easier.)

■ Then, finally, continuing all the movements above, start singing a song like "Old MacDonald Had a Farm" or "Twinkle, Twinkle Little Star."

■ Stop and rest. Notice what has happened to you. What has this "turned on" in you?

Control of Body "Pre-programmed" Movements

We also have entire routines and patterns of pre-programmed actions that automatically "kick into gear," with little or no thought or conscious intention. Many of these were once voluntary, consciously practiced actions, which once learned and internalized, moved into the "pre-programmed" status of movements. Others are instinctively learned. Pre-programmed action includes walking, steadying ourselves when we lose our balance, jumping out of the way of danger, or catching something that is thrown to us. The fact of the matter is that we can be consciously involved in both controlling and improving these actions if we train ourselves to carefully observe them.

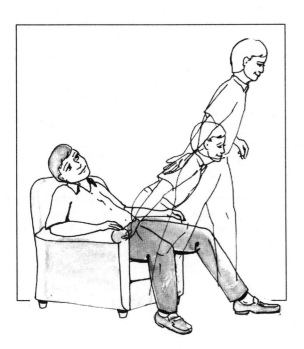

Once we learn a physical movement, we rarely think about it again. This exercise involves creating a conscious awareness of how we perform various physical tasks. Give each of them a try and see how much you can learn!

■ Sit in a chair. Now *think* your way through the process of standing up. See if you can recall every distinct action you make to come to a standing position.

■ Now actually stand up and check your accuracy. What did you leave out when you only thought about standing up?

■ Sit back down and try it again. First *thinking* the process through, then doing it. Keep repeating this until you have improved, bringing your mental awareness more in line with the body's actual movement.

■ Now begin walking around the room very slowly. As you walk, try to become aware of everything that goes on in the walking process; including how you balance yourself; how the feet work; notice the role of the knees and hips; how are the chest, shoulders and arms involved? See if you can even become aware of the brain sending signals to the body to walk! (Do this for 10 minutes.)

■ Stop and write observations and reflections from both the standing up and walking exercises.

■ Make a list of five different patterns of routine behavior you perform each day. Practice careful observation of at least one of these each day and see if you can improve your mental awareness of the body's movement.

Expanding Awareness Through the Body

Biofeedback laboratories have documented the fact that our awareness or consciousness can be extended through our bodies and through careful attention to physical movement. Some of the results of increased body awareness include improved health as we learn to cooperate with and listen to our body; fewer accidents due to greater attentiveness to how we are moving and using our bodies; and the ability to perceive, know, and understand with our whole being rather than just with the part above the neck.

This exercise can help you expand your experience of living throughout your body. It integrates physical, mental, and emotional being. It can help you get a "whole in one" with everything you do!

■ Begin by walking briskly all over the room, breathing deeply as you go. After about one minute, STOP. Focus your attention on the bottom of your feet. What do they feel like?

■ Now, start walking again keeping your focus on the bottoms of your feet as you walk. What goes on there? How do they feel? After another minute, STOP. Do you know what your arms and hands were doing as you were walking?

■ Start walking again, keeping your attention on both the bottoms of your feet and your hands and arms. Walk for another minute then STOP. Do you know with certainty what your hips do when you walk?

■ Walk again, giving special attention to the involvement of your hips in walking. However, don't loose awareness of the bottoms of your feet and of your arms and hands. Then STOP. What about your head? What does it do when you're walking?

■ Once again, start walking and try to be fully aware of your head, your hips, your arms and hands, and the bottoms of your feet. After a minute or so STOP once again. Are you aware of the sound of your walking as well as other sounds around you?

■ Start walking again and add the awareness of sound. After a minute STOP and be aware of other senses of which you may have lost track— sight, touch, taste, smell, as well as inner feelings and/or thoughts.

■ For one last time, start walking again trying to add to your conscious awareness all of the senses and inner experiences of walking, while at the same time staying keenly aware of your head, your hips, your arms and hands, and the bottoms of your feet.

■ Now rest for a minute. When you are ready, record your reflections and observations. Note especially what you learned about your body awareness.

The Mind and Body Connection

The relationship between the images we form in our mind and our physical being is one of the most fascinating areas of contemporary research. It is quite possible to produce profound changes in the body through both words and sensory images. For example, vividly imaging your favorite food will trigger a number of physical responses such as salivation in the mouth and anticipatory movements in both the throat and stomach. Likewise, it is possible to alter the body with the emotions. Consider the physical sensations when you sense fear or anxiety (even if it's only while watching a TV thriller) or how you can use "pleasant" images and thoughts to help achieve body relaxation. Think about the physical components connected with images of intense joy.

The content of images in our heads has a profound affect on our bodies. Try the following exercise and see what you can discover about this mind-body connection.

■ Close your eyes and vividly imagine the following things in your mind. Notice where and how each of these images affects your body:

  - the smell of fresh cookies baking

  - the taste of a lemon slice

  - the sound of finger nails on a blackboard

  - the touch of velvet against your face

  - the sight of a new puppy

■ Close your eyes and visualize the following scenes as vividly as you can. Again notice both where and how they affect your body:

  - You see yourself lying on the beach in the warm sun.

  - You are walking down a dark street late at night and sense you are being followed.

  - You have just seen a romantic Broadway musical with someone very special to you.

  - You see a young child about to be hit by an oncoming car.

  - You have just made a very successful presentation that thrilled your boss.

■ Finally, make a list of words that produce a physical response in you. Try to get a variety of words that produce fear, joy, excitement, anger, anticipation, disgust, etc.

■ Spend a few minutes recording your experiences, observations, and reflections as you worked with this exercise.

Mimetic Abilities

In our lives we learn many things simply by watching others and imitating them until we learn to do it on our own. Children playing house, actors playing a role on stage, learning how to perform such physical feats as high diving into water, skating backwards on ice, various gymnastics routines, and cooking a fine dinner are examples. Teachers have long known the importance of "learning by doing," especially in such subjects as science, typing, home economics, industrial arts classes, and of course physical education. Professional mimes, like Marcel Marceau, have taken this aspect of body/kinesthetic intelligence and turned it into a high art.

This exercise involves several types of "role-playing" to help you explore some of the possibilities of using your body to express yourself. Go ahead, give 'em a try. It's OK to risk feeling a little strange!

- On a blank piece of paper, list at least one life experience you associate with each of the following emotions: happiness, fear, uncertainty, anger, and satisfaction.

- Standing in front of a mirror, think of the life experiences you associate and then "embody" each emotion in the following ways:

  - Create a facial expression that communicates the emotion.

  - Try various body postures to dramatize the emotion.

  - Experiment with a style of walking to communicate the emotion.

  - Make up a physical gesture that you could associate with the emotion.

- Still working in front of a mirror, in Marcel Marceau fashion, try to mime/act out the following situations (this is like the game "Charades," but only for yourself):

  - Someone baking a cake

  - A very old man climbing a flight of stairs

  - A woman riding on a bumpy bus

  - An rent collector trying to get a tenant to pay

- Spend a couple of minutes recording your reactions to this exercise. What surprised you? What was difficult? What did you learn?

Improved Body Functioning

One of the most interesting areas of research dealing with body/kinesthetic capacities is what has been called the "psycho-physical" approach to physical exercise. We can re-educate our central nervous system through mindfulness in body movement and thus dramatically improve the functioning of our bodies. When we learn conscious awareness of body movement and how the body works, not only do we decrease possibilities of injury to the body (due to lack of awareness), but much of the physical deterioration assumed to "naturally" accompany aging can be halted!

In the following exercise you will be working to improve the functioning of your non-dominant hand. It may seem a little strange at first, but bear with me—**it really does work!** I have created the following adaptation of a longer exercise from *Listening to the Body* by Robert Masters and Jean Houston.

- Place the palms of your hands flat on the table. Starting with the little finger of each hand rap on the table several times. Then move to the next finger, the middle finger, the index finger, and the thumb. Notice the differences between the hands.

- Focus now on your non-dominant hand.

- Take your dominant hand off the table and place the index finger of your dominant hand in between the little finger and the ring finger of your non-dominant hand. Rub the index finger back-and-forth in the crack between the fingers 25 times using a sawing motion. You are trying to get as much stimulation as you can with this movement.

- Then do the same thing between the ring finger and the middle finger, the middle finger and the index finger, and the index finger and the thumb.

- Now repeat the above sequence rubbing the side of the palm of your dominant hand back and forth between the fingers of the non-dominant hand.

- Repeat the above sequence rubbing the forearm of your dominant hand back and forth between the fingers of the non-dominant hand.

- Grasp the thumb of the non-dominant hand with the dominant hand and gently rotate it 25 times. Repeat this with each finger of the non-dominant hand respectively.

- Rub the palm of your non-dominant hand on your thigh up and down 50 times.

- Place the palms of both hands on the table as you did in the beginning. Again, starting with the little finger of each hand rap on the table several times. Then move to the next finger, the middle finger, the index finger, and the thumb.

- Notice the differences between the hands. What has changed?

- Compare this with your observations at the beginning of the exercise.

- Write your observations on what has happened during this exercise. Brainstorm a list of 10 different ways you could use/ exercise the non-dominant side of your body each day.

BODY/KINESTHETIC INTELLIGENCE AND THE BRAIN

Our body/kinesthetic capacities comprise a complex, intricate, highly integrated network of brain/body operations. The motor cortex of the brain executes specific muscular movements, with the right side of the brain controlling the left side of the body and the left side of the brain controlling the right side of the body. The cerebral cortex acts as a perceptual feedback mechanism, which both feeds information to the spinal cord and receives input from the rest of the body through the spinal cord. Once information has been sent and/or received and interpreted, the motor cortex brings about the appropriate body responses to match the information received by the cerebral cortex (see diagram).

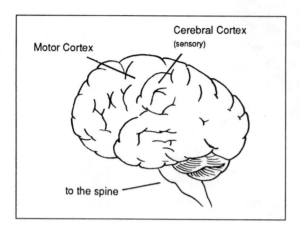

One of the key aspects in learning to use body/kinesthetic intelligence for knowing and to use it in teaching is to change our current attitudes toward the body. In *The Possible Human* Jean Houston states :

> Ironically, we are all too often educated *out of* rather than *into* an awareness of our body. The active, indeed the wriggling child's body is urged to 'sit still,' to restrain its natural impetus toward movement and exploration as it is confined to chair and school desk. . . .

> Even when we would direct attention to training the body, we often provide methods for doing so that result in a dangerously distorted body image. Thus we are often guilty of regarding the body as something to be "brought into line." The resulting rigidity of posture is often mirrored in a similar rigidity of perception, of feeling, and cognition.[35]

It appears that four major images dominate Western culture's attitudes and approaches to the body:

☐ It is a *wild beast that must be tamed*, thus the wriggling child must learn to control the spontaneous and natural urges to run, jump, and dance around.

☐ It is a *disobedient slave that must be disciplined*, thus we drive our bodies beyond comfort in physical exercise and have almost deified physical endurance sports which push the body beyond its limits.

☐ Our religious traditions have taught us that the body is a *vile thing that must be brought under subjection* of the spiritual, and thus we do not trust our bodies and at the greatest extremes are filled with disgust for "things that are *merely* physical."

☐ It is an *intricate mechanical instrument,* and like all machines you can pour certain things into it to make it run better, occasionally some malfunctioning parts must be replaced, and it is continually moving to a state of ultimate, irreparable breakdown.

Until these metaphors are replaced and our attitudes about the body change, the fullness of this way of knowing will not be available to us.

Awakening Body/ Kinesthetic Intelligence

The exercises above provide a starting place for getting in touch with your body/kinesthetic intelligence. In general, body/kinesthetic intelligence is awakened by physical movement. As mentioned earlier, any physical movement activates an immense amount of activity in the brain/mind/body system; through the cerebral and motor cortex. Every part of this system affects every other part. In *Listening to the Body*, Robert Mas-ters and Jean Houston illustrate this:

> Everyone knows that mind and body interact, the one affecting the other. Sexual fantasies and dreams, for ex-

ample, trigger complicated body changes. Drugs act upon the mind through the body, releasing emotions, ideas and images. . . .Even as children we learn, or somehow know, that we can alter our mental states by rocking, whirling, and by other means. Many children also know that physical pain can be banished by intense involvement in either mental or physical activity.

As people go through life they acquire either random or specialized knowledge of mind-body interactions which they can apply in a variety of ways. Some learn to relax by "thinking pleasant thoughts." Others run, swim, or walk as much for the mental and emotional benefits as for any physical ones.[36]

Amplifying Body/ Kinesthetic Intelligence

Once you have awakened body/kinesthetic intelligence as a way of knowing, you can start working to further expand and strengthen it, and to develop and refine its "knowing skills," along with your own ability to trust and understand its wisdom. Again Masters and Houston describe how:

> In some important respects, children generally possess greater self-knowledge and awareness than adults. The child is more in touch with his body— his movements, his sensations, his needs, and his desires. He moves and expresses his thoughts and his feelings more freely. His unblunted senses respond to a world that is more colorful and vital, and this perceived reality, in turn, enlivens him... Fairly early in life, the child's orientation shifts simultaneously away from the body and toward the external world. Mental processes are now experienced almost as though there were no concomitant changes occurring in the body. There should be an increasing orientation toward the external world, but it need not, and must not, be achieved at the cost of a diluted and distorted awareness of one's own psycho-physical [mind-body] reality.[37]

Following are several practices you can use to recover some of this "body knowing" and sensibility you had as a child. They work with developing awareness of the body and its intricacies. They are designed to access things you can learn and know through physical movement that can't be learned any other way. They can help you begin training your body to work for you today and every day as an adult. Try these and see what happens. Chances are you will experience your life unfolding on many more levels.

The Imaginal Body

The first two practices use both real and imagined physical movement to improve the quality of bodily action, your awareness of it, and to activate the plethora of senses, feelings, and thoughts connected with the body. These are based on exercises designed by Jean Houston in *The Possible Human* and are examples of psychophysical exercises.

The first practice works with the idea of the "imaginal body." This is the image of the body that is encoded in the motor cortex of the brain. It can be experienced with as much reality as our physical body. Sound strange? Give it a try and see for yourself!

- Stand in a relaxed, comfortable manner with your eyes closed. Take several deep breaths to help you relax.

- Spend a few minutes with your attention focused on your breath, carefully watching the inhalation and exhalation. This will help you direct your attention inward.

- Mentally scan your body. How are you feeling? Is each part of your body equally available to your awareness or are some parts difficult to sense? Try to remember these things for at the end of the exercise you will compare how you feel then with now.

- With as much attention and mindfulness as possible, raise your right arm over your head and stretch. If you are left-handed, raise your left hand. Pay careful attention to everything that happens—the shifting alignment of your body, the stretching in your chest, shoulders, arms, hands, and fingers.

- Now, lower your arm, again paying close attention to everything that happens throughout your body.

- Repeat this several times, each time trying to become more and more conscious of what goes on in your body when you raise your arm.

- Now, stretch your *imaginal* arm (the arm of muscular imagination) over your head, experiencing this with as much feeling and attention as when you raised your *actual* arm. Then lower your *imaginal* right arm, watching, feeling, and experiencing every move.

- Stretch again with your *actual* right or left arm, and then with your *imaginal* arm. Continue working with this, alternating between your *actual* and *imaginal* arms until you can feel the *imaginal* arm with as much reality as the *actual* arm.

- Now, repeat the same sequence above with your other arm and your *imaginal* arm. Remember to always experience your *imaginal* arm with as much reality as your *actual* arm.

- Using the same pattern above, try several other activities, practicing them first with your *actual* body and then with your *imaginal* body. Some things you might try to include:

  - circling your *actual* arms and shoulders like the wheel of the windmill, then doing it with your *imaginal* arms and shoulders

  - jumping forward and back with your *actual* body, then with the *imaginal* body

  - walking suddenly to the right or left and coming back to your starting place with your *actual* body, then repeating this with your *imaginal* body

- Try these and other routines you create.

- After about 15 minutes, stop and close your eyes as at the beginning of the practice. Once again, mentally scan your body. Notice how you are feeling. Is there a greater awareness in your body now? Open your eyes and begin to walk around. What has happened to your awareness? To your senses?

■ Pause now and record your observations, feelings, and thoughts about this practice. What effect do you think continuing to practice this over time could have on you?

Practice

Skill Practice with a Master

Olympic athletes use a version of the following practice to improve performance of their sport. After performing the skill with the actual body, they perform it with their imaginal bodies, *imagining themselves going through every part of the skill, performing it perfectly.* After practicing several times with their imaginal bodies, they do it again with their physical bodies and discover they have improved!

This practice is an extension of the "Imaginal Body" practice above.

■ Think of several skills you possess that you would like to improve, such as your serve in tennis, playing the piano, parallel parking, and so forth. Choose one to work with in this practice.

■ Now, with your *actual* body go through all of the physical movements involved in performing the skill, playing careful attention to what happens all over your body as you perform it. Do this for several minutes.

■ Now, perform the skill with your *imaginal* body only, making sure that you experience this performance with as much reality as when you did it with your *actual*, physical body.

■ For several minutes, alternate between doing the skill with your *actual* body and your *imaginal* body until the performances of the *actual* and *imaginal* bodies are almost identical.

■ Stop and rest for a moment. Then imagine you are standing before the Master Teacher of the skill. Close your eyes and visualize the Master of the skill performing it with absolute perfection. Continue to watch the Master until you have a real feeling for what it takes to perform it with real precision.

■ Now, practice the skill with your *imaginal* body several times, "em-bodying" the perfect movements you observed as you watched the Master Teacher. Then practice it with your *actual* body trying to "em-body" what you have learned from your Master Teacher and your imaginal rehearsal.

■ Stop and record what happened.

Reflection on "The Imaginal Body" and "Skill Practice with a Master" Practices

These practices can strengthen attentiveness to your body and its movements. Some researchers speculate that what is happening in this kind of exercise is that one part of the brain is training another. Reflecting on the "Imaginal Body" practice, as she has used it in many seminars and workshops around the world (NOTE: Jean Houston says she calls it the "kinesthetic body"),

The activation of the kinesthetic imagination serves to enable the part of brain functioning that stores optimal images of performance to re-educate, as it were, the part of the motor cortex that informs the usual performance. The motor cortex is then able to release the inferior performance patterns and incorporate the improved patterns, with substantial improvement in the skill needed to perform the task.[38]

Examples of ways to work with the imaginal body in your everyday life include:

☐ Rehearse any routine task you perform on a daily basis in your imaginal body before you perform it with your actual, physical body. (Chances are that it will be easier and more interesting!)

☐ Imaginally rehearse a difficult situation you will face in the near future such as an interview, a test, or a major challenge you must face. Rehearse it until it seems both real and realizable. (This will help you deal with it better when you actually face it.)

☐ When you are bedridden with an illness, exercise imaginally: tap your fingers, wiggle your toes, flex your arm, raise your leg, and so on a number of times with your actual body; then alternate this "micro-exercise" by doing it with your imaginal body. (This can help reduce muscle atrophy and poor circulation while you are confined.)

Practice

Unblocking Future Goals

The wisdom that our bodies possess is immense. Think of an activity like riding a bike or roller skating. Once the body has learned how to do these things, it never forgets—even if we neglect to continue practicing and don't do it for many years. The mind may think that it can't still perform the task, but the body knows it can. This practice involves psycho-physical work with things that are blocking us or that are major challenges we are facing. Often the body can find a way through a dilemma or problem situation that baffles the mind.

In this practice students have an opportunity to work with their goals for the future. They will use the physical body to help them more fully understand their goals and to achieve what they want. Have fun!—this is a lively one!

■ Begin by making a list of five to seven goals you have for the immediate future. Include such things as your future family life, your future job, friends, community, education, church, and so forth.

■ Select one with which you would like to work during the exercise. For this goal, brainstorm several obstacles that are blocking its achievement and/or challenges that you must meet if the goal is to be realized.

■ For each block and challenge, create a metaphor that describes the kind of block or challenge it is.

Example: some obstacles may be *like a brick wall* that has to be broken through or *like a rock in the road*, a *blockage* that must somehow be gotten around or moved out of the way. Some challenges may be *like jumping across a deep ravine* or *like white-water rafting*. Create metaphors that are appropriate to the obstacles and challenges you are facing.

■ Continue this work until you have dramatically dealt with all of the blocks/ challenges related to your selected goal.

■ Then be seated, close your eyes and relax for a few minutes.

■ Spend some time thinking and writing about the goal you selected at the beginning of the exercise.

- What has changed as a result of the work you've been doing?

- How do you see it differently?

- What new insights/reflections do you have?

Reflection on Unblocking The Future Goals Practice

Researchers have discovered that when you physically engage in the kind of symbolic, dramatic activity suggested in this exercise, you are at the same time doing very real neurological work. The medieval morality plays are an example of the power of symbolic, dramatic activity to shape the thinking and living of a culture. The Greek tragedies played a similar role in more ancient times. By acting out the major challenges and problems facing humanity, an entire culture received a profound kind of therapy. People attending the theatre would kinesthetically or imaginally become Oedipus or Medea and live their own tragedies, challenges, and problems through the enactment on the stage.

Examples of daily practices for continuing to work with body/kinesthetic knowing and for strengthening this way of knowing could include such things as:

☐ Intentionally express your ideas and feelings through actions, gestures, and physical movement. Watch others' "body language" and see what you can learn and know from this.

■ Now, with these images in your mind, stand up and start playing some lively, energizing music. Begin with the block/challenge you feel is the easiest to deal with. Visualize or imagine the block/challenge and its metaphor as vividly as you can.

■ As soon as you are ready, physically act out dealing with the block/challenge. In other words, if it is a wall to break through, act out breaking through it and keep working on breaking through until you know the wall is down. If it is a leap over a ravine, then leap and keep leaping until you know you have made it to the other side. If it is a dragon to be slain, then slay it, and so on.

[Note: it is important to work with as much physical and mental intensity as you can. Pretend that you are actually doing these things.]

■ When you feel you have dealt with one block/challenge, return to your paper and choose another and proceed in the same manner.

□ First, try physically acting out a challenge/problem you're facing. Then imaginally try to get as much reality with the kinesthetic enactment as with the physical. Then try it again physically. Do this several times and see what new knowledge you gain regarding the challenge/problem.

□ Try walking in different ways to express your current feelings and ones that you want or need for a given situation; for example, try various styles of walks which could help you get ready for a meeting with your boss, taking a test, or participating in a planning meeting that requires creative thinking.

□ At several different times during the day, practice "physical mindfulness," carefully observing your body involved in various actions or motions.

Teaching and Learning with Body/Kinesthetic Intelligence

So far we have tried to awaken body/kinesthetic intelligence as a valid way of knowing and understanding life. And we have done some work to familiarize ourselves with it. We have begun to learn how to use it and to strengthen it. In the next section we will work with body/kinesthetic capacities as a way of learning and teaching content-based information and as a step to remedy the following problem presented in *Listening to the Body* by Masters and Houston:

Education should, but does not, teach us to make effective use of our bodies and our minds. We are not taught the inter-relatedness of movement, sensing, thinking and feeling functions, or how mind and body interact to determine what we are and what we can do. We are

not even taught how to use our bodies efficiently so as to avoid damage to the organism. . . .Adequate awareness of body-mind interactions is basic self-knowledge, and until these defects are remedied, education will always fail—fundamentally.[39]

Here I am reminded of a story about a friend of mine who was a dance major in college. He was not only an excellent dancer in his own right, but a fine original choreographer. I can remember an occasion when he created a new dance routine. One evening he performed it for me. At the end of the performance I asked him what was the meaning of the dance. What was he intending to communicate through the dance? In response to my question he simply performed the dance again! At the end he said, "*That is* the meaning of the dance. The dance itself is what I was intending to communicate. If I could have said it in any other way I would not have created the dance!"

Following is a content lesson that utilizes body/kinesthetic intelligence as the primary way of knowing and learning. This is a lesson I learned from one of my daughters when I was helping with her homework one evening. Try it with your students and see what happens.

Kinesthetic Vocabulary

This is a vocabulary lesson that uses physical movement to help students learn the meaning of words. They will literally learn to "em-body" the verbal definitions.

SUPPLIES: Fifteen vocabulary words written on flash cards, one word per card with the definition on the back of the card. You will need one set of cards for each team of three students, with the words divided into packets of three. Also, you'll need to create a match-the-words-with-their-definitions quiz (i.e., words listed on the left and scrambled definitions on the right).

■ Begin by modeling for the students what you want them to do with each other. Choose three words from the list (one from each packet of divided words) and use the following sequence to teach them to the class:

- Show one of the words on a flash card to the class

- Say the word for them, and have them repeat the word

- Embody (act out) the meaning of the word for the class

- The class then embodies the word using the same movements

- When you have completed teaching all three words, test the class by simply showing them the word, pronouncing it, and having the class act it out. DO NOT verbally tell them the meaning.

■ Divide the students into teams of three. Pass out the flash cards giving each student a packet of five cards. AT NO POINT, UNTIL THE END OF THE LESSON, ARE THEY TO SHOW OR TELL THEIR TEAMMATES THE WRITTEN DEFINITIONS OF THEIR WORDS. [*NOTE: You will have already taught one of their words as you modeled the lesson above. All they have to do with this word is review your embodiment.*]

■ Give each individual team member 10 minutes to learn the definitions of their words and to plan a way to teach the meaning of the word to the other members of the team using physical gestures and body movement only.

■ At the end of the individual study time each student will teach his/her words to the others by helping them "em-body" the meanings of the words using the following sequence:

- Show the word on one flash card to the other team members.

- Say the word for them, and have them repeat the word.

- The individual embodies (acts out) the meaning of the word for the team.

- The team then embodies the word using the same movements.

- When the first person has completed teaching all five words, he/she tests the group by showing them the word, pronouncing it, and the team acts it out.

- Then proceed to the second person in the group, using the same sequence, and then the third.

■ When each individual has taught his/her words to the team, give them 5 minutes to check for understanding, making sure each person knows the meanings *with their body*—STILL NO TALKING!

■ Now have everyone sit down. Pass out the matching quiz, to test what they have learned. Tell them, "The key to this quiz is remembering the movements you were taught. Your body knows the meaning of these words! Let these movements tell you which written definition goes with which word."

■ At the end of the quiz have students return to their teams and check each other's work. At this point they may show each other the definitions on the reverse side of the flash cards.

■ After a reasonable amount of time bring the class together as one group and lead them in the following discussion:

- What did you like about using your body to learn? Why?

- What did you not like? Why?

- What was interesting?

- What did you learn about your own way(s) of learning?

- What are other times in our class would you like to use the body to learn?

Reflection on Vocabulary Lesson

For many people, the involvement of the body and physical movement is a critical part of their ability to learn. With children this often means providing opportunities to "act out" or to "embody" what they are learning, as in the kinesthetic vocabulary lesson above.

Attaching a physical gesture or motion to something being learned can accelerate and deepen learning for it moves the knowing beyond simply "facts in the head." It literally encodes the learning in the whole body/mind system, thus creating a greater integration and application of the knowledge with the rest of life. Just consider what happens when kids do science projects, use math to create something useful, or when they act out a play rather than just read it.

Other ideas for using body/kinesthetic intelligence in content-based lessons include:

☐ Role play important moments from history, key scenes from literature, or simulate situations from "life in the real world," beyond the classroom, for discovering applications of present learning.

☐ Use the learning of folk dances from various cultures to deepen cross-cultural understanding in social studies.

☐ In mathematics, put a number of students together in a group and have them increase/decrease the group size by adding, subtracting, dividing, and multiplying.

☐ Have the class form itself into different shapes such as a circle, square, triangle, or polygon for learning some of the principles of geometry by embodiment.

Transferring Body/ Kinesthetic Intelligence to Life

In *Frames of Mind* Howard Gardner makes the following observation regarding the knowledge of the body:

> The body is more than simply another machine, indistinguishable from the artificial objects of the world. It is also the vessel of the individual's sense of self, his most personal feelings and aspirations, as well as that entity to which others respond in a special way because of their uniquely human qualities. From the very first, an individual's existence as a human being affects the way that others will treat him, and very soon, the individual comes to think of his own body as special.[40]

The following exercise deals with the transfer of body/kinesthetic intelligence to our daily living. It involves exercising body/kinesthetic ways of knowing and perceiving to amplify and deepen our experience and understanding of life.

Transfer Strategy

Changing Awareness Through Breathing and Walking

The ability to maintain a sense of balance or "centeredness" in our life is a very important skill for our times. This is especially true when one considers the number of unbalancing, uncentering, and stressful things that happen in the midst of our complex modern lives.

The following transfer strategy is one in which you can experiment with shifting your awareness to fit the needs of situations you encounter in your daily life. It involves conscious use of breathing and walking. It is a powerful practice and can make an immense difference in your ability to creatively cope with the different situations in which you find yourself.

The imagery of the exercise is taken from various Native American Medicine Wheel traditions. It uses the four cardinal directions and the four basic elements. Work with each section until you sense the change it can bring about in your awareness.

[NOTE: Most people find that if they close their eyes during the "Breathe" parts of the exercise it is easier to imagine what is suggested and that the results/effects are more noticeable.]

THE EARTH (the West)

Restores a sense of stability & groundedness

■ Breathe: Breathe in and out through the nose. Think of the earth below you. As you breath in, imagine you can draw the earth's life-giving energy up your spine. As you breathe out, feel yourself attracted to the earth beneath, like being drawn by a magnet. Continue breathing in this way as you start the walk.

■ Walk: As you walk be very aware of where your foot is going. Place it exactly where you want it. Walk with purpose and intention. Walk as if there were a strong hand behind you, supporting you. It is the walk of an irresistible force. Nothing can stop you!

■ Pause for a moment and think of a situation in your life that needs this kind of walk—purposeful, grounded, clear in direction. Now begin walking again, imagining or visualizing yourself walking into that situation with the walk of the Earth.

THE WATER (the South)

*Restores a sense of openness,
flexibility, and love*

- **Breathe:** Breathe in through your nose and out through your mouth, the lips just slightly parted. Imagine the breath to be a fine stream of cleansing, water flowing through you. Feel the clean, fresh flow as you become the water of life. Continue breathing in this way as you start the walk.

- **Walk:** Walk with great sensitivity, great gentleness. Walk as if you are walking on soft grass in your bare feet. Walk "in tune" with everything around you, like a deer in the forest—totally aware, harmless, at one with the environment. There is no self. Just harmony with everything.

- Pause for a moment and think of a situation in your life that needs this kind of walk— flexible, open, compassionate. Now begin walking again, imagining or visualizing yourself walking into that situation with the walk of Water.

THE FIRE (the East)

*Restores energy, will, confidence,
& motivation for action*

- **Breathe:** Breathe deeply, in through the mouth and out through the nose. Imagine that each inhalation is blowing on hot coals in your solar plexus in the "pit" of your stomach. On the exhalation, feel the energy from this fire radiating throughout your body. Sense this energy pouring out from you in all directions. Continue breathing in this way as you start the walk.

- **Walk:** As you walk, imagine the sun in your heart. Let its energy drive your walk. Become a torch so bright and full of light that all darkness disappears. Walk with clear vision, like a sunbeam or a ray of bright light. Set your sights on where you want to go, and walk straight for that point with confidence, courage, and no sense of limitation.

- Pause for a moment and think of a situation in your life that needs this kind of walk— confidence, clear direction, passionate. Now begin walking again, imagining or visualizing yourself walking into that situation with the walk of Fire.

THE AIR (the North)

*Restores inner vision, intuition,
and connection with all above the earth*

■ **Breathe:** Breathe in and out through the mouth, the lips barely parted and the breath very refined. Use the exhalation to blow your mind, thoughts, and emotions way out into the universe. Use the inhalation to bring your mind, thoughts, and emotions back together again. Then blow them out again. Continue breathing in this way as you start the walk.

■ **Walk:** Focus your full attention on a point 8-10 inches above your head and begin to walk. This is like floating or flying. You're not sure how you even get from one place to another. It's like being transported. Walk without any intention—just follow your intuition. Feel yourself expanding in all directions. Let yourself become vast and all-encompassing.

■ Pause for a moment and think of a situation in your life that needs this kind of walk—vast, panoramic, full of insight. Now begin walking again, imagining or visualizing yourself walking into that situation with the walk of Air.

After practicing each of the breaths and the walks, spend some time recording your reflections on what happened.

I suggest that you first of all practice each of the breaths and walk at home until you get a feel for them, and then try them in other situations such as walking down the hallway at work, walking to the bus, walking for your morning coffee break. While sitting in various situations, at your desk, or riding the train you might try different breaths and see what happens to your energy and awareness.

Reflection on Breathing and Walking Strategy

This exercise is not really as strange as it may seem at first glance. Think of how you breathe and walk when you are depressed. You probably do a lot of heavy sighing and walk slowly with your head and eyes down cast. Now think of how you breathe and walk when you are filled with happiness and are excited. And what about when you are frightened? The exercise merely demonstrates that you can use your breathing and body movement to shift your awareness, thus intentionally putting yourself into more optimal states to face different situations in your daily life. For example, how do you need to breathe and walk to prepare yourself for a difficult, probably stressful meeting? How can you use the breath and walking to help you get ready for a situation where you need to be highly creative? What about situations that demand a great deal of sensitivity?

In ancient times, people believed that the body was a sacred vehicle for journeying into greater understanding, wisdom, and knowledge. Maybe we can rediscover this today for our era!

Personal Reflection Log
Body/Kinesthetic Intelligence

Observations made—what happened?

_____

_____

_____

Emotional/feeling states:

_____

_____

_____

Reflections, insights & discoveries:

_____

_____

_____

Self-evaluation (comfort zone/skill ability):

├ — ┤

Like a fish in water   Like landing on another planet

Practical strategies for fully activating/developing this intelligence within myself:

_____

_____

_____

Application ideas for my classroom, family, community, or organization:

_____

_____

_____

Chapter 5

I've Got Rhythm, You've Got Rhythm…Who Could Ask for Anything More?

Explorations of Musical/Rhythmic Intelligence

Just as humus in nature makes growth possible, so elementary music gives to the child powers that cannot otherwise come to fruition.… The imagination must be stimulated; and opportunities for emotional development, which contain experience of the ability to feel, and the power to control the expression of that feeling, must also be provided. —Carl Orff, *The Schulwerk*

Music and rhythm have played an important part in the development of every culture, from the drums of Africa to the simple complexity of the Gregorian chant in the early Middle Ages, to the intricacies of Mozart's compositions, to contemporary synthesizer music, to the sonic vibrations of the modern disco. Of all the intellectual capacities, none develops earlier. This is true both in terms of the evolution of the human species and in the development of the child.

Studies have shown that at birth a child responds positively and specifically to the tones of the human voice. This implies that even while the child is in the womb, some musical capacities are growing. Think about sounds that affect the fetus in the womb, the vibrational effect of the mother's speech, laughter and singing, music from the radio, the muffled sounds of others talking, the sound of the mother's beating heart. Even after birth, the sound of the mother's heart has a soothing, calming effect on most babies.

Over the past 30 years, teaching music has played a significant role in our schools. Don Campbell, author of *Introduction to the Musical Brain*, has suggested that there may be no other country in the world where the public has been so exposed to musical skills as the United States. Just consider marching bands, church choirs, the overwhelming variety of music available even at the corner drugstore, music in elevators, restaurants, offices, hotel lobbies, and supermarkets. And yet, Campbell asks if music's survival in our educational system is being endangered as more and more school districts quickly eliminate music from the elementary school curriculum the instant there are financial problems:

> Has music earned a permanent place in the fundamental nature of education or is it still considered an ornament? **The question of music as a part of leisure, pleasure and entertainment, versus its power as an enabling agent for human learning at large, is now at hand.** Are we going to be able to keep the public and financially-ruling boards interested in music by presenting a few concerts per year and an enjoyable class where students have the attitude of non-learning?[41]

In many ways music and rhythm are more foundational to our species than language. They have a power to evoke and express that no other medium possesses. Mothers use it to lull their children to sleep. Armies march to war to the beat of drums and national anthems. The use of chanting as a religious practice has been a part of every major world religion. And of course, the development of a wide variety of folk music has been used for entertainment, for dancing, as an expression of grief, and as a declaration of love.

What are some of the dimensions and capacities related to our musical/rhythmic intelligence?

The following exercises illustrate capacities connected with musical/rhythmic intelligence. Some have called these our auditory capacities,

however, sounds that cannot be heard can often be felt through vibrations. Recall how Helen Keller learned to speak; she sensed and imitated the vibrational patterns of Ann Sullivan's voice. Give some of the following exercises a try with your students (and yourself) and see if you and they can get a sense of this amazing intelligence.

Appreciation for the Structure of Music

Musical/rhythmic intelligence includes the ability to notice different factors in a musical composition, such as tones, phrases, rhythms, and how they fit together in a larger piece. You can see the informal operation of this ability when you watch your reaction to music, when you are aware of why you appreciate certain kinds of music and not others. The formal training of this capacity occurs in various kinds of "music appreciation" classes taught in elementary school through college levels.

This first exercise presents students with a variety of musical selections and asks them to "track" their responses, impressions, and images of each. For the exercise you'll need an audio-cassette player and eight tapes of different kinds of music, such as classical, country-western, lively rock, new-age, sounds from nature (e.g. ocean waves), religious, march music, music from another culture, or something quite dissonant. Give it a try and see what you can learn about how music affects different people.

■ Have students divide a blank piece of paper into eight sections (one for each musical selection) and then number the boxes.

"Schemas" or "Frames" for Hearing Music

Any time we hear a piece of music we are filled with certain anticipations about it. We learn to recognize its repeating themes. We have expectations about how it will end. We have come to associate things with different kinds of music, such as the kind of music played to signal impending danger in a movie, music associated with death, comical music played for the performance of a clown at the circus or with Saturday morning cartoons, and the rousing, uplifting feeling of a John Phillips Souza march. These "schema" also allow us to recognize similarities and differences between various musical phrases.

This is a "what if" exercise in which you will be connecting musical/rhythmic patterns with various things in everyday life. Be creative. You may find there is more music in your life than you think!

- Play about 1 1/2 minutes of the first tape. In the first box, have students write their immediate impressions, feelings, images, reactions, and how the music affects them. Allow 30 seconds for this.

- Now continue in the same fashion, playing each tape in turn for about 1 1/2 minutes and giving students 30 seconds to respond on their charts after each.

- When they have completed their reflection on the last selection, have them compare their reactions with two other people sitting close to them. Note similarities and differences in responses. Why do you think this is?

- Think about a normal workday in your life. On a blank piece of paper write down your feelings/moods for each part of the day; for example, the early morning, midday, and the end of the workday.

- Now imagine that you could have a musical background for each part of your day. What kind of music would you play for the different parts of the day? (Note its loudness, speed, intensity, and rhythm.)

- Close your eyes and try to hear each part of the day with the musical background you have imagined as vividly as you can.

- For each of the following situations see if you can imagine a piece of music and/or a rhythmic beat that would be an appropriate accompaniment. Write down your ideas; then close your eyes and try to hear the music playing in your head.

- rush-hour traffic

- the beginning of summer

- eating a wonderful chocolate bar

- a small child's first steps

- unexpectedly seeing your beloved

- holding a warm, cuddly puppy in your arms

- eating cooked liver

- watching the leaves turn color in the fall

■ If possible, have another person do the same list then share and discuss your answers.

xercise

Sensitivity to Sounds

Musical/rhythmic intelligence also involves awareness of different sounds made at various frequencies. In music sounds are usually grouped

in a prescribed manner, as illustrated in formal compositions. We can also see this capacity operating when we listen to our natural and humanly-made environments; for example, sometimes we know what is going on in the next room because we can hear the activities. And while sitting at our desk, we may know what the traffic and weather conditions are outside, just by listening. You'll need a partner for this exercise; it's a sound guessing game.

How much can you tell about what is going on just by hearing the noises that accompany an activity? OK, let's test it and see if you're as good as you think!

■ Ask your partner to number a piece of blank paper from 1 to 10. Then have your partner close his or her eyes (no peeking) while you perform 10 different tasks. After each task, give 30 seconds for them to jot down notes about what they think you were doing. Then have them close their eyes again and move on to the next task.

■ Ideas for tasks you can perform:

- look up something in a book

- get a glass of water

- move a piece of furniture

- tear a page out of a magazine

- count the coins in your pocket/purse

- comb or brush your hair

- scratch your arm as if you have an itch

- turn on a lamp

- dial the telephone

- do a physical exercise (e.g. push up)

■ When you have finished all of the actions, have your partner tell you what you were doing in as much detail as they can.

■ Reverse roles and repeat the process. Your partner will need to think up a different set of tasks to perform.

Recognition, Creation, and Reproduction of Melody/Rhythm

Early in our lives we learned to mimic sounds that adults made to us as we were lying in our cribs. Infants begin exploring sound using only a few basic notes. They are also able to match a rhythmic structure given to them, such as clapping. This is the core of the development of language, namely being able to reproduce strange sounds at a prescribed pitch, frequency, and melodic pattern (sometimes called "words").

Again, you will need a partner for this exercise. You will be working with the capacity to imitate tunes and rhythms made by someone else. It could be called the "Instant Replay" exercise. Don't be intimidated—it's fun and you can learn a lot!

■ Each partner is to make a secret list of two melodies, tunes, or songs that they think are unfamiliar to their partner. These can be anything from a church hymn, to a childhood song, to a popular melody from the past, to an obscure part of a piece of classical music.

■ Make a second secret list of two different rhythmic patterns that you can remember and perform for your partner. (HINT: Try beating out a popular nursery rhyme or a Christmas carol as a pattern of beats you could readily remember.)

■ Finally, make a list of two different sounds you can make with your vocal chords that you would be willing to do for your partner.

■ Now, beginning with the melodies, hum the first melody for your partner. When you are finished, your partner is to try to hum it back just as you hummed it. Work with your partner until he or she gets it.

■ Continue through each melody/tune on your list. Then reverse the roles and have your partner hum for you and you try to reproduce the melody/tune.

■ Repeat the same process with the rhythmic patterns you have listed, each time making sure your partner learns the beat.

■ Finally, repeat the process with the vocal chord sounds, again teaching your partner how to make the sound as best you can.

■ Discuss with each other what you have learned in this exercise.

Sensing Characteristic Qualities of Tone

In formal musical training, tonal quality is called *timbre*. This involves sensitivity to such things as a shrill, piercing tone, a deep, soothing resonant tone, and a grating, guttural one. Each of these can produce very different emotional and physical reactions; for example, consider your reaction when someone scrapes their fingernails on a blackboard. Likewise, we can tell a great deal about another's mood, the intended meaning in what they are saying, and what they are anticipating or hoping for by simply listening carefully to the quality of the tone in their voice and to their breathing (especially their sighs).

Again, you will need a partner for this exercise. In the exercise you will be exploring some of the communicative aspects of music, sound, and rhythm. Try to imagine what it would be like if we had no formal language but could only express ourselves through sound and rhythm. Interesting, huh?

- Divide students into teams of two. Have them designate one of them as person A and one as person B.

- On four large cards write the following emotions (do not show these to the students):

    SORROW

    EXCITEMENT

    ANGER

    CONTENTMENT

- Begin with person B. Person A is to close his or her eyes in order to rely on sound only. Hold up the first card and tell person B they are to communicate this emotion to their partner using only sounds from the vocal chords—NO WORDS! Person A is to try to guess the emotion being communicated.

- When person A has guessed it, try the second emotion using the same process.

- Then reverse roles with person A communicating emotions three and four to person B using only sounds from the vocal chords. Person B's eyes are closed.

- On four large cards write the following (do not show these to the students):

    NATIVE AMERICAN

    LATIN AMERICA

    BUSY DOWNTOWN

    SUBURBAN or RURAL AREAS

- Begin with person B. Person A is to have his or her eyes closed. Hold up the first card and tell person B to communicate this culture to his or her partner using only rhythm and beat—again, NO WORDS! Person A is to try to guess the culture by sensing its beat.

- When person A has guessed it, try the second culture using the same process.

- Then reverse roles with person A communicating a part of the city (cards three and four) to person B using only rhythm and beat. Person B's eyes are closed.

- Have partners share their experience of the exercise and discuss what they have learned.

MUSICAL/RHYTHMIC INTELLIGENCE AND THE BRAIN

The sampling of capacities you have been working with, plus others in the remainder of this chapter, are known as the *figural* approach to music and rhythm. This is the experiential approach. It is intuitive, based on what is heard in the music and what is "naturally" perceived and enjoyed. These abilities are mostly located in the right hemisphere of the brain, although the roots of music, especially its emotive power, are located in a much older part of the brain known as the *limbic system* (see diagram below). In evolutionary history the limbic system developed with the appearance of mammals. Still intact within our brain, we share this old mammalian brain with other animals. It is primarily concerned with the processing of emotions. In *Introduction to the Musical Brain*, Don Campbell describes its role in music as follows:

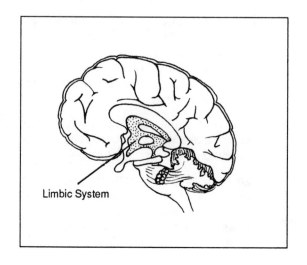

Limbic System

The limbic system is essential in the emotional processing of a musician. Both learning and motivative behavior are seated here. Often, classifications are made to the right and left hemispheres of the brain which belong in the limbic system. This system has no words, no self-evaluation or criticism. It is deeper, stronger and more elemental to our basic nature than the opinions expressed by the higher parts of the brain. The urge to make music, to dance and to imitate movement are seated in the limbic system.[42]

On the other hand, the *formal* approach to music is a disciplined, analytical study based on propositional knowledge about music as a system. It is the left hemisphere that is primarily engaged in the formal approach. The formal approach involves such things as the development of musical form, the sophisticated analysis of musical/rhythmic structure, and an understanding of harmonies, timbre, phrasing, technique, and various musical styles.

How can we account for the powerful impact of music and rhythm on us?

Contemporary brain research has discovered that the brain produces different kinds of electrical frequencies, or patterns, called "brain waves." These frequencies help us cope with various activities and situations in our lives. When we are asleep, for example, the activity of the brain is much slower, more open, flexible, and relaxed than when we are driving in the middle of rush hour traffic.

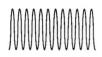 **Beta Level.** The most familiar level of brain waves is called the beta level. This is the level of mental activity in which we usually operate in our everyday lives. It tends to be rational, analytical, and relatively organized. It is verbal and filled with continual chatter, random ideas, lists, data, and thinking about anything and everything. It is quite predictable and subject to routine.

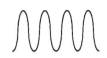 **Alpha Level.** The alpha level is the level of mental activity present in times of deep relaxation. It involves a sense of "letting go" of cares and concerns. It tends to be more holistic and open to multiple perspectives and possibilities beyond the rational, analytical limits imposed by the beta level of awareness. Our intuitive sensibilities are high and keen in this state of awareness.

 Theta level. The theta level is the level of mental activity just prior to sleep or full wakefulness. It is sometimes called "twilight imagery," like day-dreaming, because the mind is open to images, symbols, and patterns. It's a kind of relaxed, almost floating awareness—awake, but barely. It is a world of metaphor, analogy, archetypes, symbol, and myth.

 **Delta level.** The delta level is the level of mental activity present in deep sleep. It deals almost exclusively with the realm of the unconscious, which tends to frequently manifest itself in dreams. Most researchers agree that this is the language of the unconscious. In our dreams some of the deepest levels of the human psyche are reaching out trying to build bridges and linkages with the conscious mind.

The most important aspect of these findings is that we can control these frequencies. We can learn to orchestrate the functioning of our own brains! For example, depending on what is needed for a given situation we are facing, we can intentionally alter our brainwave patterns to place ourselves in optimal states of being thus maximizing our effectiveness. Researchers say that **the primary factors that influence and modulate brainwave patterns are sound, es-**

pecially music, and vibrational patterns, especially rhythms or beats. For example, think of the different moods you experience when you listen to the sound and rhythm of the ocean waves on the shore, the beat of a popular song, a jackhammer tearing up the sidewalk outside your office, or the rhythm of rush-hour traffic.

This research takes us to the very heart of musical/rhythmic intelligence, for it is made of sounds, tones, and vibrations. Commenting on music's impact on the brain, Campbell says:

> Millions of neurons can be activated in a single [musical] experience. Music has an uncanny manner of activating neurons for purposes of relaxing muscle tension, changing pulse and producing long-range memories which are directly related to the number of neurons activated in the experience.[43]

It is through the activation of these neural connections that learning takes place. The more neurons that can be "turned on" in any given situation, the greater the learning potential of the situation. Music and rhythm can be used to create more connections than would ordinarily happen within a given learning experience, thus more fully charging the brain. Music can be used not only to increase memory, but also to improve perception in other fields of study.

Awakening Musical/ Rhythmic Intelligence

The previous exercises are good examples of what is involved in awakening musical/rhythmic intelligence. Hopefully you were able to get a sense of this intelligence within yourself as you worked with them. Generally speaking, musical/rhythmic intelligence is awakened by sound and vibration. This can include birds chirping outside your window, sounds from a musical instrument

or the radio, the vibrations and the quickening of your pulse when a marching band goes by in a parade, a bell chiming in the distance, and a jet airplane flying overhead. In *Frames of Mind* Howard Gardner makes the following observation regarding efforts to understand the phenomenon of music:

> From the point of view of 'hard' positivistic science, it would seem preferable to describe music purely in terms of objective, physical terms: to stress the pitch and rhythmic aspects of music, perhaps recognizing the timbre and the permissible compositional forms; but taking care to avoid the pathetic fallacy, where explanatory power is granted to an object because of the effects it may induce in someone else. . . . Yet hardly anyone who has been intimately associated with music can forbear to mention its emotional implications: the effects it has upon individuals; the sometimes deliberate attempts by composers (or performers) to mimic or communicate certain emotions; or, to put it in its most sophisticated terms, the claim that, if music does not in itself convey emotions or affects, it captures the *form* of these feelings.[44]

Amplifying Musical/ Rhythmic Intelligence

Once we have awakened this vibrational, sound-loving intelligence, the next task is to find ways to strengthen it, and improve its ability to work for us. We must also learn how to appropriately use it, to understand it, and to trust it as both a natural and familiar way of knowing. It is well worth our while to take time to develop these capacities within ourselves and our students, for music can activate the creative imagination of the listener in ways that few other things can.

The benefits of a strong musical/rhythmic intelligence are many as stated by Zolton Kodaly:

> Music education contributes to the many-sided capacities of a child, affecting not only specifically musical aptitudes but his general hearing, his ability to concentrate, his conditional reflexes, his emotional horizon, and his physical culture.[45]

Following are four practices that work with different aspects of developing and training our musical/rhythmic intelligence, especially as it relates to the stimulation of more neural connections in a learning situation.

Speaking in Musical Tongues

Remember the childhood game of making up a new language or speaking a foreign language? It was basically gibberish or verbal babble, but you pretended you were talking and could understand each other perfectly.

I designed the following practice based on an exercise of the same name in *Introduction to the Musical Brain*. In it you have an opportunity to explore the impact of sound and vibration. Drop your inhibitions and give this a try!

- Ask students: "Have you ever been someplace where you couldn't speak or understand the language around you? What was this like?"

- After several responses to these questions, start talking in a completely made-up language. For example, on the board explain how to find the area of a rectangle. Make up words for rectangle, numbers for its length and width, and the process of multiplying length times width to get the area.

- Carry on as if students are understanding. After a couple of minutes, try to get them into the act by asking them questions. See if you can get them to pick up on some of the terms you have invented.

- Try to get them into teams of two, still using the original language to give the directions.

- Once they are in their teams, stop and ask them (in English!) what some of the terms were in this language you made up. "How did you know what I was talking about?"

- Now with their partner, the students should make up a language and carry on a discussion. Tell them to see how they can communicate through the quality of their voices, tones, the rhythm of what they are saying, and the pitch of their voices. There is only one rule—NO ENGLISH OR ANY OTHER LANGUAGE THAT ALREADY EXISTS! The topic for the discussion is favorite foods.

- Let the discussions go on for at least 5 to 7 minutes so they get past the initial discomfort and really get into trying to understand and communicate with each other. Then have the group come to silence.

- Have them now reflect with each other, in English, on what this was like. Ask them to check with each other and see if they knew what they were talking about. "How did you know? If you didn't know, what could you have done differently?"

- Have several teams share their experience with the whole group. "What have you learned from this practice?"

Reflection on Musical Tongues Practice

A great deal of neurological activity is catalyzed in this practice. First, there is the *tonal* impact of the imaginary words on the auditory center of the brain. Second, there is the *vibrational* impact of the speaking. A resonance is set up in the brain by simply speaking the "language." These vibrations can have a very relaxing effect, one which creates an openness, flexibility, and desire to be creative in the brain. In terms of our earlier discussion, it can modulate brainwave frequencies to alpha levels. Third, there is the fun of making strange sounds and words, which further quickens the brain and its *release of endorphins*—the chemical present in the brain during states of great joy, pleasure, and ecstasy (the opposite of the release of adrenaline).

To continue "speaking in musical tongues":

☐ Experiment with injecting appropriate sound effects for emphasis when you are talking with another person or in a speech you are giving.

☐ After reading a story, go back through it and illustrate it with sound. Reread the story and have students make the appropriate sounds and noises at various places in the story.

☐ Also in reading, make up a sound for each punctuation mark in a story. Then read the story, making the sounds at the appropriate places.

☐ Practice "thinking musically" about things in your daily life. What sound would different objects around you make if they could make a sound? For example, what sound would the paperweight on your desk make, or what's the sound of the trash can in the corner?

Practice

Improving the Musical Center of the Brain

The second practice works with improving your inner ability to hear, appreciate, understand, and produce music. The practice is a music visualization in which you will imagine that you are improving your auditory and musical/rhythmic capacities in the brain. You will need an audio-cassette player and a tape of a piece of music that is highly inspirational, such as "Chariots of Fire" or Pachelbel's "Cannon in D."

This practice is based on one created by Jean Houston in *The Possible Human* called "Cleaning the Rooms of Perception." In it you have an opportunity to work on improving the center of hearing and music in your brain. See how imaginative you can be.

■ Before beginning the visualization below, spend a few minutes thinking about your sense of hearing. What things are involved in this sense? How many factors can you think of?

■ Now, close your eyes and allow yourself to relax. Take several deep breaths and let go of worries, concerns, problems, or anxieties you may have on your mind. Focus your full attention on the process of your own breathing for several minutes, relaxing more with each breath.

■ Now imagine that your right ear is a hallway to a place in your brain that is "the room of hearing."

■ As vividly as you can, imagine that you are small enough to walk into your right ear and down this hallway to the room of hearing. Imagine yourself doing this now. (PAUSE)

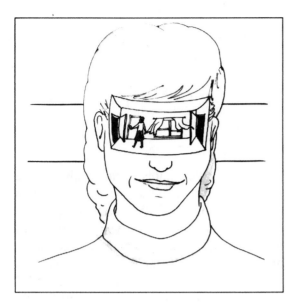

■ When you arrive in the room of hearing you are overwhelmed by the mess: cobwebs on the walls and ceiling, a thick wax buildup on the floor, the windows boarded, and piles of trash in every corner. (PAUSE)

■ In one corner, behind a pile of trash, you see a cleaning closet. Open the door and see all of the supplies you need to clean this room. Now go to work, knowing that as you work you are improving the quality of your hearing—

- Sweep away those cobwebs!

- Get rid of the trash!

- Take the boards down from those windows so that the fullness of sound can enter this room once again!

- Scrub the floors, removing all the old wax! (PAUSE)

■ When you have finished cleaning the room, open the window and let the wind blow through. Hear it swooshing through, blowing away any dust that may still remain. Listen to the birds in the trees and the children playing outside the window. (PAUSE)

■ As you move about this freshly cleaned room you suddenly notice a set of double doors at the far end of the room. On the door is a sign. You go to the door and read the sign. It says "Music Room."

■ You decide to enter this room, taking your cleaning supplies with you because you know that it will need cleaning as well. Make sure you leave the door open to the room of hearing as you enter the Music Room.

■ As you enter you are aware of a musty, dusty smell. The room is dark and depressing. Old music stands are stacked in the corner; crumpled, wrinkled, pieces of sheet music yellowed from age are scattered everywhere; an old baby grand piano covered with a thick layer of dust is in a corner; and a worn sofa is in another corner.

■ You decide to go to work cleaning this room. Find the windows. Clean them and open them wide so that light fills the room. Go to work dusting everything in sight. Pick up the sheet music and put it on the piano. Scrub the floor. Do whatever else you need to refurbish and renew the Music Room so that it is a place of great pleasure and joy. (PAUSE)

■ Enjoy being in this room that hasn't been used for so long. Notice the fresh wind from the room of hearing blowing through the Music Room. (PAUSE)

■ Turn on the musical selection you have chosen and allow yourself to hear and experience music more fully and more completely than you ever have before. Sit on the sofa and allow the sound of the music to carry you away.

■ When you are ready leave the Music Room, making sure to leave the windows open. Re-enter the room of hearing, leaving the doors between the rooms open wide. Find the hallway to your ear and slowly make your way back, remembering with each step that you can return to the these rooms at any time.

■ Now open your eyes. Stretch, and as you reflect on the exercise, play your musical selection once again.

Reflection on Musical Center of the Brain Practice

One of the strange things about the brain is that it apparently does not know the difference between something that is actively and vividly imagined and the real thing. People who have worked with this exercise over time report on the improvement of their sense of hearing, along with a much greater sensitivity to many of the subtle sounds about us (especially in nature), and a greater enjoyment of and appreciation for formal music. There is likewise often a sense of wonder, similar to what we possessed in childhood, that accompanies this exploration of sound. It can also lead to greater awareness of the impact of various kinds of music on us.

Here are some other ways you can continue to develop and work with your Music Room every day:

□ When sitting at your desk, imagine that your sense of hearing has a dial on it that you can turn up or down. It is now at the setting 3. Slowly turn it up until it reaches 10. With each turn of the dial see what you can hear that you couldn't before. Then slowly turn it back down to 3.

□ At least once a day, find a moment to go to the Music Room in your brain and listen to one piece of music. Practice experiencing it as fully and completely as you can.

□ Try listening to music and drawing at the same time. Put into visual patterns what the music is doing and saying. Work with colors, shapes, and interesting designs.

Listening to Music with the Whole Body

The third practice in this section deals with the experience of music in the body. Music often touches us so deeply that there are physical changes produced, such as tears, a quickened heartbeat, a desire to get up and dance, or a sense of humility as in worship. For the practice, you will need an audio-cassette player and a tape of several instrumental musical pieces, preferably ones with which you are unfamiliar.

The practice is based on a technique used in *Introduction to the Musical Brain*. It gives you an opportunity to experience a piece of music on multiple sensory levels. Give it a try. It can be a very pleasurable experience.

■ Close your eyes and take several deep breaths. Allow yourself to relax as fully as possible, letting go of other concerns and thoughts so you can be fully present at this moment.

■ As you relax, picture your ears and imagine that you can extend them throughout your whole body so that every part of your body can hear. Think of yourself as covered with ears!

■ Start the music that you have selected. Let it flow over you, under you, and all around you. You are surrounded by the sound of the music, almost as if you were wrapped in a blanket of music.

■ Imagine that the sound of the music is everywhere and that you can hear it with every part of your body, with every cell of your being. Notice its movements, tones, rhythms, pitches, and its effects on you.

■ Do not only hear the music, but see, smell, taste, and touch it. Allow nothing to disturb you during this whole-body listening experience. Let the sound "carry you away."

■ When the music is over, sit or lie quietly for a few minutes and savor the experience. Then try it again with a second piece, using the same process outlined above.

■ At the conclusion of listening to both pieces of music, draw, paint, or write your reactions and observations about listening with your whole body and all of your senses. What was this like?

Reflection on Listening to Music Practice

Since music, like all sound, comes to us through the air which surrounds the entire body, it is not strange to talk about music as "flowing over us" and interacting with the body. Consider how we sometimes say that a piece of music "gave us goose bumps" or "caused shivers to go up and down our spine." And just think of your physical reaction when chalk scrapes on the blackboard or when someone drops a tray full of dishes. This is also an excellent practice for enlivening other senses which are "brought into the act" as you experience music as fully as possible throughout your entire brain-mind-body system.

For further everyday practice:

☐ At least once a day try listening to what is going on around you with your whole body. Listen to what others are saying in a meeting, to the normal sounds around your office or home, or a song on the radio.

☐ Several times during the day focus your attention on a particular sound and bring all the senses to bear on it for a few minutes. Try to not only hear it, but see, taste, touch, and smell it as well.

☐ While sitting at your desk, focus your attention on a particular sound you hear. Stay focused on the sound then draw its pattern, shape, design, and color on a piece of paper.

☐ Reverse the previous process. Focus on an intriguing design, pattern, or color in your office or classroom and try to imagine as vividly as you can the sound it would make.

Superlearning Experiment

The final practice in this section is based on the research of the Bulgarian scientist Georgi Lozanov. He pioneered the creation and testing of a relaxed, deep-learning technique for teaching foreign languages. Known popularly as "optima learning," "super learning," or "suggestopedia," the technique can increase the rate at which children and adults are able to learn languages. It employs such things as internal imagery, music (especially largos and adagios), and an adjustment of brain waves to alpha levels—a more open and receptive state for learning such things as vocabulary words and their pronunciation. You will need a tape of baroque music—largos and adagios—and an audio-cassette player for this exercise. If you are doing this alone, you will need a second cassette player and a blank tape.

Following is a glimpse into the world of "superlearning." A full training course in these methods is obviously required for anyone who wants to use this seriously in the classroom. But for our purposes here, give this a try and see if you can get a sense of the possibilities.

■ Create a list of new vocabulary words, math concepts or definitions, historical facts, or social studies data that you want students (or yourself) to learn. If you are working alone on this exercise, record the list of information to be learned three separate times on a blank audio-cassette before you begin the exercise.

■ Sit quietly in a chair. Take several deep breaths and systematically relax every part of your body. Beginning with your feet, move up your legs to the calves, knees, thighs, and hips, intentionally relaxing each part.

■ Now move up to your upper body, relaxing the stomach, chest, and shoulders. Move the relaxation down your arms, to your wrists, and into your hands.

■ Finally, relax your neck, face, and head. Pause for a moment and enjoy the experience of total body relaxation.

■ Start the tape of the baroque music. Give your full attention to the music and use it to help you relax even more.

■ If you are doing this with a group, simply begin quietly reading the information in the background as people are enjoying their relaxation and listening to the music. Read the "input" information three separate times. If you are working alone, turn on the second cassette player on which you have recorded the information you want to learn.

■ As the information is being read, do not try to focus on the material. Rather, keep your attention on the music. The informational tape is the background for the music!

■ When the information "input" is finished, turn off the music and slowly "bring yourself back" to a more ordinary state of awareness and review the list or give students an informal quiz to see how much they know. The information they know is probably a result of the input during the relaxation.

Reflection on Superlearning Practice

When we engage in the kind of learning suggested in this practice, the neural activity in the right hemisphere of the brain is dramatically increased. In the relaxed alpha brainwave state, the mind is able to absorb and assimilate information much more readily and quickly than in more "ordinary," beta states of awareness. Experts working in the field of super-learning have observed students who systematically use these techniques, learn material (such as foreign language vocabulary) at significantly accelerated rates.

To experiment with the Lozanov technique every day:

☐ Use the superlearning practice to help you with any list of things you want to remember, such as groceries, things that must be done during the day, etc. Simply "input" the list once you have achieved a relaxed alpha state. Record the list and play it along with the music.

☐ Try using different kinds of music to enhance your performance during the day. For example, what music would prepare you for a potentially stressful meeting? What music could promote creativity in a planning session?

☐ Experiment with shifting to an alpha state of brain activity using baroque music and deep, relaxed breathing. Then approach some routine, fairly mechanical, generally boring activity in this different state of awareness.

Teaching and Learning with Musical/Rhythmic Intelligence

So far we have tried to awaken musical/rhythmic intelligence as a valid way of knowing and understanding life. We have done some work to familiarize ourselves with it. We have begun to learn how to use it and to strengthen it. Now we will work with musical/rhythmic capacities as a way of teaching and learning content-based information. Many researchers believe that there are countless possibilities for helping children improve their reading, mathematical, and writing skills through activating the musical/rhythmic capabilities of the brain. Campbell elaborates on this in *Introduction to the Musical Brain*:

> Music may serve to facilitate the logical studies of our students rather than make them more aesthetically sensitive. History and mathematics may have more to gain from music than our performance techniques. While we are aware that biochemical research has proven that certain foods release important brain chemicals, it is just as possible that music, the sound food, is providing us similar nutrition. Perhaps there is junk music, as there is junk food. Some music is truly not healthy for us....There is also the probability that certain music has no effect on some people and, on the other hand, dynamically brings about peace of mind, even exhilarating religious experiences, with others.[46]

While music can be, and most often is, a subject that is taught in its own right, it can also be used to enhance learning and as a means for acquiring information in other subject areas.

esson

Mnemonic Possibilities of Music/Rhythm

This is a lesson that uses musical/rhythmic intelligence to help students learn and remember various information, processes, and operations that are needed in other learning contexts.

SUPPLIES: Content to be learned on separate slips of paper, newsprint or large flip chart, markers, and masking tape.

■ Before the lesson, on small slips of paper, write a variety of items you want your students to learn, such as parts of speech, states and capitols, mathematical tables or operations, the digestive process, a scientific table, etc. Fold these slips of paper and place them in a hat.

[NOTE: You may want to focus on topics in the content of a particular subject. For example, if you are doing parts of speech you may have one slip for nouns and adjectives, one for verbs and adverbs, one for prepositional phrases, etc.]

■ Divide the class into teams of three. Take the hat around and have each team draw a topic.

■ The task is for each team to write a song, jingle, or rap that will teach the topic to others. Following are the steps each team should go through:

- List the different aspects of the topic that will need to be included in the song, jingle, or rap. For example, what are the parts of speech and what does each one do?

- Check the basic information with the teacher to be sure that it is correct *before* creating the song, jingle, or rap.

- Decide whether you will do a song or a rap. If you choose a song, pick a tune you think everyone will know or one simple enough

to teach. If you choose a rap, figure out a definite rhythm and pattern that will work best with your topic.

■ Give the teams time to create. Watch carefully for any team that is having trouble and be prepared to give them some special help to get them started.

■ When all teams are finished, have each write its song, jingle, or rap on a large piece of newsprint.

■ Now bring the class together as a whole group. Have each team present its creation to the class and teach it so the whole class can sing and/or rap together.

■ After all teams have made their presentations and have taught the class their songs or raps, conduct the following discussion:

- What are some things that struck you about this lesson?

- What were its pluses? What were its minuses? What was interesting?

- Did this help you learn more quickly? Why or why not?

- In what other ways could we use music in the classroom?

Reflection on Mnemonic Possibilities Lesson

This lesson utilizes the mnemonic capability of music and rhythm to help students remember important content from a lesson. The word *mnemonic* comes from the Greek word meaning "to aid in the increase of memory." Such musical/rhythmic mnemonic devices as the alphabet song, the "knee bone is connected to the hip bone. . ." song, and tapes that teach addition, subtraction, multiplication, and division tables to rap music are examples of this function. In this type of activity, memory is triggered both by the regular rhythm or beat of the song as well as by the tune and rhymes of the words.

To use musical/rhythmic capacities in teaching content-based information:

☐ Learn more about a historical era you have been studying by playing music from that particular period. Let students learn from the music itself about the feelings of the people, the mood of the times, the pace of life, etc.

- Use music before or during a test to help lower students' stress levels, thus placing them in a more optimal state for remembering the necessary information.

- Have students invent strange new musical instruments for a future they envision. Provide time for them to actually make the instruments, then work on a composition that uses what they have made.

- Deepen students' appreciation for and empathy with a culture in social studies by teaching them folk dances and songs from the culture.

Transferring Musical/ Rhythmic Intelligence to Life

Today, music and rhythm are helping thousands of people, old and young alike, keep their brains and bodies active through such things as folk dancing, crafts, and various kinds of physical exercise. Music and rhythm are the evocators *par excellence* of deep creativity within us. Let us consider one final comment from Campbell:

> Music transcends entertainment and a passive occupation when the elements of thought, action and cooperation are taking place. Creativity is reawakened by stimulating the mind with as many multi-sensory experiences as possible. Whether creativity is geriatric or pre-primer in nature, it heals! Healing is the process of becoming more than what was. The musical connections to the psyche [deep mind] of the body are deep and should be attended throughout life.[47]

Transfer Strategy

The Sound of the Future

The final part of this chapter focuses on transferring and applying musical/rhythmic intelligence to daily living. This is a transfer strategy that deals with sound as a medium of transformation. You'll need a cassette tape of good meditative music for the first and last parts of the exercise and a cassette player.

The following transfer strategy allows you to focus on your creative intentions for the future. It provides an opportunity to work with different aspects of these intentions and to bring them to fruition. Give it a try and see what happens!

- Begin playing the meditative music you have selected. Sit in a quiet place where you will not be disturbed and where you can completely relax. Breathe deeply from your abdomen several times and allow yourself to become centered and calm.

- In your mind's eye, imagine that you can see your whole future stretched out before you, as if it were a large mural.

- Use the blackline titled "Pathways" at the end of the chapter. For each stepping stone on the pathway, write one creative intention you have for your life as you consider the future. For example, think about such things as travel, pursuit of a hobby, writing, career intentions, your retirement, or intentions for your relationships.

- Now choose one of these creative intentions that you want to explore more fully, either because you have strong feelings connected to it, or because you intuitively think it might have some significance for you today.

- On the blackline titled "Creative Intention" (see end of chapter), make a list of things you now associate with the intention you have chosen, including, images, feelings, ideas, thoughts, and fears.

- As you work, staying as focused as you can, look for a phrase or thought that capsulizes why this intention is important to you. Don't worry if it is meaningful to anyone but you.

- When you find this phrase or thought, write it on your worksheet. This phrase is a window into the larger creative intention with which you have been working, as well as into your entire future.

- Start working with your phrase or thought so that it is a complete unit, but not a sentence, for example, "drinking from culture's wellspring." Work with it so that it is musically pleasing to the ear and so it flows smoothly off the tongue.

- Once you are satisfied with the phrase or thought, put the worksheet aside. Turn off the music and once again close your eyes, centering yourself as you did at the beginning of the exercise. Watch your breathing; focus your mind.

- When you feel relaxed and focused, begin repeating aloud the phrase or thought you worked on earlier. Repeat it over and over and over again, keeping your eyes closed. Concentrate your entire being on repeating the phrase. Don't engage in intellectual thoughts about the phrase, simply concentrate on its sound and rhythm.

- Experiment with saying it very softly. Slowly increase the volume, then bring it back down to very soft. What happens to your awareness as you do this?

- Try singing the phrase. Make up a pattern of notes that works with the phrase and its natural rhythm. Sing it again and again using this musical pattern.

- In this practice, it often seems as if the phrase finds its own rhythm within you; you are not sure whether you are saying the phrase or the phrase is saying you. When (and if) this happens, just "go with the flow" as long as seems appropriate.

- After working with the phrase in this way for at least 10 minutes, and longer if possible, begin to record your reflections. Try to report only on what is happening, almost like an outside observer. Steer away from rational, analytical thinking about the practice.

- When you are finished, write your answer(s) to the following question:

  What did I hear, beyond what I was saying?

Reflection on the Sound of the Future Strategy

Throughout history people have used sound in various meditation practices, often in the form of chanting. The practice above is a secular form of an ancient spiritual practice of repeating a *mantra*. A mantra is a phrase, often taken from sacred texts, which has the power to shift one's consciousness to realms of spiritual insight and inspiration. Over the centuries many people have used sound, music, and rhythm to shift awareness to the inner world: for example, the use of drums and rattles in Southern shamanistic cultures; the use of bells, gongs, and chanting in many Eastern cultures; and the use of the sung mass in the West. In light of contemporary brain research we now have some understanding about what happens in these practices. Simply stated, the vibrational patterns of the mantra, bells, or chant along with the music modulates brain waves to alpha and/or theta frequency levels. In these states of awareness we are much more "in tune with" and conscious of the deeper dimensions of the self and the universe.

Pathways

 SKYLIGHT
PUBLISHING, INC.

Creative Intention:

_____

Images	Feelings	Fears	Thoughts	Ideas

Other Associations:

Capsulizing Phrase/Thought:

_____

_____

SKYLIGHT
PUBLISHING, INC.

The Magical Multimodal Melody

The Intrapersonal Horn:

Know thy - self, be close to thy soul. Know thy-self, be close to thy soul.

The Mathematical/Logical Drum:

The pat - terns, the rea - sons, are always in season.

5 1, 1 5, 5 5 5 5 1.

The Interpersonal Clarinet:

Com- mun- i- cate, Co-op- er- ate, With oth- ers you are free to co- cre- ate,

Com- mun- i- cate, Co-op- er- ate, With oth- ers you create the new.

The Visual/Spatial Trumpet:

The art- ist in each of us is al- ways in reach of us,

The art- ist in each of us is al-ways with- in.

The Musical Violin:

The voi- ces are sing- ing, New un- i- verses bring- ing,

The voi- ces are sing- ing, New un- i- verses song.

The Verbal Bassoon:

The words paint pic - tures for the mind to see. Da da da da da da da Da da da da

With-out words what kind of peop - le would we be, Da da da da da da, Da.

SKYLIGHT PUBLISHING, INC.

Reprinted with permission
from the creator, Marie Blessing Sharp.

The Body/Kinesthetic Clap and Waltz:
Dance the waltz step as you do the following:

(Clap) - Slap - Clap - Clap - Slap - Clap - Clap

Slap - Clap - Clap - Slap - Clap - Clap

Personal Reflection Log
Musical/Rhythmic Intelligence

Observations made—what happened?

_____

_____

Emotional/feeling states:

_____

_____

Reflections, insights & discoveries:

_____

_____

Self-evaluation (comfort zone/skill ability):

├ — — — — — — — — — — — — — — — — — — — ┤

Like a fish in water   Like landing on another planet

Practical strategies for fully activating/developing this intelligence within myself:

_____

_____

Application ideas for my classroom, family, community, or organization:

_____

_____

_____

Chapter 6

Getting to Know You... and Learning Together

Explorations of Interpersonal Intelligence

WE LEARN. . . .

10% of what we read
20% of what we hear
30% of what we see
50% of what we both see and hear
70% of what is discussed with others
80% of what we experience personally
95% of what we TEACH to someone else
—William Glasser

Working with other people is virtually unavoidable and, as far as we can tell, this has always been the case for our species. In fact, some have even said that the only way we made it as far as we have in evolutionary history is because of our willingness to work together, to communicate with each other, to cooperate, collaborate, and help each other. Our very survival as a species thus far probably has depended on these things more than any other single factor.

On every front, our post-modern world is rapidly moving from a "me" to a "we" society. We see this pattern emerging in the most personal dimensions of our daily life on the micro-level and in the increasing patterns of interdependence on the global macro-scale. In the latter half of the 20th century this shift from me to we has lead many to suggest that those very skills of working together and cooperating with each other that were instrumental in getting us this far, may well be as important for our future survival. In the video version of *The Global Brain*, Peter Russell makes the following statement about this way of understanding ourselves and our world:

We are more than just biological organisms bounded by the skin. We are also unbounded, part of a greater wholeness, united with the rest of the Universe. If we are to fulfill our role, no longer will we perceive ourselves as isolated individuals. We will need to change, in the most radical way, our attitudes toward ourselves, others, and the planet as a whole.[48]

Working cooperatively and skillfully with others is not only very humanizing, it is very effective. The popular phrase "two heads are better than one" points to our culture's understanding of the importance of the interpersonal dimension of life. When people work together effectively, individual minds are wired together in such a way that the insights of each person become the insights of the whole group. Often, these insights, mingling with other insights and ideas, will lead a group to leaps in understanding that would not have been possible for an individual. When this happens, it is something like a "group mind" at work. In these cases the whole (group) is definitely MORE than the sum of its parts (individuals)! This reality is the heartbeat of interpersonal intelligence.

What are some of the dimensions and capacities related to our interpersonal intelligence?

Following are a set of exercises that illustrate capacities connected with this person-to-person way of knowing and learning. For some of them, obviously, you will need to work with another person, so find someone who is likewise interested in exploring these things with you. Give the exercises a try and see how aware you can become of your own interpersonal intelligence.

Effective Verbal and Nonverbal Communication

From the dawn of self-reflective consciousness, and probably before, humans, like all animals, have been communicating with each other. This communication ranges from our *pre-homo sapiens* grunts, groans, and babblings, to the intricate drawings on cave walls of Neanderthal humanity, to the development of the complex verbal, linguistic, and cognitive patterns of the modern human. We communicate with each other in a multitude of ways, such as facial expressions, body language (including gestures), and the inflection, tone, pitch, and intensity of our speech patterns (which often communicates much more about the *real* meaning of what we are saying than the literal meaning of the words we use).

This exercise involves keeping an observation log on person-to-person communication you experience. You can use it to analyze instances of both effective and ineffective communication in yourself and others. Go ahead and try it. It's good for you!

■　Divide a piece of paper into four equal boxes. Label the upper left-hand box *Effective Communication—Others*, the lower left-hand box *Effective Communication—Self*, the upper right-hand box *Ineffective Communication—Others*, and the lower right-hand box *Ineffective Communication—Self*.

■　For three days carry this chart with you and log things you observe regarding communication patterns between people. Look for both verbal and non-verbal patterns for each category of the chart.

- At the end of the three days, take a second sheet of paper and create a summary list of what effective communication looks like and sounds like based on your log.

- For each item of effective communication, rank yourself on a scale of 1 to 10 (10 equals "The great communicator!" and 1 equals "I might as well be a tree or a stone!").

- Brainstorm ideas of things you can do to improve your person-to-person communication skills.

Sensitivity to Others' Moods, Motivations, and Feelings

This ability involves sensitivity to another person's moods, temperaments, and feelings. It involves a highly tuned ability to "read" another person so to speak. We can learn a great deal about other people by simply training ourselves to be more attentive to "external clues" they give us about who they are what they are thinking and feeling, and their inner states of being.

In this exercise you'll be working with a partner to see how much you can tell about what's going on in each other by simply watching. It'll be strange at first, but try it. It gets easier and can even be fun!

- Each person should find something short to read to the other—a poem, something from the newspaper, a favorite quotation, etc. The listener is to react normally to what is being read but without verbal comment.

- The reader's task is to carefully watch the partner's reaction and try to sense their feelings about the reading. Tell the partner what you think he or she felt and what clues they gave that made you think that. Repeat with the other person reading—observing.

- Now use the same process as above, but this time with a favorite piece of music.

- Finally, try the same basic process, this time using a physical object. Give the object to your partner and let him or her hold it and examine it. Tell your partner what you are observing and what you think your observations mean regarding his or her feelings about the object.

■ After trying each of these, discuss what you have learned with each other.

Working Cooperatively in a Group

In many ways, the state-of-the-art research into interpersonal intelligence is represented by those who have been working in the area of cooperative learning. We grow up in a culture that does not teach us how to cooperate through the normal socialization processes. We do, however, learn how to be "rugged individuals" and how to be competitive. More and more, the skills of cooperation are being required and sought in the workplace. Like any skill, these collaborative skills or "social skills" can and must be explicitly taught and practiced if one is to successfully use them.

In this exercise each person will have a role to play that is crucial to helping the group succeed at the task. I think you will see that three heads really are better than one!

■ Before the exercise, build some kind of construction out of building blocks, Legos, Tinker Toys, or the like. Place the construction behind a screen.

■ In paper bags, put the same pieces you used to build the construction so that someone would have all the pieces needed to copy your construction. (NOTE: You'll have one bag with all the pieces for each team.)

■ Give each team a bag containing the necessary "construction pieces."

■ Divide students into teams of three. In some random manner, have them select person A, B, and C.

■ The process of the exercise is as follows:

- The "answer-giver" looks at the construction behind the screen. His or her task is to help the "builder" replicate the construction. However, the "answer-giver" may not talk. Nor may the "builder" talk.

- The "question-asker" may speak. He or she may ask yes/no questions of the "answer-giver," and the "question-asker" may give verbal instructions to the builder.

- At no time may the "answer-giver" touch the construction pieces; however, he or she may go behind the screen as often as necessary to re-observe the construction.

■ The goal of the exercise is to learn to cooperate and communicate well enough that the "builder" is able to replicate the object behind the screen.

Discerning Others' Underlying Intentions, Behaviors, and Perspectives

Often when we are talking with another person we miss what they are really trying to say because of the "mind-chatter" that goes on in our own head. Our own feelings, opinions, and beliefs get in the way of genuinely grasping "where the other person is coming from."

This exercise involves the social skill of understanding and appreciating a perspective that is quite different from your own. Don't worry; it won't hurt. Try it and see what happens!

■ Intentionally place yourself in a situation where you strongly disagree with another person or persons, whether this be over values, lifestyle, religion, or politics.

■ Start a conversation in which you ask another person to explain their viewpoint to you. Your task is to listen as fully and deeply as you can to what they are saying, trying to understand "where they are coming from."

■ After they have finished speaking, ask questions for further understanding, but keep your own opinions and viewpoints out of the conversation. This exercise may seem easier if you remember that *understanding* a different point of view is not the same as *agreeing* with that point of view!

■ Finally, see if you can paraphrase for them what they said.

■ As soon as you can after this encounter, write a brief paragraph on how your own perspective has been informed by this conversation and what "social skills" you learned (or need to improve) as a result of the experience.

 xercise

"Passing Over" into the Life of Another

As far as we know, humans are the only creatures able to consciously take on the viewpoint of another person and to "experience life through their eyes." This involves the capacity to have empathy and sympathy with another. Cutting-edge research into some of the possibilities of this capacity is being conducted by people exploring parapsychology. These investigations include such phenomena as ESP (Extra Sensory Perception, intuitively knowing with certainty unspoken things about another person) and telepathy (the ability of minds to communicate with each other over great distances).

This exercise works with our ability to deeply identify with another's experience. You will be shifting perspectives a number of times during the exercise, actually trying to see and experience through another's eyes.

■ Divide a blank piece of paper into three columns. Now familiarize yourself with the following lines:

I walked in a desert.
And I cried:
"Ah, God take me from this place!"
A voice said, "It is no desert."
I cried: "Well, but. . .
The sand, the heat, the vacant horizon."
A voice said: "It is no desert."

■ Label the first column on your paper "Self." In this column write some of your reflections on the poem. Consider the following questions to get you started:

- What word or phrase in the poem is most important to me?

- How does the poem make me feel? What emotions does it evoke?

- What are some deserts in my life I want to be taken from?

- What things have happened that helped me see "It is no desert"?

■ Now imagine that you are a young child. Close your eyes for a moment and really try to see yourself as a child. Then read the poem again from this perspective.

■ Label the second column on your paper "Child." As you did above, write some of your reflections on the poem *as a child* would see it. Use the same set of questions, but answer from the child's perspective.

■ Finally, imagine that you are a very old person. Again, close your eyes and try to see yourself as an elder as vividly as you can. Then read the poem from this perspective.

■ Label the third column "Elder" and proceed, as you did above, to reflect on the poem from the perspective of a very old person.

■ Spend a few minutes noting similarities and differences among the meanings of the poem from the three vantage points.

Creating and Maintaining Synergy

The word *synergy* comes from the Greek word *synergos*, meaning "to work together spontaneously." It implies a harmonious interaction with no coercion or deliberate effort. Our own bodies are an excellent example of a synergistic system: we spontaneously sweat when we're too hot; we shiver when we're cold; our brains release adrenaline in situations of danger or when we need an extra boost of energy; and our brains release endorphins in situations full of joy, fun, and celebration to help us achieve ecstasy! Today, something similar to "social synergy" is happening in many groups: a spontaneous give-and-take between individuals and the group in which the individual is both completely autonomous and, at the same time, an integral part of a larger whole.

This exercise deals with learning and utilizing "interpersonal strategies" to help a group function better. While synergy cannot be forced, conditions for it can be fostered.

■ Think of a group, club, or organization to which you belong and in which you are fairly active. Complete an evaluation of their interpersonal/cooperative behaviors (see chart below).

■ For each item you ranked "Excellent" or "Good," think of at least one way that you can support and encourage this behavior to continue (for example, making the group aware of its effective teamwork, asking the group to reflect on its success when high-level cooperation is happening, etc.).

■ For each item you ranked "Not Yet" think of at least one thing you can do to begin changing this ineffective group behavior into something more effective. For example, introduce a consensus-building method that has worked somewhere else, distribute articles on effective group process to members, invite members to go with you to observe a group that "works."

■ Keep a log of things you try with the group and the results you see. Don't give up no matter what happens. Just continue to think of new strategies to foster and catalyze higher and higher levels of cooperation.

	Excellent	Good	"Not Yet"
Looks for consensus			
Listens to each other			
Shares leadership responsibility			
Has a clear mission statement			
Inspires members' involvement			
Has a clear group identity			
Varies meeting methods			
Shares responsibility for work			
Welcomes new members			
Enjoys each other's company			
Others:_____			
_____			

INTERPERSONAL INTELLIGENCE AND THE BRAIN

Research into group dynamics and group process has been the domain of social psychology for the last fifty years. A major focus of this research has been on **how** people interact and relate to each other regardless of **what** they are relating about. Whenever we work with others in a group, whether in a church planning committee, a community drug task force, or a task-team in the workplace, it is our interpersonal intelligence that is operating. Interpersonal intelligence primarily involves the *neo-cortex* of the brain as well as the *frontal lobes,* also known as the *frontal cortex* (see diagram). Following is a brief summary of the functions of these parts of the brain based on Peter Russell's work in *The Brain Book* . The neocortex and frontal lobes represent the most recent growth areas in the continuing development of our neurological system as a species.

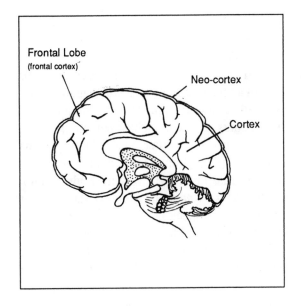

Frontal Lobe
(frontal cortex)

Neo-cortex

Cortex

The **neocortex** is the one-eighth-inch layer of brain cells that covers the whole surface of the brain. However, it is several times larger than the surface of the brain because as it developed it became more and more complex and folded back on itself many times—so much so that if it were spread out flat it would cover an area of about 400 square inches! It is responsible for many of our higher-order capacities such as language and the learning of different skills. It possesses a virtually unlimited information storage capacity and is responsible for our higher-order reasoning and thinking processes.

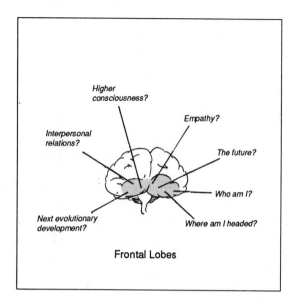

Frontal Lobes

The **frontal lobes** (frontal cortex), the most recent addition to our brain, still remains something of a mystery according to modern brain researchers. However, it has been observed that when we use our interpersonal and intrapersonal intelligence, the frontal lobes are active. Many believe that this new, evolving brain is more related to the future and the next stages of our evolution as a species than the other parts of the brain. Others feel that the frontal lobes give us the capacity to perceive higher states of consciousness, to have empathy with others, and to dream of and actualize possibilities for the future which have not yet been conceived.

Howard Gardner states in *Frames of Mind* that the "personal intelligences" (interpersonal and intrapersonal) tend to use all other forms of intelligence in their operation. Thus, they are the most complex, integrative, and synthesizing of the intelligences. In the case of interpersonal intelligence this can be seen in the many different techniques of person-to-person communication we employ, including spoken and written language, all forms of visual art, dance, hand gestures and body movements, and music.

A second insight, specifically about interpersonal intelligence, comes from the body of research on cooperative learning. Some of these researchers emphasize the importance of explicitly teaching the skills of cooperation to students since our culture does not teach us "interpersonal" skills as a matter of course. This may be the most direct way to improve and expand one's interpersonal intelligence. According to Roger and David Johnson, and Edythe Johnson-Holubec in *Cooperation in the Classroom:*

> Children are not born instinctively knowing how to cooperate with others. And interpersonal and group skills do not magically appear the first time children and adolescents are placed in contact with others. Many elementary and secondary students lack basic social skills such as correctly identifying the emotions of others and appropriately discussing an assignment. Their social ineptitude seems to persist into adulthood. . . .
>
> There is no way to overemphasize the importance of the skills required to work effectively with others. **Cooperative skills are the keystones to maintaining a stable family, a successful career, and a stable group of friends.** Yet these skills have to be taught just as purposefully and precisely as reading and math skills.[49]

Awakening Interpersonal Intelligence

As in the other chapters of this book, the exercises earlier were designed to give you a sense of your own interpersonal intelligence. Generally speaking, interpersonal intelligence is awakened by person-to-person communication and the desire to work together to accomplish something, be it a classroom lesson, a community project, a plan for a party, or a group discussion on politics. Interpersonal intelligence involves awakening and utilizing capacities such as collaborating with other people, negotiating, compromising, building on another's ideas, willingly listening, and the "give and take" of forming group consensus. The most profound experiences of interpersonal intelligence occur when we sense we have "passed over" into another person's life and are learning about and knowing the world from a new perspective, namely through the eyes of another person journeying through this human life. John Dunne describes this experience as follows in *The Way of All the Earth*:

> Passing over . . . entering sympathetically into other lives and times. . . is the way to completeness. This is not an unlikely hypothesis. For whenever a man passes over to other lives or other times, he finds on coming back some neglected aspect of his own life or times which corresponds to what he saw in the other's. Passing over has the effect of activating these otherwise dormant aspects of himself. If he were to stay fixed in himself, fixed in his own standpoint, never passing over but using the self as a vantage point from which to survey all things . . . he would never experience his own wholeness.[50]

Amplifying Interpersonal Intelligence

Once the interpersonal centers of your being have been activated, you can start working to improve your skill in using this way of knowing for understanding, learning, perceiving, and communicating. In *The Aquarian Conspiracy*

Marilyn Ferguson quotes physicist John Platt on the dynamics that naturally emerge as people work together:

> Whenever even two people start giving to each other and working for each other, these qualities and rewards immediately appear—greater mutual benefit, greater ease, and greater individual development at the same time. They appear as soon as a couple begins to work together, or a family, or a neighborhood, or a nation.[51]

Following are four practices you can use to nurture and strengthen this "interpersonal knowing." The practices work with several aspects of this intelligence, including developing collaborative skills and creating situations of positive interdependence in which you learn to rely on and trust other people. The practices focus on developing the foundational skills of interpersonal intelligence.

Empathy for Another and for Yourself

This is a practice in empathy for another and for yourself. It involves several shifts of standing point, each resulting in new knowledge and insight. Have fun and be creative with this one!

- Think of another person you know fairly well. Write this person's name in the center of a piece of blank paper and circle it.

- Draw five lines out from this circled name in different directions. On one line write "Activities," on another "Sayings," on another "Food," on another "Beliefs," and on another "Appearance."

- Now try to get as vivid a mental image of the person as possible and hold it in your head.

- On each of the lines brainstorm different things you know and appreciate about this person. Record these as if they were branches coming off the lines you have drawn out from their name. List:

  - activities you know they enjoy

  - favorite sayings or cliches they use

  - foods they like

  - beliefs you know are important to them

  - things about their appearance

  [NOTE: It is important to keep checking your list with the mental picture you're holding in your head for accuracy and objectivity.]

- When you have finished, write several sentences about the kind of person they are as represented by your diagram, and by your personal relationship with and knowledge of them.

- Now shift perspectives. Pretend you are the person you've just described, and this time they are thinking about you. On a second sheet of paper repeat the exact same steps as above, only this time your name is in the center, and it is the other person mapping and diagraming their impressions of you.

- When the other person is finished thinking about you, have them write several sentences about the kind of person you are as represented by the diagram and by their personal relationship with and knowledge of you.

- Now come back to yourself as you and compare the two sets of sentences—the one you wrote about the other person and the one the other person wrote about you. What do you notice? What did you learn?

Reflection on Empathy Practice

A practice like the one above can do a great deal to develop sensitivity to another person's perspective and feelings. When we "work on ourselves," practicing empathy, we can easily transfer this skill to real situations with other people. This practice can help us unlearn some of the poor interpersonal habits we have developed, such as getting so caught up in our own perspective and feelings we forget the other person, or getting so involved worrying about what we will say next that we completely miss what the other is trying to communicate. Learning to consciously pass over into another's life and then come back to your own with new insight and a new perspective is essential for effective person-to-person relating or knowing!

To continue to work with this practice in everyday life:

☐ In one-to-one conversations, consciously stop the "mind chatter" that is usually present. Don't sit there thinking about how the other person's clothes don't match, your opinion about what they are saying, or what you're going to do after talking with them. Discipline yourself to listen as fully as you can to what they are actually saying, deferring your judgment and evaluation.

☐ Practice seeing yourself through someone else's eyes, your students', boss', colleagues', family's, close friends', and strangers' on the bus. How do they experience what you are saying or doing in any given moment? How can you alter what you're saying or doing to have a more positive effect on them?

☐ In a group meeting, try to pass over into each person who speaks. Find something insightful or helpful in what everyone says, even if you disagree with their main point.

"ME" Concept Mapping

In our interpersonal relationships we often confine ourselves to superficial encounters with each other and thus rob ourselves of the full, rich experience of getting to know another person on a deeper level. What is required is a willingness to momentarily drop our various masks and *persona* and to simply approach others as we are. The next two practices deal with getting to know another and giving effective feedback in an interpersonal encounter. The second practice will be easier if it is preceded by the first. You will need a partner for each.

The first practice involves getting to know your partner by extending their responses in a conversation about things in which they are interested. It applies "concept mapping" to people. Enjoy knowing each other in a different way!

- Decide which one of you will go first. This person will be called the speaker. The other person is the listener. You will switch roles later in the practice.

- To the speaker: Take a blank piece of paper and write ME in the center of page and circle it. Then draw three rays out from the center in different directions. At the end of each of these lines write an area of your life you would enjoy sharing with your partner, for example, a hobby, travels, family, background, etc. After you have chosen your categories, circle the words and give your ME map to your partner.

- The listener then chooses one of the areas and asks you a question about it. Answer their question as you want to. After the answer is complete, the listener may ask you more questions about what you have said or move on to questions about other areas.

- To the listener: While your partner is talking, you are mapping what they say. To do this, draw more rays out from the circles which contain the categories the speaker has chosen. Each time they mention something new in relation to the category, write a word or phrase at the end of one of the rays and circle it. If they are elaborating on something you have already written down, then make more rays off that, continuing to expand the concept map. See the example above, which began with travel, hobby, and family.

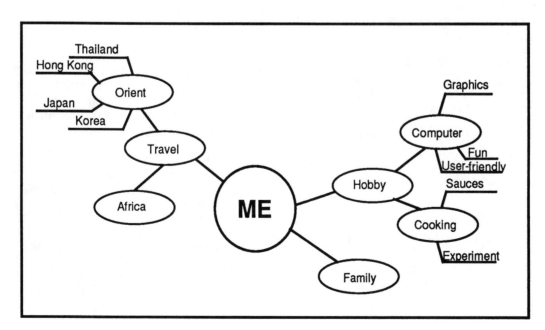

- Allow the speaker about 10 minutes. During this time keep working to extend their responses on anything that you sense they are excited about and want to share. See how much you can get to know about them in this time.

- At the end of 10 minutes, give the ME map that you have been creating to the speaker and thank them for sharing with you. Reverse roles and repeat the process.

- After each of you has completed the exercise, stop and talk with each other about your experience as both the speaker and listener. What happened? What was it like?

ractice

Affirmation of Another

In this practice you'll be working with a partner on the skills of deep acknowledgment and affirmation. You will have an opportunity to experiment with moving beyond the so-called "normal," superficial encounters we generally have with others. I created this practice based on an exercise I learned from Jean Houston. Go ahead and risk it. The benefits are wonderful!

- The first part of this practice is the preceding practice on the "ME" map. It can help you get to know each other better and can build trust between you.

- We will now try to sense and acknowledge each other at a more profound and universal level. Sit directly opposite your partner, close enough so you can comfortably touch hands.

- One of the partners now places their hands out, palms upward. The other lightly places their hands, palms down, on their partner's hands. Close your eyes and together take several deep breaths and relax.

- Spend some minutes focusing your full attention on that point of contact between you. Let go of all other thoughts, concerns, and anxieties and allow yourself to experience the presence of this other person. Feel the flow of life and energy between you.

- Open your eyes and without speaking, acknowledge your friend's presence before you. Try to express through your eyes and facial expression your appreciation and gratitude for them. (two minutes)

- Now close your eyes once again and focus on the point of contact between you and your partner's hands. Breathe deeply and relax. (one minute)

- Again, without speaking, open your eyes. As you look at your partner this time, try to imagine the whole of humanity's past sitting before you in your partner. Notice thoughts, feelings, images, and reflections that come to you as you consider your partner from this perspective. (two minutes)

- Close your eyes and let these thoughts, images, and feelings go. Again, focus on the contact in your hands, aware of the flow of life and energy between you. Breathe deeply and relax. (one minute)

- Now, for one final time, open your eyes and imagine the whole of humanity's future sitting before you in your partner. As you see the future in your partner, be aware of your own hopes, dreams, desires, and anticipations for the future, both for yourself and for your descendents. (two minutes)

- Once again, close your eyes and spend a few more minutes focusing attention on that point of physical contact in your hands and the life force flowing between you.

- When you are ready, share what you have seen, experienced, and learned in this meeting and acknowledging of each other.

Reflection on "ME" Mapping and "Affirmation of Another" Practices

Providing genuine support, encouragement, and affirmation for another person seems easy, especially when dealing with things such as hobbies, hair styles, clothing styles, and verbalized thoughts. When we move to deeper levels of this practice, however, the acknowledgment and affirmation of another's essence or core being (beyond the externals) becomes much more difficult. People who have tried meeting each other at deeper, universal levels bear witness to the fact that once you have known another in this way it is as though a door is now open and you are free to relate on this new, higher-order, interpersonal plane. This level includes, but is not limited to, the surface meeting. In fact, the so-called "surface" or "external" things are understood in the much larger context of the whole person.

To continue using concept mapping and the practice of deep acknowledgment and affirmation of others:

- Try using concept mapping to explore several aspects of personal relationships, such as student behavior problems, the process and dynamics of a group discussion, planning a party or a class field trip, or exploring your feelings about someone or something.

- Practice disciplined "people watching" and see how much you can learn and how attuned you can become to other people, their feelings, expressions, body language, tone of speech, etc.

- In talking with someone about a relatively mundane topic, practice asking questions that extend the other's responses so that you get to know them better. Ask questions of why and how and say things like "tell me more" and "that's very interesting."

- With every person you meet during the day, practice finding something you genuinely like about them and telling them what that is. Be as specific as you can. For example, rather than "I like your tie," try "I like the design on your tie. Why did you choose it?"

Can You "Zooley?"

The final practice in this section deals with learning to cooperate and collaborate with others to accomplish an assigned task. This is very different from working as an individual or in competition with others. In a situation of genuine cooperation, the goal is for each person in the group to make their best contribution to the total group effort and thus to participate in and receive full benefits from the success of the group.

The following practice "Can You 'Zooley?'"[52] comes from the IMPACT program, a National Diffusion Network project distributed through Phi Delta Kappa. It is an exercise in symbolic thinking and deductive reasoning. It generally takes a little time to get into it, but once that happens, watch out!

■ Put students into groups of three and assign one person to play the role of observer of the group's process. The observer should contribute to and participate in the task and also record things observed about how the group is working, its strategies for approaching the task, communication patterns, roles people adopt, etc.

■ Pass out copies of the "Zooley Exercise" and "Zooley Study Questions" (see blacklines at end of this chapter). There should be one exercise sheet with questions per group.

■ Introduce the exercise as follows:

- This is a game in which you are visiting a zoo in a place where you do not know the language, so you have to figure things out by other means.

- The study questions are there to help you figure out the language of this zoo. Your task is to work through the questions and agree on one answer for each question.

  CLUE: You don't have to answer the questions in order. Once you have found an answer to any of the questions, it can be used to "break the code" of the others.

- Observer, don't forget to keep track of what your group does and things you notice about how you are working together.

■ Give the teams 20 minutes to work, then hand out copies of the "Zooley Answer Key" (see blackline at end of this chapter).

■ After the groups have finished checking their answers, have the observer read what

he/she wrote down. Have other team members add to the list.

Reflection on "Zooley" Practice

This kind of exercise is powerful in helping you practice doing things together with others in a group. People are often astonished by what they were able to accomplish working together, which simply would not have been possible working individually (just consider what it would have been like to "Zooley" by yourself!). Others have said that working with a team is like "wiring individual minds together" so that what happens is the creation of a "group mind," which is more than the sum of its parts! When people work together in cooperative teams, leaps in thinking and understanding are possible that are simply not available to us when we work alone.

To work on your "collaborative spirit" every day:

☐ Put yourself in at least one situation each day where you *must* rely on someone other than yourself and where you *must* work cooperatively.

☐ Experiment with ways of helping a group you are part of improve its interpersonal skills. For example, discuss what you did to help or support each other in a meeting and how you could improve support and cooperation in future meetings. Create a group symbol, slogan, or motto. List successes and accomplishments on the wall. Plan a celebration or an outing.

☐ At the conclusion of **any** cooperative task in which you are engaged, stop for a moment to discuss what things you did that helped each other with the task and what you could do better next time you work together—how could you help each other even more?

Teaching and Learning with Interpersonal Intelligence

So far we have tried to awaken interpersonal intelligence as a valid way of knowing and understanding life. We have familiarized ourselves with it and have begun to learn how to use, nurture, and strengthen it. In the next section, we work with interpersonal capacities as a way of learning and teaching content-based information.

As mentioned earlier, state-of-the-art application of and experimentation with effectively using interpersonal intelligence is occurring through the investigation of various approaches to **cooperative learning** for our public schools. The five key ingredients specified by Sue Archibald Marcus and Penny McDonald for successful interpersonal lessons have been documented by James Bellanca and Robin Fogarty in *Blueprints for Thinking in the Cooperative Classroom*:

B = Bring in higher-order thinking so students are challenged to think deeply and to transfer subject matter.

U = Unite the class so students form bonds of trust, which enable teamwork.

I = Insure individual learning. Each student is accountable to master all skills and knowledge. The groups are a means to facilitate mastery before the teacher checks each individual through quizzes, tests, essays, or other more authentic assessment strategies.

L = Look back and debrief *what* and *how* students learned. Students are taught to "process" or "evaluate" their thinking, feelings, and social skills. This emphasis on "taught" student evaluation shifts the responsibility for learning from the teacher to student.

D = Develop students' social skills. By providing explicit training in the social skills, the teacher helps students master cooperative abilities during cooperative work.

"First this happened..."   "And then..."

Joint Storytelling in Social Studies

The following social studies lesson emphasizes the person-to-person learning and knowing that are at the heart of interpersonal intelligence. Students will work in pairs and have a chance to "pass over" into each other's thinking and imagination. It presupposes that students have had prior input and/or have studied the culture.

■ Select a particular culture that you have been studying as a class. Before the lesson, create a brief story about this culture using places, characters, situations, and the history of that culture. Make the story full of sensory-based imagery.

■ Place students in groups of two sitting close so they can hear each other speak in quiet voices. Have them designate one partner as person A and the other person B.

■ Explain the process of the lesson to the class:

- In a moment I will begin telling you a story based on a culture we have been studying. The story will be rich with images, sensations, and symbols.

- As I tell the story, fully engage your brain in imagining the story as vividly as you can, seeing, hearing, smelling, tasting, and touching what I will suggest to you.

- When I reach a certain point in the story, I will ring a bell. At that point, person B, without a break, picks up the story and tells what happens next. Try to fill your story with lots of sensory images—colors, sounds, shapes, touches, tastes, etc.

- When I ring the bell again, person A will, again without a break, pick up the story wherever person B has taken it and will tell what happens next.

- Every time the bell rings, the other person resumes the story, telling what happens next based on where your partner took the story in the last round.

■ Are there any questions? It is very important that you listen carefully to each other, trying to imagine everything your partner suggests. Don't worry about what you will say when it's your turn. When the time comes you'll know what to say!

■ Now let us begin.

[NOTE: Suggest that they keep their eyes closed throughout the exercise so that they are not distracted by things and people they might see. It is also often easier to visualize with closed eyes.]

Example story:

You find yourself on a packaged bus tour of the ancient ruins of Mexico on a cloudy day. The bus stops for a while and you have some free time, so you get off the bus. All around you are vendors selling postcards, Coca-Cola signs, candy wrappers on the ground, tourists snapping silly pictures. You feel disgusted by this and want to get away for a few moments. You start walking toward a nearby hill.

You climb to the top of the hill, away from the bus. You suddenly notice that the sky seems different; the sun has come out, and it feels warm on your skin. There is a freshness in the air that is gently blowing through your hair. You look around and notice there are no longer any telephone poles, no traffic, no roads, no planes in the sky, no sound of activity anywhere. A strange and powerful silence surrounds you.

As you continue to investigate the area, your explorations lead you to a cave in the side of the hill. It looks safe and inviting so you decide to enter it. To your surprise there is a door at the back of the cave. You decide to open the door and see what is on the other side.

As you step through the door, you find you have stepped backward in time to ancient Mexico. You find yourself in an undiscovered temple by the Great Sun Pyramid. There is a person sleeping in the far corner of the temple. You go to the person, lightly shake them and say "It's time to wake up now!"

■ At this point ring the bell and person B tells what happens next. Allow 1 ½ minutes to pass, then ring the bell again and let person A pick up the story and tell what happens next. Continue in this fashion until each person has spoken three or four times. As person A begins their last round of speaking, tell them they are to finish the story.

■ Ring the bell three times to bring the storytelling to a close. Have partners share with each other what happened and what this was like for them.

■ Group discussion:

- Would any partners like to share what this was like? What happened?

- What were some of your feelings? What surprised you?

- What new things did you learn about this culture from the exercise?

- What did you learn about each other?

- Did you like this process? Why/why not?

- What ideas do you have about other ways we could use this process in our class?

Reflection on Storytelling Lesson

Many people experience a profound merging of their thinking as they participate in this lesson, almost as if they knew what their partner would say before they said it! Others have shared what it was like being inside of each other's minds. If you continue to practice activating your interpersonal intelligence and using it everyday, your interpersonal sensitivities and abilities will grow by leaps and bounds.

To work with interpersonal intelligence in content-based, daily lessons:

☐ Group students in teams of three and divide a lesson into three parts. Have each student be responsible for learning their part and teaching it to the others.

☐ Assign research projects in which students cooperatively create their research plan, implement it, and report their findings/results to the rest of the class.

☐ Have students cooperatively create a story or write a paper, with each student having input to the story or paper. Together they write it, improve it, and present it.

☐ Try preparing for a test in cooperative groups, working until the group is confident each person knows the material. Then let students take the test individually. Return to the groups to discuss and relearn things that were missed on the test.

Transferring Interpersonal Intelligence to Life

In the *Manual for Co-Creators of the Quantum Leap*, Barbara Hubbard makes the following statement regarding where she perceives we are in the evolutionary journey:

> Humanity stands at the threshold of the greatest age in history. We have the capacity to overcome the ancient problems of hunger, disease, and violence. We can now realize new possibilities which will make us a universal species, beyond planet boundedness, self-centered consciousness, scarcity, and degeneration in a universe of immeasurable dimensions. . . .

The unity of the human race lies in our common aspiration for a stage of being beyond the current human condition. The religions of the world have laid down the template of the new stage of evolution. The sciences of the world have given us the power to self-destruct or co-create new worlds. This generation has been given the choice of a graceful or disgraceful transition to the next state of evolution.[53]

The final exercise in this chapter deals with the transfer of interpersonal intelligence to daily living. It uses interpersonal ways of knowing and perceiving to amplify and deepen our experience of life, as well as to catalyze new growth and development of unactualized interpersonal potentials. This is a good example of how interpersonal intelligence relies on all the other intelligences to do its work.

Transfer Strategy

The Self Apart and the Self as a Part

In the following exercise you have an opportunity to examine your "individualistic self" and your "interpersonal self" and discover how they can work together. I designed this transfer strategy based on a powerful process used in *Life Force* by Jean Houston.

- On a good-sized piece of paper draw a large box with arms and legs. At the top draw a stylized version of your own head.

- Now, in a random fashion all over the inside of the box, as if you were drawing the inner workings of a very complex machine, begin to list things you do as an individual for which you don't need contact and direct interaction with other people, such as reading a book, doing your laundry, working in your yard, or preparing a speech.

- For each thing you have listed, create some kind of visual image—a picture, design, or shape—that you associate with what you've listed. Work in colors. Be creative, intuitive, and have fun.

- Begin to draw connections between various items you have listed and drawn in the box. Write a word or phrase on each connecting line you draw to remind you of what the connection is. Try to get as clear a sense as possible of the workings of this individualistic self.

- Spend a few minutes looking at the picture you have drawn. Label it "The Self Apart." Ask yourself these questions:

  - What have I learned about myself by objectifying myself as an individual in this drawing?

  - What patterns of individualistic behavior are the strongest in my life? Which are weak?

  - What are the most interesting/informative connections I have seen?

  - What are the pluses and minuses about "The Self Apart"?

- Now set aside this picture of your individualistic self.

- Take a second sheet of paper and place it in front of you on the table. Then close your eyes and, as vividly as you can, imagine a group of people standing in a circle holding hands. Concentrate on this circle of people for a few minutes and see if you recognize any of them. Some may be present acquaintances, others may be from the past, others may be unknown to you, while still others may be fictional.

- As you reflect on this circle, meditate on the ancient saying: "No man is an island entire in itself; every man is a piece of the continent, a part of the main." As you continue to focus on the circle of people, repeat this saying several times.

- Let this thought subside. Now imagine that the circle of people is slowly beginning to expand until it encompasses you, and you

are in the center of the circle. See yourself in the circle and the circle in you. You are one with the circle. Spend several minutes meditating on this awareness.

- Now open your eyes and draw a large circle on the paper in front of you. Around the circle draw many stick figures so that you get the impression that the circle is made of people.

- Trying to stay in touch with what you have seen and experienced when visualizing the circle of people, begin to write and draw things inside the circle that express the interpersonal knowings and feelings you have about yourself. You are not alone; you are not an island. You are an intimate part of other people, and they are part of you. Draw things that remind you of this.

- When you have allowed yourself plenty of time to complete this drawing, label it "The Self as a Part." Reflect on your drawing in a similar manner as you did with the first drawing:

  - What immediately grabs your attention as you look at this drawing?

  - What surprises you? intrigues you? delights you?

  - What do you learn about your own interpersonal processes from your drawing?

  - Which aspects of yourself as a part are strongest? Which are weak?

  - What are the pluses and minuses of "The Self as a Part"?

- Now place the two drawings side by side. Obviously, the true picture is a blend of "The Self Apart" and "The Self as a Part." Spend a few minutes noting similarities and differences you see between the two pictures.

- Then give your full attention to the first drawing for a period of 10 seconds, staring at it intently (count the 10 seconds in your head). Then shift your full attention to the second drawing for 10 seconds. Then shift back to the first and stare at it for 7 seconds.

Then shift to the second and stare at it for 7 seconds.

- Continue shifting back and forth, giving your full attention to each picture for 5, 4, 3, 2, and 1 seconds respectively.

- Then close your eyes. Imagine a blending of the two pictures taking place within you. Know and experience yourself as an individual, and let that power flow into your relationships with other people. Know and experience yourself as an intimate part of other people. Let that power flow into your being as an individual. Allow a minimum of three minutes for this blending to occur.

- When you are ready, open your eyes and spend time recording your reflections and insights about what happened in the exercise, as well as practical implications of what you have seen, known, and experienced.

Reflection on the "Self Apart" and the "Self as a Part" Strategy

Part of the power of this exercise is its work with some of the unconscious dimensions and processes of interpersonal knowing. It allows you to "nurture the seeds" of the natural human inclination and desire to do things together with other people. However, it also provides a way to hold that in tension with another natural human inclination, namely the desire to protect the individual self, and the fear of loosing individuality in a group. The exercise can help us see that in reality there is no conflict, for a group is made up of individuals, each of whom brings their individual uniqueness. Nevertheless, in a group, or in any person-to-person encounter, individuality is transformed into corporate power! Thus the individual, through others, can become much more than is possible alone.

CAN YOU ZOOLEY?

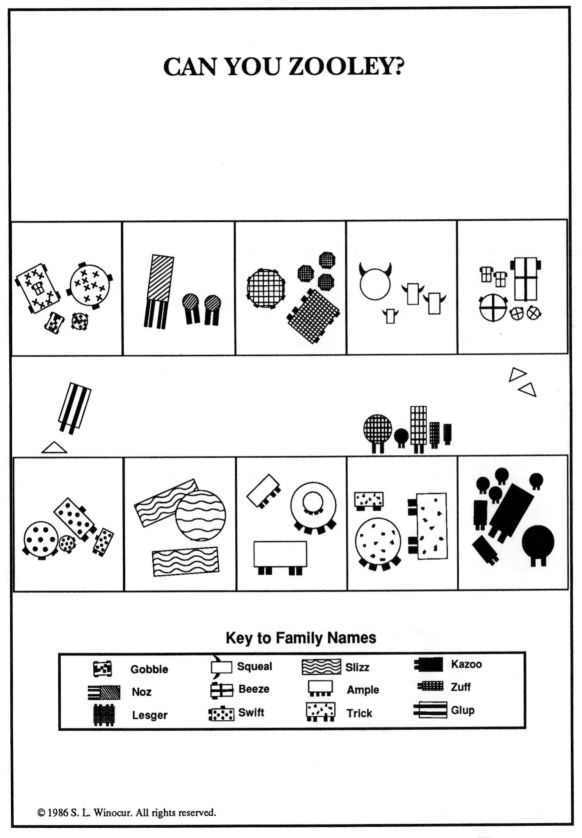

Key to Family Names

Gobbie	Squeal	Slizz	Kazoo
Noz	Beeze	Ample	Zuff
Lesger	Swift	Trick	Glup

SKYLIGHT PUBLISHING, INC.

ZOOLEY
Study Sheet

1. What family is visiting the polar bears?

2. What kind of family are they?

3. Whose family is the largest?

4. Which is the family of spiders?

5. Whose son has Mr. Crocodile just swallowed?

6. Which swimming family has only 3 sons?

7. Which family has just 3 daughters?

8. Is the polar bear's cub male or female?

9. Which family has no offspring?

10. Which is a family of snakes?

11. Which is a kangaroo?

12. What will be the surname of the elephant's baby which is soon to be born?

13. How many sons has Mr. Giraffe?

14. Which family has no father?

15. Which mother is away at the hospital?

16. Who are the neighbors of the monkeys?

17. A wee pelican has wandered into whose cage?

18. Which is a family of pelicans?

19. Give the names of each kind of animal.

20. What is the zookeeper's name?

21. What are the three other objects in the zoo?

SKYLIGHT
PUBLISHING, INC.

ZOOLEY

Answer Key

1. Zuff.

2. Humans. They are outside the cages observing other animals.

3. Kazoo.

4. Lesger. Spiders have eight legs.

5. Breeze's son was swallowed. Thus, Gobbie are crocodiles and gender of each animal is designated by shape.

6. Squeal. Note flipper and name similarity (i.e., Seal-Squeal).

7. Lesger. Spiders.

8. Male.

9. Slizz. There are only adults in the cage.

10. Slizz. See lines similar to shape of snake.

11. Swift. See pocket on side of female.

12. Ample. See baby inside female; not a Gobbie because a male is inside a male.

13. Mr. Noz has none.

14. Squeal.

15. Noz. No female is in the cage.

16. Trick. This is a family of polar bears.

17. Gobbies. This wee animal proves to be a pelican.

18. Beeze.

19. Gobbie: crocodiles   Beeze: pelicans   Trick: polar bears

    Noz: giraffes   Swift: kangaroo   Kazoo: monkeys

    Lesger: spiders   Slizz: snakes   Zuff: humans

    Squeal: seals   Ample: elephants   Glup: ?

20. Mr. Glup.

21. These symbols have no specific meaning. This question allows the student to use divergent thinking skills. Accept any answer.

SKYLIGHT PUBLISHING, INC.

Personal Reflection Log
Interpersonal Intelligence

Observations made—what happened?

_____

_____

_____

Emotional/feeling states:

_____

_____

_____

Reflections, insights & discoveries:

_____

_____

_____

Self-evaluation (comfort zone/skill ability):

├ — — — — — — — — — — — — — — — — — — — ┤

Like a fish in water   Like landing on another planet

Practical strategies for fully activating/developing this intelligence within myself:

_____

_____

_____

Application ideas for my classroom, family, community, or organization:

_____

_____

_____

Know Thyself...
Thy Cognition and
Thy Consciousness
Explorations of Intrapersonal Intelligence

Oneness and unity are qualities of our universe. Our tendency to think of the world in terms of non-interacting parts violates the most accurate descriptions of the world we have, those of modern physics . . . .

*But we keep insisting on not seeing who we really are. The human mind appears bedeviled in realizing its true affinities with the universe in which it finds itself. We cannot easily comprehend our indissoluble oneness with the cosmos . . . . We are not made up of fragments **of** the universe, we **are** that universe.*

—Larry Dossey, *Space Time and Medicine*

In 1969 humanity observed itself on the horizon of the moon. This single event catalyzed a new awareness from which there is no going back—for indeed, we saw into the very heart and soul of our planet and thus into the depths of our own being.

Today, in the West, interest in the intrapersonal dimensions of the self is on the rise. We are in the midst of something like a revolution in human consciousness or self-awareness. A number of new "consciousness disciplines" are emerging in the scientific community: **transpersonal psychology**—a psychology dealing with our capacities for self transcendence, transformation, deep insight, and unity in the midst of our otherwise fragmented lives; **parapsychology**—a psychology that investigates so-called "paranormal" or extra-ordinary capacities including telepathy (the direct interchange of information between two or more minds), precognition (the acquisition of information about the future), psychokinesis (placing a physical object in motion by will alone), and clairvoyance (the acquisition of information from inanimate objects); and **humanistic psychology**—a psychology concerned with activating latent human potentials that we all possess. In addition to these formal investigations, more and more people are turning to practices of reflective meditation and visualization. The number of self-help and self-improvement books on the shelves of even the local supermarket is at an all-time high. Peter Russell, author of *The Global Brain*, has made the following observation:

> Rapid as the growth of the information industry is, it may not be the fastest growing area of human activity. There are indications that the movement toward the transformation of consciousness is growing even faster. The number of people involved in this area seems to be doubling as rapidly as every four years or so. . . . [54]

So what are the discoveries about these intrapersonal dimensions or our "consciousness capacities?" Following is a summary of some of the research findings:

■ **Within our one mind we have hundreds of potential states of being or levels of awareness.** These include such things as an awareness of the wholeness of the universe, the mystery, depth, and greatness of our individual lives, and a sense of oneness or a deep interdependence with the natural world.

■ **We have the ability to shift from one state of consciousness to another at will.** If your present state of consciousness is not helping you deal effectively with a given situation, you can shift to a more optimal state.

■ **We have a seemingly endless capacity for improving the quality of our own thinking.** Cognitive research in the area of metacognition (thinking about thinking) has discovered countless strategies for teaching thinking skills to others, for improving our own thinking patterns, and for achieving high levels of transferring learning into everyday life.

■ **Within our unconscious mind we possess capacities for controlling many bodily functions we used to think were automatic.** These include not only heart rate, blood pressure, and body temperature, but also untapped powers for accelerating and assisting the body's natural healing processes.

■ **Creativity is not a given at birth, rather, it is a dynamic process that can be learned, taught, and improved throughout our lives.** In fact, there are things we can do to "turn on" more of our creative potential and to train ourselves to be more creative.

When dealing with intrapersonal intelligence, Howard Gardner says that we are dealing with an inward-directed intelligence that is concerned with knowledge about and the identity of the self, whereas interpersonal intelligence is externally focused and concerned about our relationships with other people. He states:

> Each form [of the personal intelligences] has its own pull, with the intrapersonal intelligence involved chiefly is an individual's examination and knowledge of his own feelings, while the interpersonal intelligence looks outward, toward the behavior, feelings and motivations of others.[55]

What are some of the dimensions and capacities related to our intrapersonal intelligence?

The following exercises illustrate capacities connected with our self-reflective abilities. Give some of them a try with your students and yourself and see if you and they can get a sense of this intelligence.

Concentration of the Mind

This capacity entails the ability to bring the mind to a single point of focus and to hold it there. Part of the discipline involved here is being able to rid the mind of extraneous thoughts so that one-pointed attention is possible. Just think about the many situations in your daily life when this skill is sorely needed, whether it be negotiating a business deal, conversing with your husband or wife over some critical family matter, or staying focused on a task or project long enough to see it through to a successful completion.

This exercise is a concentration practice. It provides you with an opportunity to experiment with bringing your mind to single-pointed focus. Why not give it a try? You may be surprised that it's not as easy as you thought it might be!

- Find a picture in which there is a circular or spiral design, such as a galaxy of stars, a flower, a picture of the earth in space, or a nautilus shell.

- Go to a quiet place where you will not be disturbed and place the picture in front of you on an otherwise clear, non-cluttered surface.

- Close your eyes and take several deep breaths from the abdomen and relax as completely as you can.

- When you are ready, open your eyes and stare at the picture in front of you, giving it your full and undivided attention. See how long you can remain focused on it without other thoughts coming into your mind. Don't think about the picture in an analytical manner. Just experience it, keeping the mind clear and open.

- When something distracts you and you loose your concentration, don't get cross with yourself. Simply acknowledge the distraction, put it aside, and return to the picture.

- After 10 minutes, stop and reflect on what this was like. What did you notice about your ability to concentrate?

- Another time try the same practice with a bell, using the tone of its ring as the point of concentration. See how long you can continue to hear it after it has been rung.

- On still another occasion, try the practice with an object from nature or an art object in your home.

Mindfulness

Mindfulness is the ability to observe your thoughts, feelings, actions, and sensations in a detached, objective way. Mind-fullness is the opposite of mind-lessness. It involves the skill of taking on the standpoint of an outside observer in relation to your own experience. Consciousness researchers call this "being a witness" to your life. Think about the situations you face every day in which it is important to be able to step back and objectively analyze your given situation, without getting caught up in emotions, opinions, intellectual ideas or theories, and immediate reactions. These include such things as situations that don't turn out the way you had anticipated; volatile, sensitive situations at work; and situations that are potentially stressful.

This exercise is a mindfulness practice. It involves learning how to pay attention to details of many routine parts of daily living. Learning how to practice "being a witness" to the many different levels of experience present, in even the most mundane encounters, can help you learn how to "take a step back" in more complex and involved encounters. It is a practice that can quickly take you beyond feeling victimized or "tossed this way and that" by the seeming capriciousness of daily living. Try it! It doesn't hurt, but pay attention!

■ Choose some routine task that you perform every day, such as washing the dishes, straightening up your room, or brushing your teeth.

■ Perform the task in slow motion so that you can watch each and every movement, and each part of the task as you do it. Keep your full attention on the task itself. Do not think about when it will be over and what you'll do after you're finished. Simply watch yourself very carefully, observing everything that goes on.

■ Do extraneous thoughts or feelings arise? Notice them, but don't allow yourself to "follow a thought" or get "caught up" in a feeling. Let them pass of their own accord, like bubbles floating on the breeze. Then return to your mindful observation of the task you are performing.

■ When you have completed the task, pause and reflect on what this action was like. What did you notice and/or learn about how your mind operates?

■ Another time, try the same practice when you are eating. Slow way down and watch everything that is involved in the eating process, from the physical movements, to anticipation in the brain, to the secretion of saliva in the mouth, and so forth.

■ On still another occasion, when you are standing in a line or waiting for a bus, direct your mindfulness to the process of waiting and/or standing, seeing how aware you can become of all that is involved in this.

Metacognition

The literal meaning of metacognition is "thinking about thinking." As far as we know, human creatures are the only ones that have this self-reflective ability, that is, the ability to step back from a situation in which they are involved and watch themselves. This capacity gives us an immense amount of freedom because in self-awareness lies the possibility of conscious change. We can observe our thinking patterns and actions in a given situation and learn from them. We can alter both our thinking patterns and our behavior for greater effectiveness the next time we are in a similar situation.

The following exercise is adapted from *Catch Them Thinking* by James Bellanca and Robin Fogarty. It involves a metacognitive technique for evaluating your own thinking. Have fun with this and see what (and **how**) you think!

■ When you have completed an assignment, whether on your job, at home, in the classroom, or for an organization of which you are a part, stop and evaluate yourself by writing your answers to the following questions:

- What was I expected to do?

- In this assignment, what did I do well?

- If I had to do this task over, what would I do differently?

- What help do I need?

- For three weeks, keep a log in which you write your answers to these questions once a day.

- At the end of the three weeks, look back over what you have written, noticing motifs of your reflections. What changes have happened in your thinking during this time? What things do you still need to work on?

xercise

Awareness and Expression of Different Feelings

This capacity involves such things as being able to communicate what you are feeling in a given moment, to express your emotions in symbolic forms such as art, poetry, song, or dance, and to understand your feelings and their impact on your behavior. Part of this capacity involves being able to get enough distance on your feelings that you can notice differences among feelings as well as predict the types of situations which evoke certain emotional responses.

The following exercise deals with understanding and expressing your feelings. Try to be as honest with yourself as you can. See how aware you can be!

- At the end of the day plot your different moods during the day on the graph below. (The vertical numbers represent high and low points and the horizontal numbers time sequence.)

- Place a mark at the high point of the day and one at the low point. Then look at the time before and after these points; think about other changes in your moods. Make marks at the appropriate places.

- Now connect the marks with a continuous curving line so that you have a visual picture of the mood changes and the "affective flow" of the day.

- For each point that you have marked along the axes, jot a brief note about what was going on that catalyzed the mood shift.

- Using colored markers or crayons, create a spectrum of colors from left to right to match the different moods you experienced.

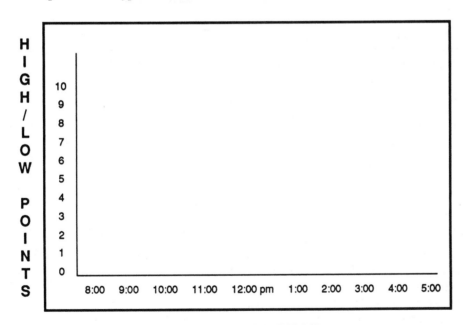

- Finally, think of the kind of music you would play as a background for each of the different moods of the day. Note these on the graph.

- Try doing this every day for a week. At the end of the week lay all of your mood graphs side by side and reflect on the week. What do you learn about yourself as you look at the week in this way?

Transpersonal Sense of the Self

This awareness involves a deep, intuitive knowledge of the solitary self as part of a larger order of things. We somehow know that we are more than just "here today, gone tomorrow." We intuitively know that, at some level, we are part of other people's lives and they are part of ours. We know that all of the things to which we cling (e.g. possessions, relationships, beliefs, and values) are temporal and therefore are not an adequate measure or definition of who we really are at deeper levels.

In the following exercise you have an opportunity to work with some of your priorities as they relate to your current self-understanding. Give it a try. Who are you, *REALLY?*

- Draw the chart below on a blank piece of paper.

- Imagine that you are going on a long journey that will last for many years. For each column list those things that you would definitely take with you.

- Now, imagine that the journey has gotten much more difficult than you thought and you must discard five items you brought with you. Decide what to throw away and cross them off the list.

- New problems have arisen and the expedition has run completely out of money so you have to get a job, but it is in a field you know nothing about. What things on the list would have to go in light of this? Once again, cross them off the chart.

Goods/Possessions	Work/Skills	Relationships	Beliefs/Values

- Finally, it has suddenly become necessary for you to become a completely new person, *totally* different from what you have been. What things would this knock off your list?

- In light of all of the above, write a brief paragraph about your current self-understanding. Begin with the sentence "My current understanding of who I *REALLY* am is. . . ."

xercise

Higher-Order Thinking and Reasoning

The most basic level of thinking and reasoning involves the recall of memorized factual information. A second, more complex level is "processing thinking" which links items from the first level into more involved thinking/reasoning processes such as comparing and contrasting, analyzing, classifying, and discerning consequences. Higher-order thinking/reasoning occurs on the third level when both factual information and process thinking are synthesized, integrated, and applied to creative thinking and problem solving in everyday situations.

The exercise is adapted from *Catch Them Thinking*. In it you will have a chance to "track your thinking patterns" as they unfold in both writing and answering higher-order questions. Don't panic. It's not as hard as it sounds!

- Begin by familiarizing yourself with the "Three Story Intellect" on the following page. Make sure you understand the differences between the three levels of recall thinking, process thinking, and synthesis or application thinking.

- With your partner, select a story, a paragraph from a textbook, a magazine article, words to a popular song, a newspaper editorial, or a recent TV show that you have both seen or know.

- Working as individuals, use the "Three-Story Intellect" and write three questions at each level about the item you have selected.

- When both you and your partner have completed these questions, exchange them and write the answers to each other's questions.

- When you are finished, return the set of questions to each other and reflect on the kind of responses your questions provoked. Did they in fact promote the level of thinking you intended? Rewrite any questions you think could be better.

- Share insights and learnings with your partner.

INTRAPERSONAL INTELLIGENCE AND THE BRAIN

The intrapersonal capacities you experienced in the preceding exercises represent an intriguing portfolio of human potentials that are, for the most part, in various states of latency in Western culture. And yet, if we are to survive, both as a species and as Planet Earth, they may well be the most important intelligence capacities we possess. As with interpersonal intelligence, intrapersonal intelligence primarily involves the *frontal lobes* of the brain as well as the *neocortex* (see Chapter 6). In *Frames of Mind*, Gardner further explains this:

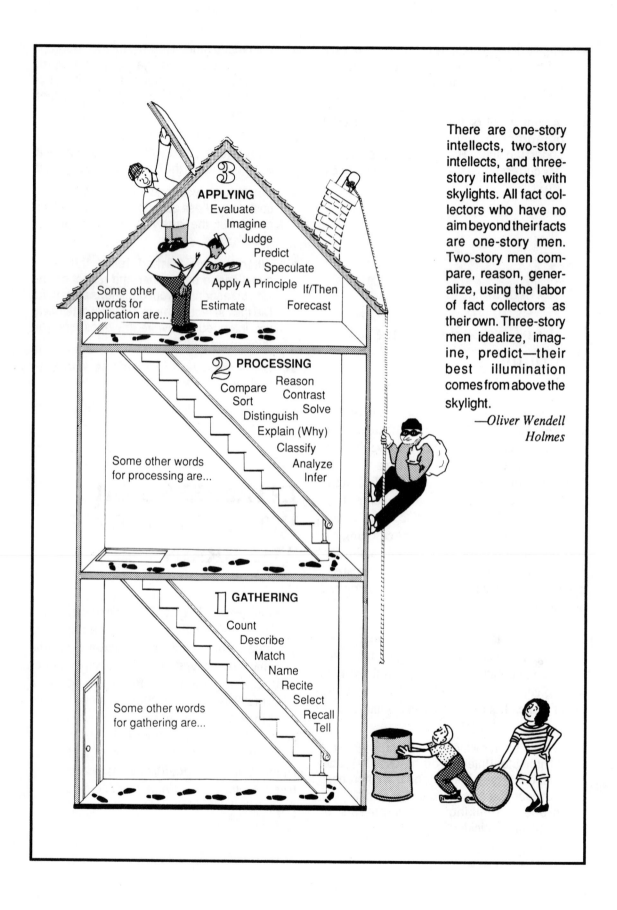

There are one-story intellects, two-story intellects, and three-story intellects with skylights. All fact collectors who have no aim beyond their facts are one-story men. Two-story men compare, reason, generalize, using the labor of fact collectors as their own. Three-story men idealize, imagine, predict—their best illumination comes from above the skylight.

—*Oliver Wendell Holmes*

The frontal lobes constitute the meeting place *par excellence* for information from the two great functional realms of the brain: the posterior regions, which are involved in the processing of all sensory information. . .and the limbic system, where individual motivational and emotional functions are housed and whence one's internal states are generated. . . .Thus, by virtue of their strategic anatomical location and connections, the frontal lobes have the potential to serve as the major integrating station—and this they do.[56]

One of the most important things in consciousness research today is the effort to create "maps" of the development of human consciousness. In many cultures outside the Western world, the existence of a wide variety of states of consciousness is commonly accepted. In these cultures, numerous "maps" of different states have been created, for example, the stages on the journey to enlightenment in the Orient, the steps for full union with higher consciousness in India, and the guidelines/practices for receiving divine guidance in the West and Middle East.

Following is a summary of five distinct stages of consciousness on which most contemporary researchers agree—both Western and non-Western. These stages can be thought of as expressions of self-identity as well as our picture of the world.

Body Awareness ("If it feels good, do it!") At this level, the self is almost exclusively identified with the physical body and with the senses. Think of an infant whose total world and awareness is one of eating, sleeping, touching, going to the toilet, and drinking—physical comfort is everything! The infant is basically unaware of the existence of a self. The only important thing is bodily comfort and a secure environment. As infants grow they begin to develop certain motor skills, such as manual dexterity, mobility through crawling and walking, the experience of getting stronger, and having the ability to defend themselves. This stage of awareness is necessary for basic survival.

Emotional Awareness ("I am I! But WHO am I?") At this stage, self-understanding is primarily identified with the emotions. We are driven by a multitude of conscious and unconscious needs, such as food, sexuality, and the desire to

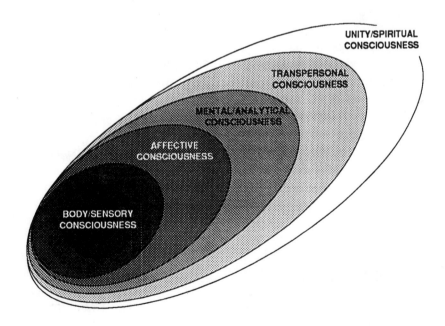

be loved. The early parts of the development are closely related to the body stage. However, with the emergence of language skills, the *ego-mind* ("I" awareness) emerges and begins to differentiate itself from the body. Think again of the infant (or the young child) who learns the meaning of the word *I*. A whole new world of awareness and experience opens, including "I want this!" temper tantrums (when things don't go MY way), and saying "No." The infant/child begins to separate from mother and the physical environment. The days of no self-consciousness are over! As this self-awareness matures in the teenage years, questions of "Who am I?" and concern with self-concept emerge for the first time, along with more subtle dimensions of feeling, thinking, and intuition.

Mental/Analytical Awareness ("I think; therefore, I am!") During this period, a full range of psychological, intellectual, and conceptual activity develops, such as human relationships, habit patterns, memory, personal history, self-image, and problem-solving capacities. A sense of self-identity comes into full bloom as a separate entity, with more or less clear concepts and beliefs about who and what one is. The struggle with authenticity, freedom, aloneness, and death emerges. We study our past, our problems, and our potentials. Think for a moment of the "identity wrestlings" of your college days—those important periods of struggle with the great questions of life's meaning and purpose, your vocational directions, and the search for an appropriate life partner. Advanced levels of the mental/analytical stage involve higher-level cognitive processes such as non-linear thinking, forecasting, the capacity for panoramic vision of history, society, the planet, and evolution, and the emergence of the "non-verbal intelligences."

Transpersonal Awareness ("I am a citizen of the universe!") At this stage, an understanding of individual existence as part of a much larger fabric and story begins to unfold. We see our life connected to and part of the larger patterns of other people, nature, and the universe. We have all had experiences of this, although they are often hard to put into words. Think about times you were listening to a great piece of music or viewing a piece of art and you were suddenly "transported to another world." Think about awe-filling encounters you have had with nature that gave you a new appreciation for being. Recall talking with another person and suddenly finding yourself overwhelmed by the sheer miracle of life embodied in this individual. And of course, there are occurrences such as death or a serious illness which "stop us in our tracks" and make us reassess our priorities and values. At this stage, the psyche reflects the whole universe. It knows no boundaries other than those that are self-imposed.

Spiritual Awareness ("I am one with all that is!") This stage involves the development of complex belief systems, including religious symbols, ritual processes, solitary spiritual practices, political ideals, aesthetic values, and philosophical presuppositions. These things tend to integrate and give meaning to the many diverse experiences of our lives. This unity is often felt as a profound and immediate sense of "the eternal" in the midst of the temporal—what some theologians call "god-consciousness." It is experienced as a purposefulness that makes sense out of the struggles, chaos, and absurdities of daily living. It is the "lure of becoming." It is "the possible" actualized today. It is the rising depth of spirit which energizes, motivates, heals, and empowers all other levels of our lives.

In all of these stages it is the "self-identity factor" which plays a vital role in our human development and which is at the heart of intrapersonal intelligence. In *The Inward Arc*, Frances Vaughn describes this process:

> Since self-concepts tend to become self-fulfilling prophecies, constricting beliefs about the self can cripple human development. Definitions of the self that expand awareness, on the other hand, can contribute to healing and

And what is more, definitions of the self which expand awareness likewise contribute to and enhance our creativity, our ability to cope with change, to sustain meaningful relationships with other people, and to promote a general sense of well-being in our lives.

Awakening Intrapersonal Intelligence

The exercises above provide a beginning place for getting an impression of this introspective intelligence. In general, intrapersonal intelligence is awakened by any exercise or activity which causes self-reflection and raises questions of self-identity, meaning, and significance. Gardner describes it this way:

> In its most primitive form, the intrapersonal intelligence amounts to little more than the capacity to distinguish a feeling of pleasure from one of pain and, on the basis of such discrimination, to become more involved in or to withdraw from a situation. At its most advanced level, intrapersonal knowledge allows one to detect and to symbolize complex and highly differentiated sets of feelings. One finds this form of intelligence developed in the novelist...who can write introspectively about feelings, in the patient (or the therapist) who comes to attain a deep knowledge of his own feeling life, in the wise elder who draws upon his own wealth of inner experiences in order to advise members of his community.[58]

Amplifying Intrapersonal Intelligence

Now that we have a sense of what it takes to awaken intrapersonal intelligence from slumber, let us begin to strengthen, nurture, expand, and improve its cognitive capabilities, and to further our understanding of this important way of knowing. The following story comes from India and is, in capsule form, "all you ever wanted to know about intrapersonal intelligence but were afraid to ask." Well, at least some are not afraid to ask:

> A young man was seeking the ultimate meaning and secret of life. He traveled the world, far and wide, seeking his heart's desire. But everywhere he turned he found nothing but shallow answers and disappointment.
>
> One day, as he was traveling, he climbed a high mountain in the Himalayas. Sitting there was one that the young man knew to be a great teacher of life's deepest wisdom. So he asked his passionate question: "Tell me, oh Wise One, what is the secret of life? What is its true meaning?"
>
> For a very long time the teacher sat in silence. So the young man again posed his question: "What is the secret and meaning of life?" And again, the teacher was silent.
>
> For three days he sat in silence. Finally, late in the evening of the third day he spoke his response: "The secret and meaning of life? THAT THOU ART!"

Following are three practices which work directly with training different aspects of your intrapersonal intelligence.

Clearing and Focusing the Mind

This practice deals with intensifying mindfulness skills. We often go through life "on automatic pilot," feeling trapped by various habit patterns and routine behaviors. The practice of mindfulness is the key to breaking the cycle of "robothood" and of giving us back our freedom of choosing what's needed in a given situation.

The following is a practice for clearing the mind of unnecessary clutter. It is a simple, but very powerful process. Try it for 10 to 15 minutes a day for about two weeks and see if it makes a difference in your ability to cope with everyday problems!

- *Attitude of the body (posture).* Sit in a relaxed yet attentive position with your feet flat on the floor. Straighten your spine and head so that your breathing is free and easy. Place your hands in your lap or rest them on your thighs. Keep your eyes open but somewhat downcast, about 45 degrees. It's best to gaze at a blank wall or a table top that is free of distracting objects, clutter, etc. You are trying to establish an awake, alert, attentive posture.

- *Attitude of the breath.* Once you have established a relaxed yet attentive posture, focus your attention on your breathing. Breathe deeply from the lower abdomen, allowing your belly to naturally expand and contract as if you were blowing up a beach ball. Just relax and watch this process. It will, of its own accord, get deeper and slower as you watch it.

- *Attitude of the mind.* Allow the mind to be free, open, and unattached. As thoughts and sensations arise in the mind, simply observe them. Let them come and go. Do not get caught up in them. When the mind wanders, as it will, gently but firmly bring it back to the task of watching the breath, watching your posture, and watching the process of the mind itself.

- After completing this practice (10 to 15 minutes), spend a few minutes debriefing yourself:

  - What are my observations about the "three attitudes"?

  - What happened to me?

  - What have I learned about my own "inner processes"?

Reflection on Clearing/Focusing Mind Practice

Consciousness researchers describe the usual operation of the mind as the "monkey mind"— jumping from here to there, swinging from one bough (thought or idea) to another, basically unable to be still and focus on one thing long enough to learn something. Any mindfulness practice cuts directly through the monkey mind by subtly interrupting the so-called "normal" thought process. The simple practice of watching the process of the mind at work can halt its usual chatter, making it possible to hear something deeper. Set a regular time and place to do this practice each day. Maintain a "beginner's mind"—don't expect too much or too little and don't continually evaluate how you're doing. Just sit, clear the mind and enjoy these moments of inner stillness.

To practice mindfulness in your everyday life:

☐ When something happens during the day that "throws you off balance," pause, take several deep breaths and become an observer watching your feelings. Don't try to change, analyze, or evaluate them. Just objectively watch the process of these feelings taking place within you.

☐ When you are involved in a necessary task, but one you don't like, such as raking leaves, doing the laundry, or washing the car, do it with acute mindfulness. If necessary, perform it in slow motion so that you can watch yourself doing the task. Turn it into an awareness game.

☐ When you are in the midst of a situation where you are surrounded by noise, chaos, and busyness, pause and practice "going inside." Take several deep breaths and just watch yourself for a few minutes. Find your point of balance, calmness, and centeredness in the midst of the whirlwind around you.

Practice

Tapping Into Your Untapped Potentials

One of the key areas of intrapersonal intelligence is intuiting previously untapped potentials in your life and working to tap them. Brain researchers claim that we use less than 1 percent of the full potential of our brains. What might be possible if we could find ways to activate and use more of the seemingly unlimited potential within us?

The following practice is a visualization for understanding and actualizing untapped potentials in your life. Go ahead and try it. You have nothing to loose, and quite possibly a whole lot to gain! You'll need an audiocassette player and a tape of some quiet instrumental music.

■ Get into a position where you can completely relax. Turn on the music and direct your attention to the flow of your breath, following it with your mind, all the way in and all the way out. With each exhalation allow yourself to get more and more relaxed. Use the breath to help you let go of all other thoughts and worries. (PAUSE)

■ In your mind, as vividly as you can, imagine that you are in a boat floating down a slow-flowing, meandering river. It is a perfect spring day. The birds are chirping in the trees that line the banks of the rivers, and the sunlight is dancing through the leaves—almost sparkling. (PAUSE)

■ As you continue, slowly winding down the river, breathe deeply and feel refreshed, somehow sensing that this is a place of renewal for the spirit.

■ As the boat continues to wind this way and that, around one bend in the river, much to your surprise, you suddenly come upon an ancient castle on the bank of the river. It looks inviting so you decide to take the boat to the shore and go for a closer look.

- As you approach the castle you are filled with anticipation and excitement at what you might find. You decide to enter it. It has no furniture. Its walls are covered with full-length mirrors. Beautiful crystal chandeliers hang from the ceiling. As you walk through its great hallways you see brilliant reflections of yourself and the whole universe. You gradually begin to feel your own powers and potentials deepened and enhanced by the effect of the reflections and the shimmering light. (PAUSE)

- You continue wandering through the many halls, knowing that this is indeed a place of renewal and transformation. Finally you reach the central chamber of the castle. There you can find a carved, jeweled box.

- As you gaze at the box, you instinctively know it contains all that you are and all that you can be as a human being. You reach out and take the box and open it.

- Now take 2 to 3 minutes and watch what happens next. (PAUSE)

- Suddenly, in the distance you hear what sounds like the chiming of an ancient bell and you realize that it is time to go. You begin making your way back through the halls and passageways of the castle, pausing often to reflect on what has happened to you here. (PAUSE)

- As you step out of the castle and return to the boat, express your gratitude for what you have known, discovered, and sensed about your life and its possibilities in this journey. Furthermore, know that you can return to the castle at any time, and resolve now that you will indeed do so in the future.

- Now, get back into the boat, pushing it back into the flow of the river and slowly, in your own time, let it carry you back to this room. Open your eyes. Stretch and move around; notice how you feel.

- Spend a few minutes recording your reflections about what you have known, sensed, and discovered about your life and its potentials in this exercise.

Reflection on Untapped Potentials Practice

The power of this practice is in the suggestion that we can come to know potentials and levels of being that have remained untapped. We can play an active role in actualizing these latent potentials. A visualization process, such as the one presented, attempts to establish a linkage or a bridge between the conscious identity of the self and the deeper, more universal identity of the unconscious self. The images suggested in the visualization literally "seed" or "program" the unconscious mind to work better for you. If you continue a practice like this, it is guaranteed that your intrapersonal sensibilities will become more highly tuned and more available to you.

To continue using and applying this exercise:

☐ At the end of the visualization, draw something that will remind you of what happened on the journey, then post the picture someplace where you will see it often. Hopefully, it will remind you that there is more to you than meets the eye!

☐ Once a week, return to the castle, or another such place where you have time to communicate with your unconscious self.

☐ Try designing other kinds of "human potential activation" visualizations, such as having a conversation with an "inner coach" who knows all about you and what you need, or imagining that you are watching the ultimate self-help TV show called "Be All That You Can Be."

Tracking Your Thinking

As mentioned earlier, metacognition is one of the key areas of cognitive research today. Metacognition is simply the awareness of and control over your own thinking and behavior. In *Patterns for Thinking—Patterns for Transfer*, by Robin Fogarty and James Bellanca, the benefits of metacognition are described as follows:

> Metacognitive processing allows the learner to step outside the situation and examine the process itself. For example, deliberately tracing the mental steps used in solving a problem propels the learner to a level of thinking that requires metacognitive behavior. She/he looks at the framework of problem solving versus the actual solution to the particular problem. Metacognition is the awareness and control over one's own thinking and behavior.[59]

You will need a partner for the following practice. In the exercise you will have an opportunity to track your thinking as you are involved in a problem-solving activity. Give it a try and see what you can learn about your thinking patterns. Which ones work well for you? Which need changing?

■ Working alone, try to solve each of the problem situations below. Visualize yourself in the situation and watch how you approach it:

- You are trying to decide on a place to go for your vacation that will be exotic, luxurious, fun, relaxing, and cheap.

- You have been writing an article for publication and find yourself blocked for ideas at the present moment. However, you're facing a completion deadline.

- The funding you were anticipating for a project has been denied, but you want to find a way to go ahead with it anyway.

■ Now, write down the distinct thinking steps you used (or would use) in each situation. Rank each thinking step or sequence on a scale of 1 to 10 with 1 meaning "doesn't work very well for me" and 10 meaning "No problem—in fact, you could learn a lot by hanging around me!"

■ Share your thinking steps for each situation with your partner, noting similarities and differences and how you ranked each one. Talk about difficulties and/or struggles you have with each.

■ Now, working together, combine your thinking steps and create a new process that includes the best features of each process (yours and your partner's) and one that eliminates the weaknesses. Together brainstorm a list of possible situations in which the new process could be used.

■ Finally, see if you can "track the thinking" you have used in this exercise concerned with tracking thinking. *Be metacognitive about metacognition!*

Reflection on Tracking Your Thinking Practice

The metacognitive processing of a learning activity has been shown to improve student achievement levels, increase motivation for school and the learning process, and develop new skills of both self-esteem and esteem for others. There are at least four different levels of metacognitive behavior: the tacit or unconscious use of a thinking strategy; the aware/conscious use of thinking; the deliberate use of particular thinking skills for particular types of learning tasks; and the reflective use of these same skills where one plans, monitors, and evaluates their use of a particular strategy. As you learn to follow and analyze your own thinking processes, you will discover that your patterns for thinking are becoming more effective. You will likewise become pro-active in the development of your own thinking.

To continue using metacognition in your everyday life:

☐ Take a couple of minutes after each task you accomplish during the day to "step back" and ask yourself "What did I do well?" and "Where do I need to improve?"—both in terms of the objectives of the task and the thinking strategies used.

☐ When you are working with a large or small group of people, try injecting as much "process awareness" as you can, such as cooperative behaviors, creativity processes, and thinking strategies.

☐ Keep a "thinker's log" to track your own thinking and reactions to things going on in your life. This is like a diary, but its focus is on how your thinking is developing and changing.

Teaching and Learning with Intrapersonal Intelligence

So far we have tried to awaken intrapersonal intelligence as a valid way of knowing and understanding life. We have worked to familiarize ourselves with it. We have begun to learn how to use it and to strengthen it. In the next section we will work with intrapersonal capacities as a way of learning and teaching content-based information.

When thinking about intrapersonal intelligence in the context of our current educational systems, one cannot help but recall Art Costa's image of what school should be in his article "The School as a Home for the Mind":

In a school that is a home for the mind there is an inherent faith that all people can continue to improve their intellectual capacities throughout life; that learning to think is as valid a goal for the 'at risk,' handicapped, the disadvantaged, and the foreign-speaking as it is for the 'gifted' and 'talented'; and that all of us have the potential for even greater creativity and intellectual power....

In a school that is becoming a home for the mind, development of the intellect, learning to learn, knowledge production, metacognition, decision making, creativity, and problem solving are the subject matter of instruction. Content is selected because of its contribution to process and thus becomes a vehicle for thinking processes.[60]

The following lesson is a fine example of Gardner's insight that the personal intelligences, especially intrapersonal intelligence, rely on all the other intelligences to express themselves.

Self-understanding Via History

This is an American history lesson dealing with the Revolutionary War. The lesson presupposes prior study and/or understanding of America's fight for independence, as well as how to mind-map (see chapter 3).

Supplies: Two sheets of blank paper and a variety of colored markers for each student.

■ Take a blank piece of paper and draw a medium-sized box in the middle of it.

■ Spend a few minutes relaxing. Close your eyes and take several deep breaths. Each time you exhale, let go of any worries, anxieties, and concerns that you may have so you can be fully present for this lesson.

■ Now, open your eyes and stare at the empty box in the middle of the paper in front of you. Keep looking at the box until an image or picture about America's struggle for independence occurs to you, for example, a liberty bell, a man on a horse, a canon, a flag.

■ When this image or picture is clear in your mind, quickly draw it in the box. Then put down your marker, but continue to stare at the object in the box.

■ Stay very focused on your image or object. We are now going to look at the image from several different perspectives:

- Pretend you are a child living during America's independence struggle. What do you see through these eyes? What does the image mean to you?

- Look at the image through the eyes of a very old person in those times.

- Look at it from the perspective of the British.

- Look at it through the eyes of one of the American patriots.

- Look at it as if you are a person living 100 years from today. What do you see?

■ Continue to concentrate on the image. As in mind-mapping, start drawing branches out from the central image. On these branches draw other images that the central image sparks. Work with colors, designs, pictures, symbols, etc.

■ These new images may spark still more images. When this happens, draw them as side branches off the main branches.

■ Watch for connections or relationships of one set of images with others in your mind-map. When you see these, draw them in.

■ When you are finished, stop and look at what you have done. Staying focused on the central image, write two or three sentences about the image and what it now means to you.

■ Now, once again focus on the central image. However, this time, pretend that the image can talk to you.

■ Ask the image what message it has for you today as a 20th-century American. (NOTE: these may be words of advice, warning, encouragement, or demand).

■ Record what the image has to say to you in two to three sentences with a dialogue balloon coming from the image.

■ Now, turn to a partner nearby and share your mind-maps and sentences with each other.

■ After a reasonable amount of time, call the class back together for a time of group reflection:

- What went on in this lesson? What things did you notice?

- What surprised you? What was exciting? What was hard?

- Who wants to share their two sets of sentences with the whole class?

- What have we learned about the struggle for independence?

- What have we learned about ourselves as Americans today?

Reflection on Self-understanding Lesson

In this lesson, one of the most powerful dimensions of interpersonal intelligence is illustrated, namely, the ability to turn our unique, self-reflective capacity back on itself to gain multiple levels of self-knowledge and understanding. When we imagine "passing over" into the lives of other people, objects, animals, and even mythical beings, seeing life from their vantage points, and then "coming back to ourselves," we do so with new eyes, new insight, and new hearts. This lesson uses a visual/spatial process to gain intrapersonal insight.

Some ideas for using intrapersonal intelligence in the midst of everyday classroom lessons include the following:

☐ After every learning activity have students reflect on how well they cooperated with and helped each other: What thinking strategies did we use and how did they work for us? If we were to do this lesson again, what could we do to improve our cooperation and our thinking?

☐ Have students keep a "thinking log" for recording their thoughts at the end of a lesson. Include sections for thinking about such things as: What did I learn? What do I find interesting? What new ideas do I have? How can I apply this outside the classroom?

☐ Use various kinds of visualization journeys to help students enter what they are studying, or "learn from the inside out." Imagine having a conversation with a historical figure; become very small and enter your own bloodstream to learn about how the body works; pretend you are a fraction and you want to be a whole.

☐ Give students an opportunity to speak into a tape recorder about how they are different at the end of an academic unit from at the beginning. How has this unit changed my understanding of myself?

Transferring Intrapersonal Intelligence to Life

Some researchers believe that our intrapersonal capacities are the cutting edge of our future development, both as a species and as a planet. In *The Global Brain*, Peter Russell states this as follows:

> With the emergence of self-reflective consciousness, the platform of evolution moved up from life to consciousness. Consciousness became the spearhead for evolution. For the first time on Earth, evolution became internalized. Thus, the urge that many people feel to grow and develop inwardly may well be the force of evolution manifesting within our own consciousness. It is the universe evolving through us.
>
> This inner evolution is not an aside to the overall process of evolution. Conscious inner evolution is the particular phase of evolution that we, in our corner of the universe, are currently passing through.[61]

Transfer Strategy

A Journey into Future Time

In this final exercise, you will have a chance to explore and clarify your intentions for the future, then to remember the future today. It may help you get in touch with a deep, abiding sense of the eternal in the midst of the many changes of your everyday life. If possible, record the instructions from the section below entitled "Walking Forward Into the Future" on an audiotape before beginning. This will allow you to simply turn on the tape at that point in the exercise and be led into the process.

FUTURE INTENTIONS FOR YOUR LIFE

SUPPLIES: Several sheets of blank paper, marking pens, crayons, or paints (your preference), two audiocassette tape players, a tape of music that evokes images and feelings of the future for you (e.g. Vangelis' *Ignatio*, or Deuter's *Ecstasy*).

■ On a blank sheet of paper make a list of things you intend and/or desire for your life as you consider the future. Use the following areas to spark your thinking if you wish:

- personal growth
- spiritual evolution
- family journey
- individual lifestyle
- professional development
- health and wellness
- civic responsibility
- financial security and flexibility
- continuing education
- other

■ Now read over your responses to these areas and reflect on what you have said about your desires and intentions for your future.

■ Look for four or five major themes or motifs which summarize your desires/intentions for the future. Try to state these as short phrases. Let your intuitions and first impressions guide you as you do this.

■ Using colored markers, crayons, or paints, create a picture, image, symbol, or some other kind of visual representation for each phrase to remind you of the inner feelings and impressions you have about these intentions and desires.

WALKING FORWARD INTO THE FUTURE

■ Begin playing the music tape that you chose earlier—music that evokes images and feelings of the future.

[NOTE: If you are doing the exercise by yourself, turn on the second tape player with the recorded instruction of this section at this point as well.]

■ Move to the center of the room where you have some space in which you can move about. Close your eyes and begin breathing deeply from your abdomen, allowing yourself to become centered, balanced, and revitalized. (PAUSE)

■ Now, as vividly as you can, imagine that you can actually walk into the future. Begin walking forward, very slowly. With each step imagine that you are walking into the future, carrying within you the fullness of your intentions symbolized by the pictures and images that you created earlier. (PAUSE)

■ Start by walking into those parts of the future that are closest to you and easiest for you to imagine—next week, next month, or an event you are anticipating during the coming

year. Move slowly, giving your attention to whatever comes to you as you walk—visual images, smells, sounds, tastes, colors, shapes, and interior sensations or moods. (PAUSE)

■ As you move into the future, you may find yourself in certain situations that are related to your intentions for the future. You will also likely meet certain people who are in some way a part of your creative intention for the future. When this happens, you may wish to pause and spend some time harvesting their wisdom, receiving gifts, or asking questions on which you feel the need for insight from the future.

■ When you are ready, continue walking forward, farther and farther into the future until you have gone as far into the future as you want, then stop and be seated on the floor or in a chair.

■ Spend a few minutes reflecting on what you have seen, heard, sensed, and known on this journey. If appropriate for you, you may want to repeat the following meditation several times:

I am the fullness of the future today!

With every breath I take I give birth to the future.

The future lives within my every movement.

- Remain still and be with this awareness for several minutes, being conscious of whatever rises within you. (PAUSE)

- Finally, standing up once again, imagine that you are returning to the present moment. Walk very slowly backward into the present moment. As you journey back into the present, bring the wisdom and insights you have gained from the future into the present moment.

- When you are ready, open your eyes and write your reflections on what you have seen, what you have known, and insights you have received from this journey into future time.

Reflection on Journey into Future Strategy

Whenever we consider the future, we have a more or less clear image of what it holds. This image is made up of our expectations, our intentions, our hopes, and our dreams, the yearnings of our hearts, our intuitions. It is shaped by our past journey and by the many factors that make up our present life, both as individuals and as a whole society.

From the perspective of our rapidly changing world, it is almost like the future is now, the past is now, and now is the past and future. When we step into this awareness, we can suddenly transgress the boundaries and limitations of   time. All time lives within us; we live and have lived in all time. When we experience this, the questions of the past and future are a matter of remembering, a matter of re-uniting ourselves with an unbounded sense of time and all of history.

Personal Reflection Log
Intrapersonal Intelligence

Observations made—what happened?

_____

_____

_____

Emotional/feeling states:

_____

_____

_____

Reflections, insights & discoveries:

_____

_____

_____

Self-evaluation (comfort zone/skill ability):

|—————————————————————————————|

Like a fish in water   Like landing on another planet

Practical strategies for fully activating/developing this intelligence within myself:

_____

_____

_____

Application ideas for my classroom, family, community, or organization:

_____

_____

_____

Chapter 8

Creating Multi-Modal Eventfulness in the Classroom and School

Teaching for Multiple Intelligences

Not only is the human brain aware of its own existence, but through it the universe has begun to know itself. Our minds have become the spearhead of evolution, and the degree to which we progress depends upon the degree to which we make use of this most incredible product of nature—the degree to which we use our intelligence and our consciousness to the full.—Peter Russell, *The Global Brain*

 The Buddha was once asked, "Sir, please tell us, exactly what are you? Are you a god?"
He replied, "Oh, no, no, definitely not!"
"Well then, are you a prophet or a great holy man?"
Again he said, "No!"
"Then please tell us. What are you?"
He said, "I AM AWAKE!"

We find ourselves standing on a threshold unlike any that has faced humanity to date. On every front the possibilities of the future are staggering: technology, health, education, environmental concerns, and trends of increasing globalization to mention but a few. One of the tasks before us is to stay awake to all that is happening in our times. Waking people up has been the commitment of educators from the beginning. At its heart, this is what education is all about.

Education is a natural process. In many ways, the evolutionary process and education are the same. Evolution is a process in which an organism changes its behavior or form in order to better compete with other organisms or to adapt to a changing environment. Evolution is the unfolding of potential. Nothing can unfold if it has no potential. Therefore, in a metaphorical sense, evolution can be described as a process of "remembering" potentials which have been forgotten or which maybe simply have not been needed previously.

Education works in the same way. Through the awakening of new knowledge, novel perspectives, and different ways of knowing, potentials that have been latent prior to this awakening process are now activated. Once this has occurred, one's perception of everything is different, for seeing, hearing, tasting, touching, smelling—in short, living itself—is happening on many more levels than before the educational encounter.

This book has been about awakening, expanding, and enhancing our intelligence capacities, and about using these capacities for knowing and understanding in our own lives and our world. In this final chapter I turn to issues about the impact of the theory of multiple intelligences on the classroom and school. We will examine such things as daily lesson planning, overall curriculum designing, and intelligence assessment. In "The Development and Education of Intelligences" from *Essays on the Intellect*, Joseph M. Walters and Howard Gardner make the following comment:

> There are important reasons for considering the theory of Multiple Intelligences and its implications for education. First of all, it is clear that many talents, if not Intelligences, are overlooked nowadays; individuals with these talents are the chief casualties of the single-minded, single-funneled approach to the mind. There are many unfilled and poorly filled niches in our society and it would be opportune to guide individuals with the right set of abilities to these billets. Finally, our world is beset with problems; to have any chance of solving them, we must make the very best use of the Intelligences we possess. Perhaps recognizing the plurality of Intelligences and the manifold ways in which human

individuals may exhibit them is an important first step.[62]

The Multiple Intelligences School: Some "Intelligent" Design Factors To Consider

In considering curriculum design for a multiple-intelligences based school, Howard Gardner invites us to remember an important piece of the contemporary research findings on human intelligences in *Frames of Mind*:

> Multiple intelligences theory posits a small set of human intellectual potentials, perhaps as few as seven in number, of which all individuals are capable by virtue of their membership in the human species. Owing to heredity, early training, or, in all probability, a constant interaction between these factors, some individuals will develop certain intelligences far more than others; but every normal individual should develop each intelligence to some extent, given but modest opportunity to do so.[63]

When we approach the educational enterprise from the perspective of teaching for multiple intelligences, a number of interesting factors come to the surface. These represent important dynamics for planning lessons, designing curriculum, and setting educational structures when working with multiple intelligences. The triangle on the following page represents an effort to present these factors in a rational construct. It is based on information in *Frames of Mind* and the chapter entitled "The Education of Intelligences."

The triangle suggests three broad areas for consideration in planning lessons, designing curriculum, and setting educational structures for working with multiple intelligences theory. Each of these represents strategic decisions teachers

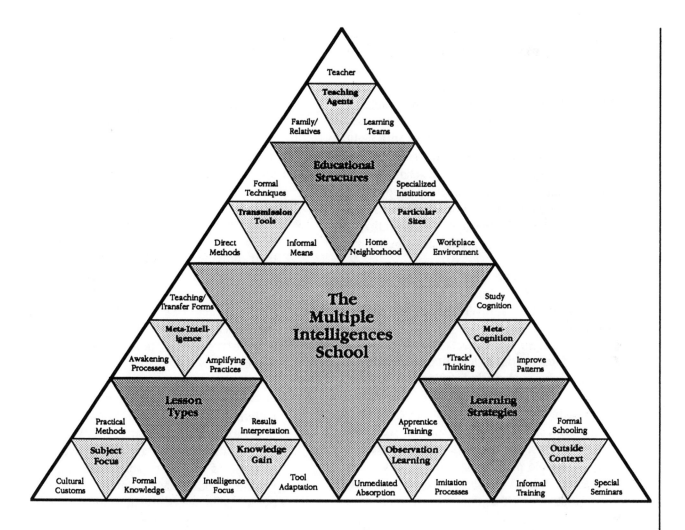

must make regarding which type of lesson, learning strategy, and structures need to be imposed on a given piece of curriculum in order to meet both the academic and intelligence objectives.

1. **Lesson Types.** There are at least three different kinds of lessons related to the intelligences:

    ☐ Each of the intelligences can be taught as a subject in its own right, such as teaching music, language, or art as a formal discipline. This course of instruction involves teaching the accumulated wisdom of a culture on the subject, the formal knowledge base, and its practical methods and/or techniques.

    ☐ The intelligences can be used as a means to gain knowledge in areas beyond themselves, such as using body movement to learn vocabulary words or music to teach math. This involves discerning the multiple intelligence possibilities of a subject, adapting particular intelligence tools or media for the instructional task, and then helping students understand and interpret the results. The lessons in this book are examples of this.

    ☐ Lessons that deal with meta-intelligence processes are concerned with teaching students about their own intelligences—how to access them, to train and refine them, and to actively use them in learning and everyday life. This has been the major thrust of this book in which we have dealt with ways of awakening each intelligence, practices for amplifying, expanding, and strengthening them, employing them in the educational process, and transferring intelligence into daily living. The multiple intelligence "People Search" at the end of this chapter is an example of a meta-intelligence process. The poster "Have You Used Your Seven Intelligences Today?" (see blackline at end of chapter) is also an example.

2. **Learning Strategies.** There are at least three different learning strategies related to teaching OF and WITH multiple intelligences:

   - **Observational learning strategies** involve students in learning by watching others perform a particular skill. Some things are learned in an "unmediated," unconscious way. That is, we learn almost by osmosis—we are around people performing a skill and we just pick it up by being exposed to it constantly. Other things are learned more by imitation, when we carefully and consciously watch others perform a skill and then try to copy what they have done. A third, more formal learning situation is that of the apprentice being trained by a master of a skill. In most observational learning the application or transfer of the skill into life is direct and immediate.

   - **Outside-context learning strategies** take students aside from daily living for a period of focused, intensive training. Obviously, our system of formal education which spans from pre-school to college and graduate-level schooling is a prime example of this "out-of-context" learning. Others include formal training seminars and workshops dealing with everything from career changes to self-improvement to learning a foreign language to learning financial investment strategies. There are likewise hundreds of informal do-it-yourself training programs available. The application or transfer of extra-context learning tends to be more remote and requires a variety of simple to complex strategies that bridge the learning into daily living.

   - **Metacognitive learning strategies** involve teaching students to think about their thinking. It is literally cognition turned back on itself! In this learning strategy students first learn to "track" their thinking in a given lesson by asking "What did I do?" so they become aware of the thinking process they used. Second, they ask "How could I improve?" so they become aware of the possibility of changing their thinking patterns to be more effective or to work better for them. Finally, they ask "What help do I need?" and are able to avail themselves of resources for increasing skillful thinking. Metacognitive processing is immediately transferable to both observational learning and extra-context learning. In fact, it relies on other content to work. There must something to think about in order to think about your thinking!

3. **Educational Structures.** When considering factors related to an effective setting for learning to take place, at least three variables need to be mentioned:

   - Various **methods for transmitting knowledge** must be considered. Direct methods of learning are largely unmediated and can involve such things as verbal descriptions and simple drawings or diagrams. Formal methods of learning, on the other hand, rely heavily on more complex and involved media to accomplish the transmission, using books, pamphlets, charts, maps, all forms of electronic communication, etc. Informal methods of learning involve people exchanging ideas and knowledge with each other in the course of normal conversation.

- The **particular sites** where learning occurs is a second factor that shapes the nature of both the teaching and learning that take place. Much of our early learning takes place at home and in our immediate neighborhood where we encounter close friends, relatives, and neighbors. Another important on-site learning situation is the workplace, which is often an apprenticeship situation in which applications of knowledge learned are immediate. Specialized learning institutions provide a third locus for education and provide opportunities to attain broad-based knowledge in a wide variety of subject areas.

- The kind of **teaching agent(s)** is the third structural factor in designing an effective learning process. The first and most influential teaching agent, at least in our early learning, is the immediate family and relatives. Another form of teaching agent is being part of a team or group in which there is a task to be accomplished; members must help and teach each other, as in Boy Scouts or Girl Scouts. A third agent is the professional teacher to whom students come for training in specific skills and/or knowledge.

Teaching FOR and WITH Intelligence

In the first chapter I posed the question *"Just what does it take to teach intelligence?"* Four stages or dynamics were suggested as an initial answer (see chart below). These stages likewise provided the framework for the presentation of the intelligences in the subsequent chapters. Let me now return to these dynamics as they apply to lesson planning for multiple intelligences.

In order to effectively teach intelligence these four dynamics must be present, although not necessarily within a single lesson. However, generally the "awakening" and "amplifying" processes are necessary prior to the effective and

I.	II.
Awakening Intelligence: activities that "trigger" an intelligence in the brain, "awakening" it from sleep.	**Amplifying Intelligence:** exercises for practicing intelligence skills, thus strengthening them.
III.	IV.
Teaching Intelligence: using multiple multiple intelligences in specific teaching/learning situations to enhance lessons and increase learning.	**Transferring Intelligence:** activities for integrating and applying the intelligences in daily life.

skillful use of an intelligence for teaching/learning content-based information. The sequence is something like this:

I. We must first of all be aware that we do in fact possess multiple ways of knowing.

II. We must learn how particular intelligences work. First is learning how to access or "trigger" each intelligence. (The exercises at the beginning of each chapter are examples of potential "intelligence triggers.") Second is learning the core capacities and skills of the intelligences, for example studying music as a subject in its own right.

III. We must learn how to use and understand different intelligence modalities. This involves both practice, to strengthen intelligence capacities that are weak because of disuse, and learning how to interpret the varying kinds of information we receive from each intelligence.

IV. Teaching content-based lessons using multiple intelligences is a matter of applying the various ways of knowing to the specific content of a given lesson, for example, learning vocabulary words kinesthetically as we did in Chapter 4.

V. Finally, there is the task of learning how to use all of our intelligences to improve our effectiveness in dealing with the issues, challenges, and problems we face in our daily lives. This is primarily a matter of approaching these things on multiple levels, with a variety of problem-solving methods that use different intelligences.

Teaching FOR...a New Look At The Curriculum

What are the skills students need so they can utilize their full intellectual potential? The Multiple Intelligence capacities wheel on p. 197 presents a set of core capacities or skills related to each intelligence. At times, Gardner has referred to these as "sub-intelligences." If we want our students to use multiple ways of knowing then these capacities or skills must be explicitly taught to them. In the past, many of these capacities were the focus of so-called "fine arts curricula." However, when schools and districts find themselves facing funding shortages and budgeting constraints, the fine arts and other "extracurricular" programs are often the first to be cut.

Of course, the alarming thing about this is that without the chance to learn and practice these capacities early on, students will be unable to perform more complex, higher-order intelligence tasks later. I believe this means carefully analyzing the so-called "academic curriculum," noting its relative strengths and weaknesses in teaching students the core capacities of the intelligences. I also believe that every academic content area has its own "fine arts" components; and thus, we have an opportunity to teach these skills in and through the academic content we will be teaching anyway.

For example, in history students can also learn the art, music, and dance of a particular period. Have them actually do it and experience it—not just read about it! Have them study the poetry of the period and write their own contemporary poetry trying to mimic the style of the period. They can enact dramas, read stories, and perform scientific experiments from the period. In other words, part of the curriculum restructuring task involves finding as many new opportunities as we can to teach FOR multiple intelligences. Let's take the "extra" out of extracurricular and make *everything* curricular!

A Developmental View of the Intelligences

It is important to recognize the fact that at different ages in our journey from infancy to adulthood, we have different capacities. The "fact sheets" on p. 198-204 provide a more detailed overview of some distinct developmental factors to consider when attempting to teach students to use their seven intelligences. Each of the intelligences follows a developmental trajectory which begins with the acquisition of the **basic skills of the intelligences.** This stage of development is more or less guaranteed for normal individuals, both by our biological make up and by the socialization process of our culture.

The second broad stage of the growth of intelligence capacities involves an expanded and more **complex development of all intelligence skills.** This stage most often begins when children start their formal education. Building on the basic intelligence patterns and skills acquired in infancy and the preschool years, children are taught to expand the basic skills and to employ them in various kinds of problem-solving tasks. Likewise, they learn the "language" and "symbol system" for each of the intelligences and to interpret and understand the information or knowledge gained.

I have called the third development stage **higher-order intelligence.** The task of this stage involves learning to synthesize, process, and integrate the intelligences into one's "repertoire for living." Students should be taught how to skillfully use the different intelligences. And they should begin to learn more about and take responsibility for the development of their own personal intelligence profile, learning when to use which of the intelligences to gain certain desired outcomes.

The final developmental stage is often directly related to one's **vocational and/or avocational pursuits.** Generally people will choose a career path based on those intelligences which they understand best and with which they are most comfortable. This is the level of mastery as well as the conscious use of one's intelligences to be of service to the larger social order, such as using visual/spatial skills to produce art to enrich the culture or using one's logical/mathematical skills to further medical research.

A second concern of this section is the question of intelligence testing, evaluation, and assessment. In *Frames of Mind,* Howard Gardner points out that intelligence assessment or evaluation should change with an individual's age and must be couched in the appropriate language and symbol system of a given intelligence. Assessment must also be appropriate to the specific developmental stages described above. Thus, during *infancy* we would test using the *raw patterning ability* (basic skill level) of each intelligence, for example, the ability to mimic certain sounds and beats for musical/rhythmic intelligence, or the recognition of different shapes, colors, textures, and designs for visual/spatial intelligence.

During *early childhood* we would test using the *expanded/complete skill levels* of an intelligence, for example, facility in using words, making sentences and telling stories for verbal/linguistic intelligence, or the ability to move the body in certain prescribed ways in physical games like sports, dance, or simple role playing.

During *late childhood* the intelligences are represented in *formal recorded symbol systems* (higher-order intelligences), such as numbers, formulas, mathematical operations, musical notes, written language skills, and so forth. At this developmental stage, intelligence testing would discern an individual's strengths and weaknesses based on his or her ability to work with and understand the "symbol systems" of a given intelligence.

Finally, during *adolescence* and *adulthood*, the intelligences often take the form of one's *voca-*

tional pursuit and various *hobbies and/or special interests*. For example, interpersonal intelligence skills may lead one to become a therapist or a teacher, while facility with logical/mathematical skills may lead one into such professions as accountant or scientist. In "The Development and Education of Intelligences" from *Essays on the Intellect*, Gardner and Walters state:

> The assessment of intellectual profiles remains a task for the future. We believe that we will need to depart from standardized testing. We also believe that standard pencil-and-paper, short-answer tests sample only a small proportion of intellectual abilities and often reward a certain kind of decontextualized facility. The means of assessment we favor should ultimately search for genuine problem-solving or product-fashioning skills in individuals across a range of materials.

> An assessment of a particular Intelligence (or set of Intelligences) should highlight problems that can be solved in the materials of that Intelligence.[64]

Gardner suggests that what we really need from intelligence testing is an individual's "intellectual profile" at a given point in their life, with the understanding that it is not static, but rather a dynamic, continually changing factor of one's growth and development. A profile would show both strengths and weaknesses along with ways to develop the fullest intelligence capacities possible within the individual. In the early years of schooling the profile could help discern ways of developing each student's full spectrum of intelligences as completely as possible. In the later years, the profile could be used to help point students in particular vocational directions for which they have exhibited an aptitude and an interest. (See p. 176-180 for some alternate "testing tools.")

Teaching WITH...a "multi-modal" look at lesson planning

It is a presupposition of this book that every lesson can and should be taught for multiple intelligences to ensure that all students benefit from the lesson. However, not all students are strong in verbal/linguistic and logical/mathematical ways of knowing, which are the basis for the majority of teaching in our current systems of education. Therefore, within a given week in a typical classroom, students need to be immersed in learning that involves all seven ways of knowing. In this way you can be relatively certain to have catalyzed interest in all students, regardless of their intelligence strengths and weaknesses. I would suggest that, *in addition* to the given verbal/linguistic and logical/mathematical bases of a lesson, that you intentionally use a minimum of two or three other ways of knowing in each lesson.

Tools for Accessing Multiple Intelligences

In the popular book of the 1960s, *The Medium is the Message*, by Marshall McLuhan, it is suggested that often the media we use to express ourselves speak louder than what we are trying to express. In some ways this is also true of the intelligences. The medium or tools used can give you almost immediate access to a particular intelligence mode. Often a certain set of tools acts as "intelligence triggers." For example, if you give students paints, crayons, or colored marking pens to use in a lesson, you will often find that little else must be done to "turn on" the visual/spatial way of knowing because this medium of expression is so much at the heart of visual/spatial intelligence.

Following is a summation of **quick ways to access the intelligences,** presented in the different chapter sections on awakening the various intelligence modes.

- **Verbal/Linguistic Intelligence** is awakened by the spoken word, by reading someone's ideas or poetry, or by writing one's own ideas, thoughts, or poetry, as well as by various kinds of humor such as "plays on words," jokes, and "twists" of the language.

- **Logical/Mathematical Intelligence** is activated in situations requiring problem solving or meeting a new challenge, as well as situations requiring pattern discernment and recognition.

- **Visual/Spatial Intelligence** is triggered by presenting the mind with and/or creating unusual, delightful, and colorful designs, patterns, shapes, and pictures, and engaging in active imagination through such things as visualization, guided imagery, and pretending exercises.

- **Body/Kinesthetic Intelligence** is awakened through physical movement such as in various sports, dances, and physical exercises, as well as by the expression of oneself through the body, such as inventing drama, body language, and creative/interpretive dance.

- **Musical/Rhythmic Intelligence** is turned on by the resonance or vibrational effect of music and rhythm on the brain, including such things as the human voice, sounds from nature, musical instruments, percussion instruments, and other humanly produced sounds.

- **Interpersonal Intelligence** is activated by person-to-person encounters in which such things as effective communication, working together with others for a common goal, and noticing distinctions among persons are necessary and important.

- **Intrapersonal Intelligence** is awakened when we are in situations that cause introspection and require knowledge of the internal aspects of the self, such as awareness of our feelings, thinking processes, self-reflection, and spirituality.

On the following page is a *Multiple Intelligences Toolbox* which catalogs various media, techniques, and methods for accessing the seven intelligences. Of course, these must be used in conjunction with other parts of a lesson and adapted for dealing with content-based information, but they can help you quickly move into emphasizing various ways of knowing in a lesson.

Designing Multiple Intelligence Lessons

I like to think of teaching for multiple intelligences as an artistic creation. Therefore, I have designed a lesson planning palette (see p. 174) to help you think about your lessons in a new way. Even though you may not use all seven intelligences in one lesson, the discipline of having figured out how you would do it is important. The following "seven-in-one" lesson is one involving adding and subtracting fractions. It shows how to integrate strategies and tools from the toolbox in designing an actual lesson. (Note: The italicized items are from the tool box.)

- A **verbal/linguistic** component could include having students create a *vocabulary* game related to fraction terminology (e.g., numeration, denominator, ratio, etc.); they could make up fraction *poetry* (e.g., limericks to explain processes) and/or fraction *jokes;* or they could engage in creative *story telling* with different fractions as the story's characters.

VERBAL/LINGUISTIC
- Reading
- Vocabulary
- Formal Speech
- Journal/Diary Keeping
- Creative Writing
- Poetry
- Verbal Debate
- Impromptu Speaking
- Humor/Jokes
- Storytelling

LOGICAL/MATHEMATICAL
- Abstract Symbols/Formulas
- Outlining
- Graphic Organizers
- Number Sequences
- Calculation
- Deciphering Codes
- Forcing Relationships
- Syllogisms
- Problem Solving
- Pattern Games

VISUAL/SPATIAL
- Visualization
- Active Imagination
- Color Schemes
- Patterns/Designs
- Painting
- Drawing
- Mind-Mapping
- Pretending
- Sculpture
- Visual Pictures

BODY/KINESTHETIC
- Folk/Creative Dance
- Role Playing
- Physical Gestures
- Drama
- Martial Arts
- Body Language
- Physical Exercise
- Mime
- Inventing
- Sports Games

MULTIPLE INTELLIGENCES TOOLBOX

MUSICAL/RHYTHMIC
- Rhythmic Patterns
- Vocal Sounds/Tones
- Music Composition/Creation
- Percussion Vibrations
- Humming
- Environmental Sounds
- Instrumental Sounds
- Singing
- Tonal Patterns
- Music Performance

INTERPERSONAL
- Giving Feedback
- Intuiting Others' Feelings
- Cooperative Learning Strategies
- Person-to-Person Communication
- Empathy Practices
- Division of Labor
- Collaboration Skills
- Receiving Feedback
- Sensing Others' Motives
- Group Projects

INTRAPERSONAL
- Meditation Methods
- Metacognition Techniques
- Thinking Strategies
- Emotional Processing
- "Know Thyself" Procedures
- Mindfulness Practices
- Focusing/Concentration Skills
- Higher-Order Reasoning
- Complex Guided Imagery
- "Centering" Practices

■ A **logical/mathematical** component could include having students use *graphic organizers* to analyze different processes (e.g., a Venn diagram to compare/contrast adding and subtracting); they could think of *problem-solving* scenarios from everyday life requiring an understanding of fractions (e.g., cutting a pizza to serve all at your table); or they could create fractions adding and subtracting *(pattern game)*.

■ A **visual/spatial** component could include having students work with sculpture, various manipulatives for adding and subtracting parts of wholes; they could solve a page of fraction problems by *drawing* or *painting* their answers; or you could teach them *active imagination* processes for seeing the operations in action.

- A **body/kinesthetic** component could include *drama* by having them act out a set of problems by physically adding and subtracting people from a whole group to make fractions of a group; they could create a *sports game* for the playground which uses adding and subtracting fractions; or they could make up a *creative dance* which involves various patterns, steps of wholes, and steps of parts of the whole.

- A **musical/rhythmic** component could have students engage in singing by making up songs and/or "raps" for adding and subtracting fractions; students could create *rhythmic patterns* to communicate wholes and fractional parts; they could participate in *music composition* and then take away from or add to the composition (e.g., remove half of the notes) and hear the new song.

- An **interpersonal** component is easily introduced by using *cooperative learning strategies*, perhaps dividing a page of problems to solve among them, working out the answers, then teaching each person in the group how to do the problems; or students could create and present a *group project* on fractions with each student responsible for a part of the whole.

- An **intrapersonal** component could use *metacognitive* techniques for comparing and contrasting the kind of thinking involved in fraction problem-solving and other types of problem-solving processes; or they could use a *"know thyself"* procedure and analyze the whole of their lives by breaking it down into fractional parts and reflecting on how each part relates to the whole.

Lesson Design Process

Let us now use the palette and toolbox to design a "seven-in-one" lesson. Following is a basic process that may help you get started with "multi-modal lesson planning." I have given you several examples for each intelligence of ways to employ tools from the toolbox in the adding and subtracting fractions lesson. Please look at my example, but more important, use one of your own upcoming lessons and take it through the process I am suggesting:

- Begin with palette (p. 174) and write title of the lesson with which you are working in the appropriate space.

- Take a couple of minutes to reflect, and write your objective for the lesson.

- Now, keeping this objective in mind, look at the Multiple Intelligences toolbox on p. 172 and choose one tool for each intelligence that you believe will help your students achieve the objective for the lesson.

- Write the tools on the palette with a description of how you could use it (i.e., what you would actually have the students do using the tool).

- Now put the lesson together using your favorite lesson-planning method.

I am NOT suggesting that each lesson should be taught for all seven ways of knowing. In your planning, however, try to figure out how you COULD teach for all seven and in light of your lesson objectives and the particular needs of your students, then make your decisions about how many intelligences to engage. In most of the teaching and training I do, I try to actively involve three intelligences BEYOND the verbal/linguistic and logical/mathematical.

In the classroom situation this would mean that within the course of a week's teaching you would include "knowing strategies" from all of the intelligences, thus reaching kids more of the time. (See p. 181 for a chart to help you track your teaching.)

Palette for Designing Multi-modal Lessons

Topic: _____

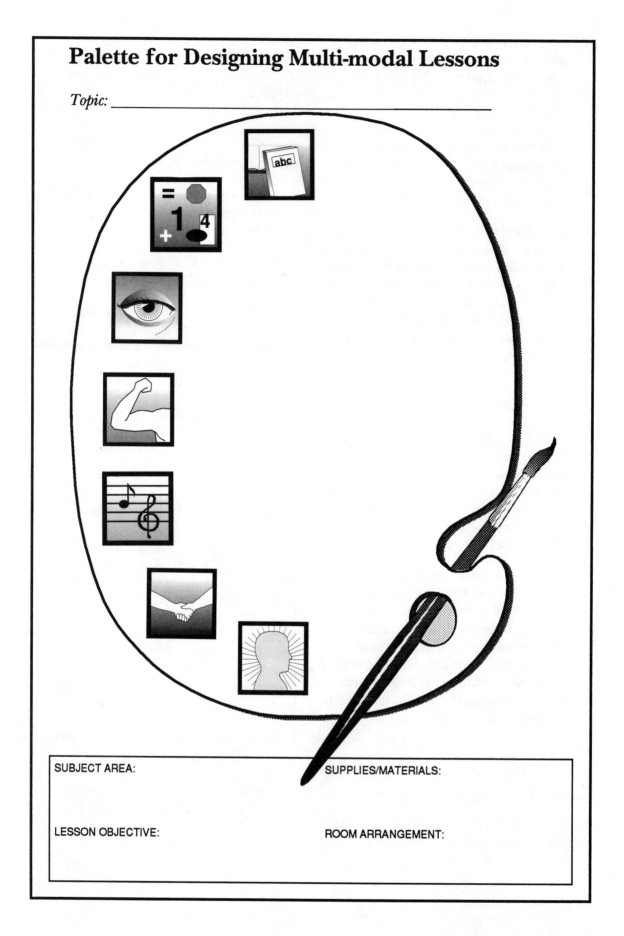

SUBJECT AREA:

SUPPLIES/MATERIALS:

LESSON OBJECTIVE:

ROOM ARRANGEMENT:

What might a test look like that evaluates multiple intelligences?

The key to designing tests for assessing different types of intelligence is that each test must itself be presented in the language and symbol system of the intelligence it purports to test. For example, a test that is presented verbally cannot accurately test for body/kinesthetic intelligence, even if one is able to describe a physical activity in minute detail! The "language" or symbol system of body/kinesthetic intelligence is physical movement itself and thus the test must be presented in these terms. Various puzzles, games, and other challenges, when couched in the unique language of each intelligence may yield the most fruitful results in trying to discern one's intelligence profile. Gardner puts it this way:

> The general idea of finding intriguing puzzles and allowing children to 'take off' with them seems to offer a far more valid way of assessing profiles of individuals than the current favorites worldwide: standard measures designed to be given within a half-hour with the aid of paper and pencil.

> My own guess is that it should be possible to gain a reasonably accurate picture of an individual's intellectual profile—be he three or thirteen—in the course of a month or so, **while that individual is involved in regular classroom activities**. The total time spent might be five to ten hours of observing—a long time given current standards of intelligence testing, but a very short time in terms of the life of that student. (emphasis mine)[65]

Part of what this means is that we must learn to observe students much more acutely in order to piece together a picture of their multiple intelligence profiles. While not scientific instruments, the "Student Watch" tools that follow can help you learn to observe factors that may be clues to reaching students by traveling down multiple pathways of knowing and learning. Give them a try for several weeks and see if you can begin to sense strengths and weaknesses. More importantly, brainstorm ways to assist each student in being all that they can be in the classroom and beyond!

STUDENT INTELLIGENCE WATCH
Behavior Patterns Log

How many of these behaviors can you find in your students?

- [ ] "Doodling" during a lecture or discussion
- [ ] Irresistible urge to discuss work with friends
- [ ] Humming quietly to self while working or while walking down the hall
- [ ] Precision in language and thought
- [ ] Difficulty sitting still or staying in seat
- [ ] Recognition of and delight in abstract patterns
- [ ] Very quiet, very self-reflective
- [ ] Quick problem solving
- [ ] Creative ideas, suggestions, and answers
- [ ] Body gestures and physical movement in expressing self
- [ ] Tapping pencil, foot, or finger while working
- [ ] Can remember thinking formulas and problem-solving strategies
- [ ] Relentless question-asking, avid curiosity
- [ ] Good at listening to and communicating with others
- [ ] Is helped by "visuals"; likes drawing, coloring, or painting
- [ ] Likes "hands-on" (manipulative) assignments
- [ ] Highly intuitive ("flies by the seat of their pants")
- [ ] Good in sports, well-coordinated physically

SKYLIGHT
PUBLISHING, INC.

SEVEN WAYS OF KNOWING

STUDENT INTELLIGENCE WATCH
Intelligence Skill Games

Set up several different "stations" around the room, each having a different type of game to perform, puzzle to be solved, challenge to be met, or task to be accomplished. Examples for stations:

- A game of "Pictionary"® and jigsaw puzzles
- Several varieties of "Rubik's Cube"® (cube, triangle, sphere)
- Books of riddles, jokes, crosswords, jumbles, and "Trivial Pursuit"®
- The game of charades and/or "Twister"®
- A variety of "sound makers" with the task to create a musical piece
- A list of intriguing tasks that are to be done cooperatively in a team
- Several "self-analysis" type of questionnaires or surveys

Give students time to explore the different stations with the understanding they can return to one for a longer period of time. Carefully observe how they deal with and respond to each station (length of time spent, kinds of activities they do, etc.).

Then allow them to return to one station to do the activities, play the game, or perform the task. Again, carefully observe where they go and what they do once at a station for a period of time.

 SKYLIGHT PUBLISHING, INC.

STUDENT INTELLIGENCE WATCH
Intelligence Attention Foci

Show students a complex film or play in which several different intelligences are dramatically portrayed. Look for ones that involve music, person-to-person relations, physical skills, clever problem-solving, vibrant colors, symbolism, and great dialogues. Some suggestions are:

- Any of the "Star Wars" series
- "To Kill a Mockingbird"
- Any of the "Charlie Chan" series
- "Alice in Wonderland"
- "A Midsummer's Night Dream"
- "A Wrinkle in Time"
- "The Miracle Worker"
- "Bambi"

After watching the movie, lead students in a structured "debriefing" discussion. Listen carefully to where different students focused their attention, what captured their imagination, and what they liked and disliked. Questions like the following may help you "listen between their answers" and catch glimpses of different intelligences watching the same movie or play:

1) What scenes do you remember? action scenes?

2) What lines of dialogue are still ringing in your ears?

3) What physical objects do you remember? what symbols?

4) What sounds (other than dialogue) do you remember?

5) What music do you recall? How was it used?

6) What feelings did you see portrayed on the screen? feelings in you?

7) Where did you see symbols used? What became a symbol for you?

8) What was the main problem or challenge in the movie? Was it solved?

9) Where have you experienced this happening in real life?

10) In a one-sentence summary, what was it about?

STUDENT INTELLIGENCE WATCH
Complex Problem Solving

The aim of this "test" is to expose students to a problem situation involving enough complexity that several intelligences are stimulated in an effort to find a solution. The following problem was presented in the Introduction to this book and is an example of a problem that stimulates several intelligences and that could be approached in multiple ways:

> A man and a woman are walking together down the street.
>
> The woman's step is 2/3 that of the man's. They start off together on the left foot. They want to keep walking together.
>
> How many steps will they each take before their left feet hit the ground at the same time again?

This problem can be approached through working with numbers, ratios, fractions, and mathematical formulas; through drawing or visualization; through physically getting a partner and stepping it out; through conversation and work with others in a group; and through intuition and meditation. Remember, from the perspective of building an intelligence profile of your students, HOW they approach the problem is far more important than if they get the "right" answer. So watch very carefully WHAT they are doing as they work.

Obviously, a problem in which students have some interest (probably **not** the one above!) will give you a better impression because they will be self-motivated to solve it. Look for potential problems in newspapers, magazines, or on TV. When you set up the situation for them to solve, make sure they know that they can use *any* means they choose to work on it (and make sure the materials are available in the classroom for more than the verbal/linguistic and logical/mathematical modes!)

SKYLIGHT
PUBLISHING, INC.

STUDENT INTELLIGENCE WATCH
Inventing

This is a "test" in which students have an opportunity to create or design something. Tell them they are scientists who are inventing things that people will need in the year 2090. You may want to create a brainstorm list of ideas making sure that items related to each of the intelligences is on the list. *[NOTE: This may take some leading questions such as what will their music be, what kinds of sports games will be popular, what will be on TV, what will stories and poetry be like, etc.]*

Now have them decide what they want to invent.

Around the room set up different kinds of "laboratories," each having the tools and materials of a different intelligence (see the Multiple Intelligence Toolbox presented earlier in this chapter). Give students time to create **whatever** and **however** they want to. Observe them carefully as they work. Note both the "lab" to which they were naturally drawn and what they do once they are in the lab.

Seven Ways of Teaching Weekly Checklist

Have I taught for the "seven ways of knowing" this week? Check yourself by listing the specific strategies, techniques, and tools you have used in classroom lessons this week.

	MONDAY	TUESDAY	WEDNESDAY	THURSDAY	FRIDAY
Verbal/ Linguistic					
Logical/ Mathematical					
Visual/ Spatial					
Body/ Kinesthetic					
Musical/ Rhythmic					
Interpersonal					
Intrapersonal					

People Search

Find Someone Who...	
Can list the different "learning styles" of his/her students. _____	Can draw a picture of symbolic representation of his/her feelings about today. _____
Loves to dance and/or is involved in some type of physical exercise. _____	Has tried and/or is currently practicing a form of meditation. _____
Has used cooperative learning groups in the classroom. _____	Sings in the shower and with the radio when riding in the car. _____
Is good at solving a variety of math problems (including a balanced checkbook!). _____	Loves to read and is good at expressing him/herself in words. _____

Conclusion

This book is not suggesting that you "add on" more "stuff" to teach in your already "over-stuffed" curriculum. It is rather suggesting and encouraging you to try new ways of teaching the old stuff!

Teaching for multiple intelligences is indeed challenging and demanding, but it is also a great deal of fun and it accesses your full creativity as an educator. And what is more, I guarantee you'll find more kids succeeding more of the time as they learn how to utilize their full intellectual potential both in school and beyond school in their everyday lives.

Remember the quote from William James which heads the table of contents:

I have no doubt whatever that most people live...in a very restricted circle of their potential being. They make use of a very small portion of their possible consciousness...much like a person who, out of the whole body organism, should get into the habit of using and moving only the little finger. We all have reservoirs of life to draw upon of which we do not dream.—William James

Research

Multiple Intelligences Theory: A Review of the Research

Our discoveries about the startling nature of reality are a major force for change, undermining common sense ideas and old institutional philosophies . . .The agenda of the coming decade is to act on this new scientific knowledge— discoveries that revise the very data base on which we have built our assumptions, our institutions, our lives.

—M. Ferguson, *The Aquarian Conspiracy*

In each chapter of this book, I have tried to provide a brief review of key research findings that support the theory of multiple intelligences. The purpose of this appendix is to pull the research together in one location for the sake of analysis and documentation. As you will see from the presentation below, *Seven Ways of Knowing* is a synthesis based on a wide range of research findings from diverse disciplines of investigation. These include such fields as psychology, medicine, education, business, cognitive patterning, sociology, anthropology, brain research, linguistics, biofeedback, and the human potential movement.

A number of the individuals mentioned have made significant contributions in several, if not all, of the intelligence areas. In the context of this book, I have cited them as research references at the particular points where they have been most helpful and informative. What appears, therefore, is not to be taken as a definitive picture of any one person's research contribution, but only as a piece of the larger puzzle I have tried to construct.

Within this research base are a variety of types of research. Ken Wilber's concept of the three ways we humans have of attaining knowledge (Chapter 2) bears repeating here, for I believe that it likewise applies to the field of triangulation research. Wilber suggests that we attain knowledge through the *eye of flesh*, the *eye of reason*, and the *eye of contemplation*.

The *eye of flesh* is the world of sensory experience—the world of what we see, hear, taste, touch, and smell with the five senses. Research methods based on the eye of flesh yield data that is quantifiable in accordance with certain accepted criteria of validity within the "scientific community."

The *eye of reason* involves the world of reason, logic, ideas, patterns, relationships, and analogy. Research methods based on the eye of reason are concerned with making connections between various pieces of knowledge and/or information, and with discovering new patterns and relationships between things that previously were not related. Thus, while it cannot be proven by hard, positivistic science (the *eye of flesh*) that the images we have in our heads control our behavior, it can, nevertheless, be validated through a process of inference, deduction, synthesis, and interpretation applied to behavioral observation and analysis.

The *eye of contemplation* involves our knowledge of "transcendent" realities; realities that go beyond what positivistic science and its sensory-based presuppositions can investigate, and that go beyond the rational, analytical abilities of the mind for understanding. Research methods based on the eye of contemplation are concerned with such things as investigating the processes of creativity, metacognition (cognitive capacities turned back on themselves), the realm of spiritual insight, intuition, values, self-consciousness, self-identity, and self-reflective abilities. The eye of contemplation examines the inner world of images, unconscious processes, self-understanding, and the like.

When examining any research, it is important to remember these "three eyes" and to know that within their own domains, they are king. Certain presuppositions of validity and invalidity apply, based on the consensus of others who are likewise operating with certain, agreed-upon presuppositions, such as what constitutes admissible data, proper "laboratory" procedures for conducting experiments, guidelines for making generalizations and/or interpretations, etc.

One falls into what Wilber calls "category error," however, when the *eye of flesh* tries to analyze data that can only be analyzed by the *eye of contemplation*—which often happens when positivistic scientists try to make pronouncements about matters of the spirit. The error here is that, by definition, the *eye of flesh* is confined to the investigation of matters of the flesh (the five senses), just as the *eye of reason* is confined to matters of reason and logic. The realm of religion, spirituality, metacognition, and the like, are beyond what can be seen, heard, smelled, tasted, and touched, as well as what can be understood and explained logically, rationally, and analytically.

The research review that follows involves all three eyes of research and, as such, there is no competition between them, as long as we guard ourselves against category error. Taken together they form an impressive and exciting base for both deepening our understanding of the theory of multiple intelligences, and for further investigation and experimentation.

Multiple Intelligences: General Research Capsule

Major Research Findings:

- Intelligence is not a static reality that is fixed at birth. It is a dynamic, ever-growing, changing reality throughout one's life. Intelligence can be improved, expanded, and amplified. The only limits to one's intelligence seem to be individual beliefs about what is possible.

- At almost any age and ability level one's mental functioning or mental processes can be improved. In fact, intelligence can be taught to others. One can learn how to be more intelligent by activating more levels of perception and knowing within daily living.

- Intelligence is a multiple phenomenon that occurs in many different parts of the brain/mind/body system. There are many forms of intelligence, many ways through which people know and understand themselves and the world.

- A stronger, more dominant intelligence can be used to train (improve or strengthen) a weaker intelligence. Much of one's full intelligence potential is in a state of latency due to disuse, but it can be awakened, strengthened, and trained.

People & Organizations	Key Concepts & Contributions
Bloom	An extraordinary, point-by-point, structured outline (a taxonomy) that describes the logical and emotional domains of the mind's various processes.
Bogen; Rico; Buzan; Russell	Two modes of information processing exist within the brain: the left hemisphere (more rational/analytical) and right hemisphere (more intuitive/artistic).
Feuerstein	Through instrumental enrichment, intelligence can be modified, expanded, and developed.
Gardner (*Project Zero*-Harvard University)	Intelligence is a pluralistic phenomenon. Seven intelligences have been tested and there are probably many more.
Guilford	There are at least 120 identifiable factors to the structure of the human intellect.
Harman (Institute of Noetic Sciences)	Creativity is learned and can be improved toward "programming" the mind for increased frequency of "breakthrough insights."
Houston (Foundation for Mind Research)	"Multiperceptual learning" utilizes body (including the full range of the senses), mind, and spirit in teaching and learning.
Machado (Ministry of Intelligence-Venezuela)	Intelligence can be taught to others; in fact, intelligence is a basic human right.
MacLean (National Institute of Health)	"Triune brain"—the brain contains, intact within itself, memories and wisdom from the journey of human evolutionary development (amphibian, reptilian, mammalian, and human).
Sternberg (IBM & Yale University)	The "triarchic theory" of intelligence identifies mental processes of various intelligences, practical ways the processes are applied to everyday life, and their transfer to new situations.

Verbal/Linguistic Intelligence Research Capsule

Major Research Findings:

- Four complex, interrelated processes within the brain comprise the neurological base of verbal/linguistic intelligence: *semantics* (recognizing meanings of words), *syntax* (sensitivity to order of words in a context), *phonics* (ability to distinguish between sounds, rhythms, inflection, and meters of words), and *praxis* (grasping the pragmatic functions of language).

- The emergence of language is the single, most important occurrence in evolutionary history. With it, for the first time, came the possibility for the human species to transcend the present situation and to anticipate and plan for the future.

- Language embodies the mood, tone, and values of a culture and, at the same time, shapes and determines its future developmental directions. Words have no *a priori* meaning. Once a consensus on meaning is reached, however, it shapes a person's perceptions of self, others, and the world around.

People & Organizations	Key Concepts & Contributions
Austin	Study of the poet's sensitivity to different, subtle shades of meaning of words in and of themselves and in the surrounding context.
Chomsky	Children are born with an innate knowledge about the rules and forms of language.
Gardner (*Project Zero*-Harvard University)	Written language "piggybacks" on oral language. It is not possible to continue reading normally if one's oral-auditory language areas have been damaged or destroyed.
Levi-Strauss; Chomsky	The acquisition of language did not occur through a gradual evolutionary process; rather, it was acquired at a *single* moment in time.
Lieberman	All of the individual components of language were present in Neanderthal humans except for the appropriate vocal apparatus or tract. When this emerged, language developed very rapidly.
Wexler & Culicover	Certain initial assumptions about the operation of language are built into the operational patterns of the central nervous system.
Wilber	The structure of a language embodies a particular culture's perceptions and this, in turn, creates the perceived limits of the self and world for its people.
Vygotsky	"Zone of potential development"—at each age and stage of development humans possess different language capacities which define the nature of social interaction and which later are internalized as self-understanding and understanding of future developmental possibilities.

Logical/Mathematical Intelligence Research Capsule

Major Research Findings:

- The mind operates through various cognitive patterns which can be improved, amplified, and changed through the explicit teaching of thinking skills and cognitive processes.

- Through metacognition (thinking about thinking) and metacognitive processing one can dramatically accelerate learning within and across the teaching/learning situation and can significantly increase the levels of transfer of learning beyond the teaching/learning situation into life.

- Logical thinking patterns occur along a spectrum of increasing complexity, including basic thinking skills, critical thinking skills, creative thinking processes, and problem-solving schemas that link "micro" thinking skills in a "macro" process. Taken together, they form a family of interrelated thinking competencies.

People & Organizations	Key Concepts & Contributions
Ambruster; Anderson; Dansereau & Davidson	Use of graphic or cognitive organizers can dramatically improve the ability to retain and recall information.
Ausubel	The theory of meaningful reception learning. Information is stored hierarchically in the brain from general to specific.
Beyer	Thinking skills must be explicitly taught through focusing attention on a skill, defining the skill, guided practice of the skill, reflection on the practice, and extended practice in other areas.
Costa (California State University)	Restructuring school curriculum so the process of thinking is the subject matter of instruction: learning to learn, creativity, metacognition, decision making, and problem solving.
de Bono (Cognition Research Trust)	"Lateral thinking" is a creative thinking skill that encourages the interaction of new ideas with old ones, deferring judgment; thus, divergent and creative thinking is promoted.
Fogarty & Bellanca (The IRI Group)	Key elements for teaching thinking: teaching FOR (setting the climate), OF (explicit teaching of thinking skills), WITH (structuring student interaction cooperatively), and ABOUT (metacognitive processing) thinking.
Lyman & McTighe	Use of "theory-imbedded tools" for cognitive instruction aids in the development of logical thinking and organization skills.
Piaget	All knowledge first comes from one's actions upon the world thus the course of development is from objects to statements, action to relations among actions, from sensory-motor to pure abstraction, ultimately to the realms of logic and science.

Visual/Spatial Intelligence Research Capsule

Major Research Findings:

- The mind naturally thinks in images. It "programs" and "reprograms" itself through images.

- Inner images (both conscious and unconscious) control one's behavior. They are comprised of every life experience one has had. They form an "inner guidance" system related to one's identity and understanding of the world.

- Images can change. The bombardment of various "messages" on images brings about the possibility of someone deciding to change their images. No one can change another's image for them.

- Since the capacity for imagination is inherent in the central nervous system, imaginistic abilities can be improved, strengthened, and extended through regular, focused, and intentional practice.

People & Organizations	Key Concepts & Contributions
Boulding (University of Indiana)	Images determine and control one's behavior, but they (images) can change through the impact of "messages"; a changed image equals changed behavior.
Gendlin (University of Chicago)	"Focusing" is a step-by-step approach to help people discover inner insights/knowings which can bring about immediate and lasting changes in one's life.
Harman (Institute of Noetic Sciences)	Whatever is vividly and energetically imagined or visualized by the mind, the brain believes to be true and present reality. This is the key to the practice of affirmations.
Houston (Foundation for Mind Research)	The ability to use internal imagery processes (visualization and guided imagery) can be improved even in so-called "non-imagizers" through working with "eidetic images" in the mind.
Samuels & Samuels	The most basic mental process is the ability to visualize; the mind naturally thinks in images.
Shone	All people possess a wide variety of "inner guides" or "inner teachers" which can be accessed and called upon at any time.

Body/Kinesthetic Intelligence Research Capsule

Major Research Findings:

- Through conscious, focused attention one can learn to control many seemingly "automatic" or "non-voluntary" physiological processes such as body temperature, heart rate, and brain-wave patterns.

- Any mind-body process can be worked with and improved. Few limits can be found to the central nervous system's capacity to modify (i.e., to educate and re-educate) both the mind-body and the system itself. Humanity is almost infinitely malleable.

- The content of the various images in the mind has a profound, physiological influence on the body. These images can be used to change bodily experience. The body can be used to change or alter images in the mind.

- By gaining awareness of how the body works, as well as various patterns of muscular abuse, one can inhibit negative reflexes and replace them with positive ones, thus creating a new situation of optimal body functioning.

People & Organizations	Key Concepts & Contributions
Alexander	Bad posture is in reality a profound misuse of the self that often results in the malfunctioning of the whole system.
Bartlett	Procedures for translating intention into action involve linking diverse receptive and performing functions in a continuous flow, which takes signals from "outside" and translates them to an action carried out.
Benson (Harvard Medical School & Hypertension Section, Beth Israel Hospital)	The "relaxation response" is a well-defined set of innate, physiological processes which balance the potentially harmful effects of stress and anxiety.
Feldenkrais	"Functional integration" or "freedom through awareness" increases the movement potential of the body, which simultaneously frees inhibited cells of the motor cortex in the brain.
Institute for the Development of Human Potential	The damaged brain can be re-patterned and re-trained to compensate for many lost physical capacities due to accidents, stroke, etc.
Masters & Houston (Foundation of Mind Research)	Through increased mental awareness one can learn to rid the body of tension and stress, improve the ability to concentrate and absorb information, and reverse physical symptoms of aging that come from misuse of the body.

Musical/Rhythmic Intelligence Research Capsule

Major Research Findings:

- The brain produces different electrical patterns or frequencies called "brain waves." Brain waves can be controlled and modulated thus creating optimal states of being and awareness for performing various tasks and for dealing with different situations.

- It is through the activation of neurons in the brain that learning takes place. The more neurons that can be activated in a given situation, the greater the learning potential of that situation; for example, increased memory, greater relaxation, and improved perception. Music and rhythm generally activate millions of neural connections.

- By modulating brain-wave frequencies to "alpha" or "theta" states of functioning, the brain is placed in a state of receptiveness to the assimilation of new information and in a state of flexibility/openness for creative thinking and inventing.

- The representation of musical/rhythmic intelligence in the brain involves the limbic system (emotional seat of music/rhythm), the left hemisphere (the more formal/analytical aspects of music as a system), and the right hemisphere (the figural/experiential aspects).

People & Organizations	Key Concepts & Contributions
Campbell	Use of music in the teaching/learning situation to improve long-term memory, to enhance, deepen, and accelerate other learning, and to increase perception in all the senses.
de Beauport (Mead School)	Use of art, music, crafts, and poetry to increase the role of less dominant parts of the brain thus improving achievement in other subjects such as reading, science, and math.
Gardner; Orff; Kodaly; Bernstein	The universal "Ur Song" is the basic melody given to children by nature. It is comprised of three notes—*so, mi, la*. Children in all cultures sing this basic melody in their early play.
Kimura	"Asymmetry of audio perception" involves dichotic listening techniques used to evaluate hemispheric dominance of musical and non-musical sounds.
Lozanov	"Suggestodedia" (popular "superlearning") is the use of music to modulate brain-wave patterns to relaxed, receptive states during which foreign languages are taught.
Monroe (Monroe Institute)	Use of "hemisynch synthesized music" to modulate brain waves so realms of the unconscious, archetypes, and altered states of consciousness are available in visualization journeys.
Orff & Guenther	Development of right-brain musicality (music based on the natural rhythms of the body and language) is basic to elemental rhythmic education where music, movement, and speech are taught together and supplement each other.
Steiner (Waldorf Schools)	"Eurythmics"—understanding the human form and the world as a blend of external physical aspects and internal musical forces. Music can be found anywhere.

Interpersonal Intelligence Research Capsule

Major Research Findings:

- When people work together in situations of positive interdependence achievement levels are higher, self-esteem and esteem of others are raised, motivation for and enjoyment of the task is increased, and creative/higher-order thinking processes naturally occur.

- Something like "synergy" (a spontaneous working together) is happening in many groups today where individuals are autonomous and independent, but at the same time are an integral, inseparable part of a larger whole.

- The skills of cooperation/collaboration, basic human relations, and group process can be learned and taught at any age level, the earlier the better. In order to teach these skills one must be made aware of the need for a skill, define the skill, and have multiple opportunities to consciously use and practice the skill.

- The greater one's awareness about what is involved in successful cooperation with others, and the greater the awareness of personal patterns of cooperation/non-cooperation, the greater are the possibilities for change and improvement.

People & Organizations / Key Concepts & Contributions

People & Organizations	Key Concepts & Contributions
Bellanca & Fogarty (The IRI Group)	The linking of the collaborative skills from various cooperative learning models with cognitive instruction, including thinking skills, cognitive organizers, metacognitive strategies, and explicit teaching for transfer.
Institute of Cultural Affairs (ICA)	Internal human development organization which utilizes and teaches teamwork, creating a "corporate culture," and methods of group strategic planning to local communities and businesses around the world.
Johnson & Johnson (Cooperative Learning Center, University of Minnesota)	Humans are not born instinctively knowing how to cooperate with others. Therefore, interpersonal and group skills must be explicitly taught and opportunities must be given to practice cooperation.
Kagan (University of Southern California)	A repertoire of interactive structures/strategies to force collaboration in group process, such as "round-robin" discussions, the curriculum "jigsaw," and the "think-pair-share."
Marcus & McDonald (The IRI Group)	Key elements for structuring successful cooperative lessons include **BUILD**: **B**= bring in higher-order thinking, **U**= unite the teams, **I**= insure individual learning, **L**= look over and discuss learning, **D**= develop social skills.
Slavin (Johns Hopkins University)	"Curriculum packages" for the classroom which prescribe specific cooperative strategies for use with heterogeneously grouped teams (alternatives to tracking and ability grouping practices).

Intrapersonal Intelligence Research Capsule

Major Research Findings:

- Within the mind are hundreds of potential states of awareness. These include such things as an awareness of the wholeness of the universe, the mystery, depth, and greatness of the individual self, and a sense of oneness with the natural world. The mind can shift from one state of consciousness to another at will.

- The mind has a seemingly endless capacity for improving the quality of its own thinking. Through the strategic use of "metacognition" (thinking about thinking) and metacognitive processing techniques, complex thinking skills can be taught to others and all thinking patterns can be improved.

- Within the unconscious mind are capacities for controlling many bodily functions previously thought to be automatic. These include not only heart rate, blood pressure, and body temperature, but also untapped powers for accelerating and helping the body's natural healing processes.

- Creativity is not given at birth; it is a dynamic process that can be learned, taught, and improved. There are practices that can "trigger" more of the brain's natural creative potential and exercises that can train the brain to be more creative.

People & Organizations	Key Concepts & Contributions
Assagioli	"Psychosynthesis"—the resources and guidance needed to attain wholeness in life are already naturally present in the psyche; they can be accessed for assistance in daily living.
Fogarty; Perkins; Beyer	"Teaching for transfer" includes analysis of different levels and dynamics of transfer. There are various strategies to increase transfer within specific curriculum content, across curriculum areas, and beyond the school classroom into life.
Harman (Institute of Noetic Sciences)	"The 3rd metaphysic"—civilization is currently shifting from a materialistic understanding of reality to one in which reality is grasped as primarily spiritual at its core.
Houston & Masters (Foundation for Mind Research)	"Altered states of consciousness" means one's consciousness can be altered from ineffective states to ones that more fully actualize innate human potentials and that promote optimal functioning.
Markley (Futures Department, University of Houston)	Use of depth intuition in creative problem solving and strategic planning. It is possible to access the depth intuition in a systematic, sustained fashion.
Vaughn	Self-concepts (identity) determine the limits of one's world, perspective, lifestyle, values, beliefs, and self-understanding about what is and is not possible.
Wilber	Consciousness development occurs along a spectrum that moves to ever-higher levels of unity, beginning with the body, emotions and rational/mental awareness, and ending with transpersonal and unity consciousness.

Multiple Intelligences Summary Wheel

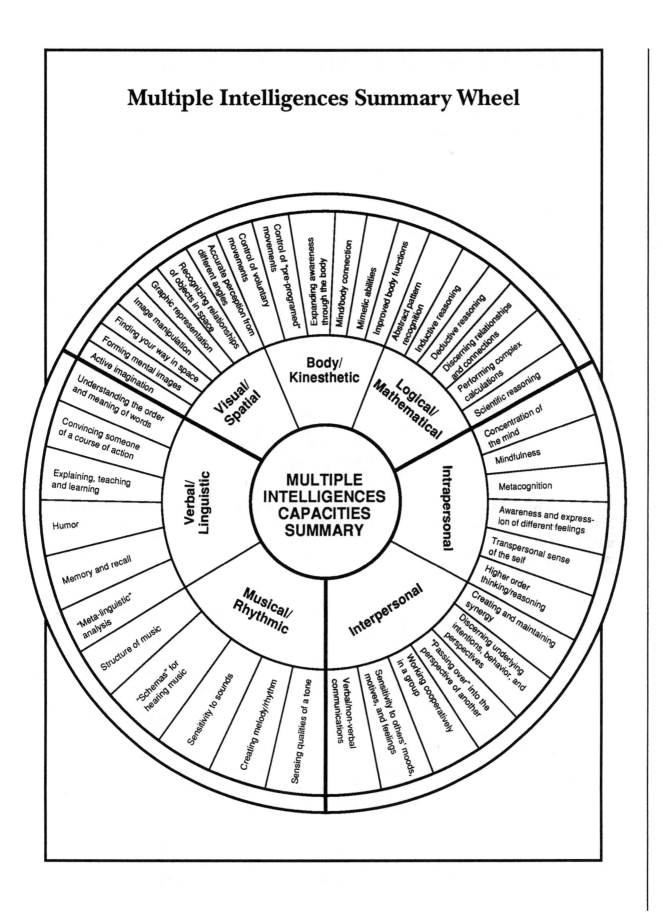

MULTIPLE INTELLIGENCES CAPACITIES SUMMARY

Body/Kinesthetic
- Control of "pre-programed" movements
- Control of voluntary movements
- Expanding awareness through the body
- Mind/body connection
- Mimetic abilities
- Improved body functions

Logical/Mathematical
- Abstract pattern recognition
- Inductive reasoning
- Deductive reasoning
- Discerning relationships and connections
- Performing complex calculations
- Scientific reasoning

Intrapersonal
- Concentration of the mind
- Mindfulness
- Metacognition
- Awareness and expression of different feelings
- Transpersonal sense of the self
- Higher order thinking/reasoning

Interpersonal
- Creating and maintaining synergy
- Discerning underlying intentions, behavior, and perspectives
- "Passing over" into the perspective of another
- Working cooperatively in a group
- Sensitivity to others' moods, motives, and feelings
- Verbal/non-verbal communications

Musical/Rhythmic
- Structure of music
- "Schemas" for hearing music
- Sensitivity to sounds
- Creating melody/rhythm
- Sensing qualities of a tone

Verbal/Linguistic
- Understanding the order and meaning of words
- Convincing someone of a course of action
- Explaining, teaching and learning
- Humor
- Memory and recall
- "Meta-linguistic" analysis

Visual/Spatial
- Accurate perception from different angles
- Recognizing relationships of objects in space
- Graphic representation
- Image manipulation
- Finding your way in space
- Forming mental images
- Active imagination

Verbal/Linguistic Intelligence Fact Sheet

Capacities Involved

- Understanding Order & Meaning of Words
- Convincing Someone of a Course of Action
- Explaining, Teaching, and Learning
- Humor
- Memory & Recall
- "Meta-linguistic" Analysis

Verbal/Linguistic Intelligence is awakened by the spoken word, by reading someone's ideas, thoughts, or poetry, or by writing one's own ideas, thoughts, or poetry, as well as by various kinds of humor such as "plays on words," jokes, and "twists" of the language.

Neurological Process

- Mostly located in temporal cortex of left hemisphere of brain ("Broca's Area")
- Sensitivity to shades of meanings of words (semantics)
- Sensitivity to sounds, rhythm, inflection, and meter of words (phonology)
- Sensitivity to order among words (syntax)
- Sensitivity to different uses of language (praxis)

Strengthen verbal/linguistic practices through creative writing, impromptu speaking, learning and using new words, formal speech, debate, formal composition, and story telling and invention.

Developmental Journey

Basic:
- infant babblings
- pairs of words/meaningful phrases
- simple sentences (poor syntax)
- imitation writing (letters/name)

Higher-Order:
- creative/expressive writing
- story-telling/inventing
- poetry creation/appreciation
- debate/formal speaking
- use/understanding of figures of speech
- meta-linguistic conversation

Complex:
- grasp of grammar/expanded vocabulary
- complex sentence creation (good syntax)
- reading (stories and other narratives)
- humor (telling and understanding jokes)
- self-initiated writing

Vocational/Avocational Pursuits:
- public speaking
- novelist, poet, journalist
- comedian
- play writing
- newscasting
- story-telling/writing

Logical/Mathematical Intelligence
Fact Sheet

Capacities Involved

- Abstract Pattern Recognition
- Inductive Reasoning
- Deductive Reasoning
- Discerning Relationships & Connections
- Performing Complex Calculations
- Scientific Reasoning

Logical/Mathematical Intelligence is activated in situations requiring problem solving or meeting a new challenge, as well as situations requiring pattern discernment and recognition.

Neurological Process

- Ability to read and produce mathematical signs (left hemisphere of brain)
- Ability to understand numerical relationships and concept (right hemisphere)
- Search for abstract patterns and design
- Love of order and harmony for its own sake

Strengthen logical/mathematical intelligence by learning and using various "patterns for thinking" (e.g., prediction, intuitive and deductive thinking, etc.); working with symbolic language; using complex problem solving; and learning and using number patterns.

Developmental Journey

Basic:
- manipulation of objects in outside world
- simple abstraction/number recognition
- pattern recognition
- cause/effect thought patterns

Higher-Order:
- finding unknown qualities (e.g., algebra)
- linking operations for complex problem solving (e.g., geometry, profits)
- inductive/deductive reasoning processes
- metacognitive processing skills
- logic

Complex:
- performing standard math operations (+, -, +, x)
- problem-solving skills
- math process understanding
- critical thinking pattern development
- complex abstraction (e.g., math symbols)

Vocational/Avocational Pursuits:
- scientific research
- accounting/business
- legal assistance
- banking
- computer programming
- mathematician
- medicine

Visual/Spatial Intelligence Fact Sheet

Capacities Involved

- Active Imagination
- Forming Mental Images
- Finding Your Way in Space
- Image Manipulations
- Graphic Representation
- Recognizing Relationships of Objects in Space
- Accurate Perception from Different Angles

Visual/Spatial Intelligence is triggered by presenting the mind with and/or creating unusual, delightful, and colorful designs, patterns, shapes, and pictures, and engaging in active imagination through such things as visualization, guided imagery, and pretending exercises.

Neurological Process

- Mostly located in the parietal lobes of the right hemisphere
- Sense of sight also involved (occipetal lobes)
- Search for/love of balance and harmony
- Power of vivid, active imagination on the brain ("virtual reality")

Strengthen visual/spatial intelligence using active imagination to picture things that are outrageous or fantastic, using visual media such as paints, colored markers, or clay. Use mind-mapping skills, and drawing patterns/designs.

Developmental Journey

Basic:
- sensori-motor exploration of physical world
- color discernment
- shape discernment
- simple drawing
- getting from one place to another (e.g., crawling/walking to desired location)

Complex:
- recognition of spatial depth and dimension
- drawing, sculpting, painting (reproduction of scenes/objects)
- use of active imagination
- decentration (seeing from different perspectives)
- map reading/understanding spatial implications

Higher-Order:
- building (blueprints)
- map making
- impressionistic/expressionistic art-form creation
- abstract spatial imagery (e.g., geometry)
- complex visual/spatial relationships (e.g., chess)

Vocational/Avocational Pursuits:
- architecture
- graphic design artistry
- cartographer
- drafting
- painting (art)
- sculpting (art)
- advertising

Body/Kinesthetic Intelligence
Fact Sheet

Capacities Involved

- Control of "Voluntary" Movements
- Control of "Preprogrammed" Movements
- Expanding Awareness Through the Body
- The Mind and Body Connection
- Mimetic Abilities
- Improved Body Functioning

Body/Kinesthetic Intelligence is awakened through physical movement such as in various sports, dances, and physical exercises, as well as by the expression of oneself through the body, such as inventing, drama, body language, and creative/interpretive dance.

Neurological Process

- Cross-lateral motor functions (right controls left/left controls right)
- Cerebral cortex of brain feeds information to spinal cord (perceptual system feedback mechanism)
- Motor cortex of brain executes specific muscular movements
- Brain repatterning potential
- Power of kinesthetic body awareness

Strengthen body/kinesthetic intelligence through physical gestures and body movement, role-playing, drama, mime and charade games, kinesthetic skills (e.g., sports, exercise, dance), or inventing something with the hands.

Developmental Journey

Basic:
- "automatic reflexes" (infant sucking, looking, reaching)
- basic motor skills (turning over, crawling, holding, sitting up, walking)
- gaining physical independence
- goal-oriented actions

Complex:
- expressive gestures/body language
- physical exercise/education routines
- role playing/charades
- folk/cultural dance
- sports games (basic skills)

Higher-Order:
- complex motor coordination (gymnastics/roller skating/typing)
- creative/expressive dance (e.g., ballet)
- dramatic enactment of complex scenes
- sports games (skilled execution)
- inventing

Vocational/Avocational Pursuits:
- athletics
- dramatic acting/mime
- physical education instruction
- inventor
- professional dancing/choreography

Musical/Rhythmic Intelligence
Fact Sheet

Capacities Involved

- Appreciation for the Structure of Music
- "Schemas" or "Frames" in the Mind for Hearing Music
- Sensitivity to Sounds
- Recognition, Creation, and Reproduction of Melody/Rhythm
- Sensing Characteristic Qualities of a Tone

Musical/Rhythmic Intelligence is turned on by the resonance or vibrational effect of music and rhythm on the brain, including such things as the human voice, sounds from nature, musical instruments, percussion instruments, and other humanly produced sounds.

Neurological Process

- Mostly in the right hemisphere of the brain (right frontal, temporal lobes)
- Figural processing (intuitive, based on what is heard, "natural" perception)
- Formal processing (analytical, based on propositional knowledge about music as a system)
- Modulation of brain waves patterns or frequencies by vibration and tone (*beta, alpha, theta*, and *delta* frequencies)

Strengthen musical/rhythmic intelligence by practicing listening to music and other sounds, expressing feelings through tones, beats, and vibrations, creating songs/jingles to communicate thoughts, and using music, humming, and rhythm to alter moods.

Developmental Journey

Basic:
- basic "Ur Song" (universal song of babies)
- tonal recognition and reproduction
- rhythm recognition and reproduction
- sound association forming

Complex:
- song/melody production
- rhythm/beat production
- "reading" music/rhythm
- enjoyment of different types of music
- musical technique development

Higher-Order:
- music composition/performance
- teaching music to others
- basic understanding of music theory
- grasp of the meanings of music symbols
- music appreciation skills

Vocational/Avocational Pursuits:
- advertising
- performance musician
- music composer
- music teacher
- environmental sound engineering
- film making
- musical theatre
- television

Interpersonal Intelligence Fact Sheet

Capacities Involved

- Effective Verbal/Non-Verbal Communication
- Sensitivity to Other's Moods, Temperaments, Motivations, and Feelings
- Working Cooperatively in a Group
- Ability to Discern Other's Underlying Intentions and Behavior
- "Passing Over" into the Perspective of Another
- Creating and Maintaining Synergy

Interpersonal Intelligence is activated by person-to-person encounters in which such things as effective communication, working together with others for a common goal, and noticing distinctions among persons are necessary and important.

Neurological Process

- Mostly involves the frontal lobes of the brain, as well as the neo-cortex
- Integrates all other forms of intelligence in gaining knowledge about and relating to other human beings
- Catalyzes group creative processes ("mind linkages" with others)
- Individual self-transcendence in social relations (self is more than alone)
- Positive interdependence/reliance on others (feedback for self understanding/ preservation of the larger social order and culture)

Strengthen interpersonal intelligence by practicing reflective listening, working as a member of a team, giving and receiving empathetic feedback, being aware of others' feelings, motives, and opinions, and effective person-to-person communication.

Developmental Journey

Basic:
- parental bonding
- recognition/acceptance of "familiar others"
- imitation of sounds, words, gestures, and facial expressions (simple communication with others)
- emergence of affective empathy
- social role playing (e.g., playing "house," "office," etc.)

Higher-Order:
- consensus-building skills
- basic understanding of effective "group process"
- cooperative problem-solving abilities
- recognition of differing cultural values/ norms
- recognition of various "social ideals"

Complex:
- establishing meaningful peer relationships (beyond the family)
- development of effective "social skills" (collaboration)
- empathy for others
- being-part-of-a-team skills

Vocational/Avocational Pursuits:
- counseling/therapist
- professional teaching
- politics
- sociologist/anthropologist
- religious leader

Intrapersonal Intelligence Fact Sheet

Capacities Involved

- Concentration of the Mind
- Mindfulness
- Metacognition
- Awareness and Expression of Different Feelings
- Transpersonal Sense of the Self
- Higher-Order Thinking and Reasoning

Intrapersonal Intelligence is awakened when we are in situations that cause introspection and require knowledge of the internal aspects of the self, such as awareness of our feelings, thinking processes, self-reflection, and spirituality.

Neurological Process

- Involves mostly the frontal lobes of the brain, as well as the neo-cortex
- Integrates all other forms of intelligence in gaining knowledge about the self
- Catalyzes awareness of a purposefulness about one's life/role ("entelechy")
- Higher-order reasoning/thinking (synthesis, application, transfer strategizing)
- Altered states of consciousness to produce spiritual intuition, insight, unity

Strengthen intrapersonal intelligence and practice metacognition by using higher-order critical and creative thinking processes, the skills of "focusing and centering" the mind, mindfulness exercises, and self-conscious emotional or affective processing techniques.

Developmental Journey

Basic:
- expression of a range of body states, different feelings at different times
- awareness of separate self-identity ("the terrible twos")
- ability to correlate certain emotions/feelings with specific experiences/situations (2-5 years)

Higher-Order:
- conscious control of emotional states
- identity search (e.g., who am I, *raison d'être*)
- symbol understanding/creation
- emerging personal belief/philosophy system
- conscious use of higher-order thinking processes (metacognition)
- self-understanding (including psychological aspects of the self, e.g., motivation, aspiration, cultural role)

Complex:
- development of concentration skills
- "why" questioning (trying to "make sense" of life)
- self-improvement skills acquisition/concern
- defining personal likes/dislikes
- correlation of others' behavior with self-understanding/feelings

Vocational/Avocational Pursuits:
- psychiatry
- spiritual counseling
- human potential exploration
- philosopher
- guru
- cognitive patterns research

End Notes

Introduction

1   Gardner, H., & Walters, J.M. "The Development and Education of Intelligences." *Essays on the Intellect.* Alexandria, Virginia: Association for Supervision and Curriculum Development, pp. 3-4, 1985.

2   Houston, J. *Life Force.* New York: Dell, p. 84, 1980.

Chapter 1. In the Beginning Was the Word...

3   Wilber, K. *The Atman Project.* Wheaton, Illinois: Quest Books, p. 22, 1980.

4   Wilber, K. *The Atman Project.* Wheaton, Illinois: Quest Books, p. 22, 1980.

5   Lawrence, D.H. "Search for Love." *The Complete Poems of D.H. Lawrence,* V. de Sola Pinto & F.W. Roberts (Eds.). New York: Viking Press, p. 118, 1959.

6   Gardner, H. *Frames of Mind.* New York: Harper & Row, p. 77, 1985.

7   Laird, C. *The Miracle of Language.* New York: Fawcett Publications, p. 101, 1957.

8   Wilber, K. *The Atman Project.* Wheaton, Illinois: Quest Books, p. 29, 1980.

9   Houston, J. *The Possible Human.* Los Angeles: J.P. Tarcher, p. 55, 1982.

10   Kazantzakis, N. *Saviors of God.* New York: Simon & Schuster, p. 94-95, 1960.

11   Bacon, F. "Of Studies." *Century Readings in the English Essay,* Wann Louis (Ed.). New York: Appleton-Century-Crofts, p. 76, 1939.

12   Laird, C. *The Miracle of Language.* New York: Fawcett Publications, p. 224, 1957.

Chapter 2. As Easy as 1, 2, 3

13   Bellanca, J., & Fogarty, R. *Catch Them Thinking.* Palatine, Illinois: Skylight, p. 27, 1986.

14   Wilber, K. *Eye to Eye.* New York: Anchor Books, p. 3, 1983.

15   Wilber, K. *Eye to Eye.* New York: Anchor Books, p. 4, 1983.

16   Gardner, H. *Frames of Mind.* New York: Harper & Row, p. 147, 1985.

17   Harman, W. *The Global Mind Change.* Indianapolis: Knowledge Systems, p. 27, 1988.

18   Gardner, H. *Frames of Mind.* New York: Harper & Row, p. 129, 1985.

19   Fogarty, R., & Bellanca, J. *Patterns for Thinking—Patterns for Transfer.* Palatine, Illinois: Skylight, p. 127, 1989.

20   Fogarty, R., & Bellanca, J. *Patterns for Thinking—Patterns for Transfer.* Palatine, Illinois: Skylight, p. 152, 1989.

21   Gardner, H. *Frames of Mind.* New York: Harper & Row, p. 141, 1985.

22   Gardner, H. *Frames of Mind.* New York: Harper & Row, p. 148, 1985.

Chapter 3. Seeing Is Believing...and Knowing!

23   Samuels, M., & Samuels, N. *Seeing with the Mind's Eye.* New York: Random House, p. xi, 1975.

24   Shone, R. *Creative Visualization.* New York: Thorson's Publishers, p. 18-19, 1984.

25   Samuels, M., & Samuels, N. *Seeing with the Mind's Eye.* New York: Random House, p. 59. 1975.

26   Harman, W., & Rheingold, H. *Higher Creativity.* Los Angeles: J.P. Tarcher, p. 84, 1985.

27 Houston, J. *The Possible Human*. Los Angeles: J.P. Tarcher, p. 144, 1982.

28 Harman, W., & Rheingold, H. *Higher Creativity*. Los Angeles: J.P. Tarcher, p. 82, 1985.

29 Graham, I. "Mindmapping: An Aid to Memory." *Planetary Edges*. Toronto: The Institute of Cultural Affairs, p. 22, April/June 1988.

30 Russell, P. *The Brain Book*. New York: E.P. Dutton, p. 175-179, 1976.

31 Graham, I. "Mindmapping: An Aid to Memory." *Planetary Edges*. Toronto: The Institute of Cultural Affairs, p. 22, April/June 1988.

32 Russell, P. *The Brain Book*. New York: E.P. Dutton, p. 179, 1976.

33 Boulding, K. *The Image*. Ann Arbor: University of Michigan Press, p. 47-48, 1966.

Chapter 4. Practice Makes Perfect or Learning by Doing

34 Houston, J. *The Possible Human*. Los Angeles: J.P. Tarcher, p. 2, 1982.

35 Houston, J. *The Possible Human*. Los Angeles: J.P. Tarcher, p. 2-3, 1982.

36 Masters, R., & Houston, J. *Listening to the Body*. New York: Dell, p. 3-4, 1983.

37 Masters, R., & Houston, J. *Listening to the Body*. New York: Dell, p. 29-30, 1983.

38 Houston, J. *The Possible Human*. Los Angeles: J.P. Tarcher, p. 20, 1982.

39 Masters, R., & Houston, J. *Listening to the Body*. New York: Dell, p. xi-xii, 1983.

40 Gardner, H. *Frames of Mind*. New York: Harper & Row, p. 235, 1985.

Chapter 5. I've Got Rhythm, You've Got Rhythm... Who Could Ask for Anything More?

41 Campbell, D. G. *Introduction to the Musical Brain*. Richardson, Texas: Magnamusic-Baton, p. 4, 1983.

42 Campbell, D. G. *Introduction to the Musical Brain*. Richardson, Texas: Magnamusic-Baton, p. 22, 1983.

43 Campbell, D. G. *Introduction to the Musical Brain*. Richardson, Texas: Magnamusic-Baton, p. 17, 1983.

44 Gardner, H. *Frames of Mind*. New York: Harper & Row, p. 105-106, 1985.

45 Campbell, D. G. *Introduction to the Musical Brain*. Richardson, Texas: Magnamusic-Baton, p. 8, 1983.

46 Campbell, D. G. *Introduction to the Musical Brain*. Richardson, Texas: Magnamusic-Baton, p. 59, 1983.

47 Campbell, D. G. *Introduction to the Musical Brain*. Richardson, Texas: Magnamusic-Baton, p. 67, 1983.

Chapter 6. Getting to Know You...and Learning Together

48 Russell, P. *The Global Brain*. (video) Los Angeles: J.P. Tarcher, 1983.

49 Johnson, D.W., Johnson, R., & Holubec, E.J. *Cooperation in the Classroom*. Edina, Minnesota: Interaction Book Company, p. 5:2, 1988.

50 Dunne, J. *The Way of All the Earth*. New York: MacMillan, p. 180-181, 1972.

51 Ferguson, M. *The Aquarian Conspiracy*. Los Angeles: J.P. Tarcher, p. 215, 1980.

52 Winocur, S.L. *Zooley*. IMPACT Program (Improve Minimal Proficiencies by Activating Critical Thinking). Huntington Beach, CA: Phi Delta Kappa, 1986. The activity presented here is an excerpt from a lesson in deductive logic, and does not in any way reflect the intention of the original author. As presented, the activity assumes the student possesses the skills of deductive logic and will apply them correctly. The IMPACT program requires that the student be taught these skills directly prior to the presentation of the general practice activity thus "enabling" the student to focus on cooperative processes.

53 Hubbard, B. *Manual for Co-Creators of the Quantum Leap*. Irvine, CA: Barbara Mary Hubbard, Inc., p. I-2, 1985.

Chapter 7. Know Thyself...Thy Cognition and Thy Consciousness

54 Russell, P. *The Global Brain*. Los Angeles: J.P. Tarcher, p. 183, 1983.

55 Gardner, H. *Frames of Mind*. New York: Harper & Row, p. 240-241, 1985.

56 Gardner, H. *Frames of Mind*. New York: Harper & Row, p. 262, 1985.

57 Vaughn, F. *The Inward Arc*. Boulder, Co: The New Science Library, Shambhala, p. 25, 1986.

58 Gardner, H. *Frames of Mind*. New York: Harper & Row, p. 239, 1985.

59 Fogarty, R., & Bellanca, J. *Patterns for Thinking—Patterns for Transfer*. Palatine, Illinois: Skylight, p. 204, 1989.

60 Costa, A. "The School as a Home for the Mind." *Developing Minds* (second edition). Alexandria, Virginia: Association for Supervision and Curriculum Development, p. 22, 25, 1991.

61 Russell, P. *The Global Brain*. Los Angeles: J.P. Tarcher, p. 159-160, 1983.

Chapter 8. Creating Multi-Modal Eventfulness in the Classroom

62 Gardner, H., & Walters, J.M. "The Development and Education of Intelligences." *Essays on the Intellect*. Alexandria, Virginia: Association for Supervision and Curriculum Development, p. 20, 1985.

63 Gardner, H. *Frames of Mind*. New York: Harper & Row, p. 278, 1985.

64 Gardner, H., & Walters, J.M. "The Development and Education of Intelligences." *Essays on the Intellect*. Alexandria, Virginia: Association for Supervision and Curriculum Development, p. 20, 1985.

65 Gardner, H. *Frames of Mind*. New York: Harper & Row, p. 387-388, 1985.

BIBLIOGRAPHY

Alexander, F. (1984). *The use of the self: Its conscious direction in relation to diagnosis, functioning, and the control of reaction.* Downey, CA: Centerline Press.

Ambruster, B., & Anderson, T. (1980). *The effect of mapping on the free recall of expository tests* (Tech. Rep. No. 160). Urbana-Champaign, IL: University of Illinois, Center for the Study of Reading.

Anderson, R., & Biddle, W. (1975). On asking people questions about what they are reading. In G. Bower (Ed.) *The psychology of learning and motivation.* New York: Academic Press.

Arlin, P. (1990). Teaching as conversation. *Educational Leadership, 48(2).*

Armstrong, T. (1987). *In their own way: Discovering and encouraging your child's personal learning style.* Los Angeles: J.P. Tarcher.

Assagioli, R. (1973). *The act of will.* New York: Viking Press.

Ausubel, D. (1968). *Educational psychology: A cognitive view.* New York: Holt, Rinehart, and Winston.

Bacon, F. (1939). Of studies. In W. Louis (Ed.) *Century readings in the English essay.* New York: Appeton-Century-Crofts.

Bartlett, F. (1958). *Thinking.* New York: Basic Books.

Bellanca, J., & Fogarty, R. (1991). *Blueprints for thinking in the cooperative classroom* (rev. ed.). Palatine, IL: Skylight Publishing.

Bellanca, J., & Fogarty, R. (1986). *Catch them thinking.* Palatine, IL: Skylight Publishing.

Benson, H. (1975). *The relaxation response.* New York: Morrow.

Beyer, B. (1987). *Practical strategies for the teaching of thinking.* Boston: Allyn & Bacon.

Bloom, B. (1956). *Taxonomy of educational objectives.* New York: David McKay.

Bogen, J. (1979, February). Some educational aspects of hemispheric socialization. *Dromenon.*

Boulding, K. (1966). *The image*. Ann Arbor: University of Michigan Press.

Bruner, J., Goodnow, J., & Austin, G. (1956). *A study of thinking*. New York: Wiley.

Buzan, T. (1991). *Use both sides of your brain*. New York: Dutton.

Caine, R., & Caine, G. (1990). Understanding a brain-based approach to learning and teaching. *Educational Leadership, 48*(2), 66-70.

Campbell, D. (1983). *Introduction to the musical brain*. Richardson, TX: Magnamusic-Baton.

Campbell, J. (1989). *The improbable machine: What the upheavals in artificial intelligence research reveal about how the mind really works*. New York: Simon and Schuster.

Campbell, L. (1985). *Tomorrow's education today*. Seattle: The Pegasus School.

Chomsky, N. (1968). *Language and mind*. New York: Harcourt, Brace, Jovanovich.

Coles, R. *The spiritual life of children*. Boston: Houghton Mifflin, 1990.

Costa, A. (Ed.) (1991). *Developing minds* (rev. ed.) Alexandria, VA: Association for Supervision and Curriculum Development.

Costa, A. (1991). The school as a home for the mind. In A. Costa (Ed.), *Developing Minds, Volume 1* (rev. ed.) pp. 47-54. Alexandria, VA: Association for Supervision and Curriculum Development.

Costa, A. (1984). Mediating the metacognitive. *Educational Leadership, 42*(3), 57-62.

Costa, A. (1981). Teaching for intelligent behavior. *Educational Leadership, 39*(1), 29-31.

Culicover, P., & Wexler, P. (1980). *Formal principles of language acquisition*. Cambridge, MA: MIT Press.

Curry, L. (1990). A critique of the research on learning styles. *Educational Leadership, 48*(2), 50-52.

Dansereau, D. et al. (1979). Development and evaluation of a learning strategy training program. *Journal of Educational Psychology, 71*(1).

Davidson, J. (1982). The group mapping activity for instruction in reading and thinking. *Journal of Reading, 26*(1),52-56.

de Bono, E. (1973). *Lateral thinking: Creativity step by step*. New York: Harper & Row.

Demillle, R. *Put your mother on the ceiling*. New York: Viking-Penguin, 1976.

Dickinson, D. (1987). *New developments in cognitive research*. Seattle: New Horizons for Learning.

Dunne, J. (1972). *The way of all the earth: Experiments in truth and religion*. New York: MacMillan.

Feldenkrais, M. (1977). *Awareness through movement: Health exercises for personal growth*. New York: Harper and Row.

Ferguson, M. (1980). *The Aquarian conspiracy: Personal and social transformation in the 1980s*. Los Angeles: J. P. Tarcher.

Feuerstein, R. (1980). *Instrumental enrichment*. Baltimore, MD: University Park Press.

Fogarty, R., & Bellanca, J. (1989). *Patterns for thinking: Patterns for transfer*. Palatine, IL: Skylight Publishing.

Fogarty, R., & Bellanca, J. (1986). *Teach them thinking*. Palatine, IL: Skylight Publishing.

Gardner, H. (1987). Developing the spectrum of human intelligences: Teaching in the eighties, a need to change. *Harvard Educational Review*.

Gardner, H. (1983). *Frames of mind: The theory of multiple intelligences*. New York: Harper and Row.

Gardner, H. (1982). *Developmental psychology: An introduction*. Boston: Little Brown.

Gardner, H. (1981, December). Do babies sing a universal song? *Psychology Today*.

Gawain, S. (1978). *Creative visualization*. New York: Bantam Books.

Gazzaniga, M. (1988). *Mind matters: How mind and brain interact to create our conscious lives*. Boston: Houghton Mifflin.

Gendlin, E. (1978). *Focusing*. New York: Everest House.

Glasser, W. (1986). *Control theory in the classroom.* New York: Perennial Library.

Graham, I. (1988) Mindmapping: An aid to memory. In *Planetary Edges.* Toronto: The Institute of Cultural Affairs.

Guilford, J. (1979). *Way beyond IQ.* Buffalo, NY: Creative Education Foundation.

Harman, W. (1988). *The global mind change.* Indianapolis: Knowledge Systems.

Harman, W., & Rheingold, H. (1985). *Higher creativity.* Los Angeles: J.P. Tarcher.

Houston, J. (1987). *The search for the beloved: Journeys in sacred psychology.* Los Angeles: J.P. Tarcher.

Houston, J. (1982).*The possible human: A course in extending your physical, mental, and creative abilities.* Los Angeles: J.P. Tarcher.

Houston, J. (1980). *Lifeforce: The psycho-historical recovery of the self.* New York: Delacorte Press.

Hubbard, B. (1985). *Manual for co-creators of the quantum leap.* Irvine, CA: Barbara Mary Hubbard, Inc.

Institute of Cultural Affairs (1981). Imaginal training methods. *Image: A Journal on the Human Factor.*

Institute of Cultural Affairs (1968). *5th city preschool education manual.* Chicago: Author.

Johnson, D., Johnson, R., & Holubec, E. J. (1988). *Cooperation in the classroom.* Edina, MN: Interaction Book Company.

Johnson, D., Johnson, R., & Holubec, E. J. (1986). *Circles of learning.* Edina MN: Interaction Book Company.

Kagan, S. (1990). *Cooperative learning resources for teachers.* San Juan Capistrano, CA: Resources for Teachers.

Kazantzakis, N. (1960). *The saviors of god.* New York: Simon & Schuster.

Laird, C. (1957). *The miracle of language.* New York: Fawcett Publications.

Langer, S. (1979). *Reflections on art.* New York: Arno Press.

Lawrence, D. (1959). Search for love. In V. de Sola Pinto & F. Roberts (Eds.)*The complete poems of D.H. Lawrence.* New York: Viking Press.

Lazear, D. (1991). *Seven ways of teaching: The artistry of teaching with multiple intelligences.* Palatine, IL: Skylight Publishing.

Lederer, R. *Anguished English.* New York: Dell Publishing, 1987.

Loye, D. (1983). *The sphinx and the rainbow: Brain, mind, and future vision.* Boulder, CO: New Science Library.

Lozonov, G. (1978). *Suggestology and outlines of suggestology.* New York: Gordon & Breach.

Machado, L. (1980). *The right to be intelligent.* New York: Pergamon Press.

MacLean, P. (1977). On the evolution of three mentalities. In S. Arieti & G. Chryanowski (Eds.) *New dimensions in psychiatry: A world view,* (*Vol. 2*). New York: Wiley.

Markley, O. (1988). Using depth intuition in creative problem solving and strategic innovation. *Journal of Creative Behavior, 22*(2), 85-100.

Masters, R., & Houston, J. (1978). *Listening to the body: The psychophysical way to health and awareness.* New York: Delacorte Press.

Masters, R., & Houston, J. (1972).*Mind games.* New York: Delacorte Press.

McTighe, J. (1987). Teaching for thinking, of thinking, and about thinking. In M. Heiman & J. Slomianko (Eds.), *Thinking skills instruction: Concepts and techniques.* Washington, D.C.: National Education Association.

McTighe, J., & Lyman, F. (1988). Cueing thinking in the classroom: The promise of theory-embedded tools. *Educational Leadership, 45*(7), 18-24.

Monroe, R. (1985). *Far journeys.* Garden City, NY: Doubleday.

Nat Hahn, T. (1988). *The miracle of mindfulness.* New York: Beacon Press.

Orff, C. (1978).*The schoolwork.* (M. Murray, Trans.). New York: Schott Music Corporation.

Perkins, D. (1986). *Knowledge as design.* Hillsdale, NJ: Lawrence Erlbaum Associates.

Piaget, J. (1972).*The psychology of intelligence.* Totowa, NJ: Littlefield Adams.

Pribram, K. (1974). *Holonomy and structure in the organization of perception.* Stanford, CA: Stanford University Press.

Pribram, K. (1971). *Languages of the brain: Experimental paradoxes and principles in neuropsychology.* Englewood Cliffs, NJ: Prentice-Hall.

Progoff, I. (1975). *At a journal workshop: The basic text and guide for using the intensive journal.* New York: Dialogue House Library.

Rico, G. (1983).*Writing the natural way: Using right-brain techniques to release your expressive powers.* Los Angeles: J.P. Tarcher.

Rosenfield, I. (1988). *The invention of memory: A new view of the brain.* New York: Basic Books.

Russell, P. (1983). *The global brain: Speculations on the evolutionary leap to planetary consciousness.* Los Angeles: J. P. Tarcher.

Russell, P. (1976). *The brain book.* New York: E.P. Dutton.

Samuels, M., & Samuels, N. (1975). *Seeing with the mind's eye: The history, techniques, and uses of visualization.* New York: Random House.

Schmeck, R. (Ed.) (1988). *Learning strategies and learning styles.* New York: Plenum Press.

Shone, R. (1984). *Creative visualization.* New York: Thorson's Publishers.

Slavin, R. (1983). *Cooperative learning.* New York: Longman.

Snowman, J. (1989). Learning tactics and strategies. In G. Phy & T. Andre (Eds.) *Cognitive instructional psychology: Components of classroom learning.* New York: Academic Press.

Springer, S., & Deutsch, G. (1985). *Left brain, right brain.* New York: W. H. Freeman.

Steiner, R. (1925). *Music in light of anthroposophy.* London: Anthroposophical.

Sternberg, R. (1986). *Intelligence applied: Understanding and increasing your intellectual skills.* San Diego: Harcourt Brace Jovanovich.

Sternberg, R. (1984). *Beyond I.Q.: A triarchic theory of human intelligence.* New York: Cambridge University Press.

Sternberg, R., Okagaki, L., & Jackson, A. (1990). Practical intelligence for success in school. *Educational Leadership, 48*(1), 35-39.

Striker, S. with Kimmel, E. *The anti coloring book.* (Series) New York: Holt, 1982-1990.

Vaughn, F. (1986). *The inward arc.* Boulder, CO: The New Science Library.

von Oech, R. (1986). *A kick in the seat of the pants: Using your explorer, artist, judge, & warrior to be more creative.* New York: Perennial Library.

von Oech, R. (1983). *A whack on the side of the head: How to unlock your mind for innovation.* New York: Warner Books.

Vygotsky, L. (1986). *Thought and language.* Cambridge, MA: MIT Press.

Walsh, R., & Vaughn, F. (Eds.) (1980). *Beyond ego: Transpersonal dimensions in psychology.* Los Angeles: J. P. Tarcher.

Walters, J., & Gardner, H. (1984, September). *The development and education of the intelligences* (position paper). Chicago: Spencer Foundation; New York: Carnegie Corporation.

Weinstein, M., & Goodman, J. (1980). *Playfair.* San Luis Obispo, CA: Impact.

Wilber, K. (1983). *Eye to eye: The quest for the new paradigm.* Garden City, NY: Anchor Books.

Wilber, K. (1980). *The atman project.* Wheaton, IL: Quest Books.

Index

M

Whitehead, Alfred North, 75

Whole brain, xxiv

Wilber, Ken, 1, 2, 10, 29, 30, 187-88

Words, understanding order and meaning of, 2-3

Z

Zone of potential development, 190

log

Toto, I've a feeling we're not in Kansas anymore.
—Dorothy, *The Wizard of Oz*

Reflection Log

"An insight/thought
I've had today is. . ."
(Write it!)

"An interesting pattern I'm
noticing is. . ."
(Think about it!)

"An image/picture I
have of this day is. . . "
(Draw it!)

"A body movement/
gesture for today is. .
(Do it!)

"If today were a song
it would be. . ."
(Sing it!)

"I want to talk with
someone about_____."
(Discuss it!)

"My inner feelings
about today are. . ."
(Meditate on it!)

Reflection Log

"An insight/thought
I've had today is. . ."
(Write it!)

"An interesting pattern I'm
noticing is. . ."
(Think about it!)

"An image/picture I
have of this day is. . . "
(Draw it!)

"A body movement/
gesture for today is. . .
(Do it!)

"If today were a song
it would be. . ."
(Sing it!)

"I want to talk with
someone about_____."
(Discuss it!)

"My inner feelings
about today are. . ."
(Meditate on it!)

Reflection Log

"An insight/thought
I've had today is. . ."
(Write it!)

"An interesting pattern I'm
noticing is. . ."
(Think about it!)

"An image/picture I
have of this day is. . . "
(Draw it!)

"A body movement/
gesture for today is. . .
(Do it!)

"If today were a song
it would be. . ."
(Sing it!)

"I want to talk with
someone about_____."
(Discuss it!)

"My inner feelings
about today are. . ."
(Meditate on it!)

Reflection Log

"An insight/thought
I've had today is. . ."
(Write it!)

"An interesting pattern I'm
noticing is. . ."
(Think about it!)

"An image/picture I
have of this day is. . . "
(Draw it!)

"A body movement/
gesture for today is. . .
(Do it!)

"If today were a song
it would be. . ."
(Sing it!)

"I want to talk with
someone about_____."
(Discuss it!)

"My inner feelings
about today are. . ."
(Meditate on it!)

Reflection Log

"An insight/thought
I've had today is. . ."
(Write it!)

"An interesting pattern I'm
noticing is. . ."
(Think about it!)

"An image/picture I
have of this day is. . . "
(Draw it!)

"A body movement/
gesture for today is. .
(Do it!)

"If today were a song
it would be. . ."
(Sing it!)

"I want to talk with
someone about_____."
(Discuss it!)

"My inner feelings
about today are. . ."
(Meditate on it!)

Reflection Log

"An insight/thought
I've had today is. . ."
(Write it!)

"An interesting pattern I'm
noticing is. . ."
(Think about it!)

"An image/picture I
have of this day is. . . "
(Draw it!)

"A body movement/
gesture for today is. . .
(Do it!)

"If today were a song
it would be. . ."
(Sing it!)

"I want to talk with
someone about_____."
(Discuss it!)

"My inner feelings
about today are. . ."
(Meditate on it!)

Reflection Log

"An insight/thought
I've had today is. . ."
(Write it!)

"An interesting pattern I'm
noticing is. . ."
(Think about it!)

"An image/picture I
have of this day is. . . "
(Draw it!)

"A body movement/
gesture for today is. .
(Do it!)

"If today were a song
it would be. . ."
(Sing it!)

"I want to talk with
someone about_____."
(Discuss it!)

"My inner feelings
about today are. . ."
(Meditate on it!)

LEARN FROM OUR BOOKS
<u>AND</u> FROM OUR AUTHORS!
Bring Our Author-Trainers To Your District

Now that you have benefited from IRI/Skylight's high-quality publications, extend your learning by meeting the actual authors. IRI/Skylight authors are seasoned professionals with a wealth of knowledge and experience. They offer dynamic, exciting presentations. Many authors are available to visit your site and discuss their particular areas of expertise!

Training of Trainers

IRI/Skylight provides comprehensive inservice training for experienced educators who are qualified to train other staff members. IRI/Skylight presenters possess years of experience at all levels of education and include authors, field experts, and administrators. IRI/Skylight's training of trainers program is the most powerful and cost-effective way to build the skills of your entire staff.

Training Programs

IRI/Skylight training is available in your district or intermediate agency. Gain practical techniques and strategies for implementing the latest findings from educational research. No matter the topic, IRI/Skylight has an experienced consultant who can design and specially tailor an inservice to meet the needs of your school or organization.

Network

An IRI/Phi Delta Kappa partnership, *The Network of Mindful Schools* is a program of site-based systemic change, built on the core values advocated by Arthur L. Costa. Each member school is committed to restructuring itself to become a "home for the mind." The network is built on three elements: a site leader, a faculty that functions as a team, and an external support system to aid in school transformation.

To receive a free copy of the IRI/Skylight Catalog, find out more about The Network of Mindful Schools, or for more information about trainings offered by IRI/Skylight, contact:

IRI/Skylight Publishing, Inc.
200 E. Wood Street, Suite 274, Palatine, Illinois 60067
800-348-4474
FAX 708-991-6420

There are
one-story intellects,
two-story intellects, and three-story
intellects with skylights. All fact collectors, who have
no aim beyond their facts, are one-story men. Two-story men compare,
reason, generalize, using the labors of the fact collectors as well as
their own. Three-story men idealize, imagine, predict—
their best illumination comes from above,
through the skylight.
—*Oliver Wendell*
Holmes